CAPABILITY M
Monitoring and Impr... ...g Capabilities

CAPABILITY MANAGEMENT
Monitoring and Improving Capabilities

Dr M S Saxena

GLOBAL INDIA PUBLICATIONS PVT LTD
NEW DELHI
www.globalindiapublications.com

Copyright © 2009 by Global India Publications Pvt Ltd.

All rights reserved. No part of this book may be reproduced or utilized in any form or by any means, electronically or mechanically, including photocopying, recording, or by any information storage and retrieval system, without the prior permission in writing from the publisher.

Published by :

Global India Publications Pvt Ltd
11, Darya Ganj, New Delhi - 110 002
Phone : +91-11-41563325 (Customer Service)
+91-11-41562846 (Editorial)
E-mail (orders): info@globalindiapublications.com
Website: www.globalindiapublications.com

ISBN: 978-93-80228-43-3

Published and Printed by Mr. Pranav Gupta on behalf of **Global India Publications Pvt Ltd** at Mohit Enterprises, Delhi.

Preface

The first is that for many organisations the task of assessing strengths and weaknesses has become an annual charade of little meaning, so much so that some organisations give little thought to this basic step in strategic thinking.

Corporate strengths and weaknesses do not of themselves make good strategies, but they are an essential foundation. If you want a tree to grow, you ensure that its roots are sound and that it is planted in a carefully prepared hole. Then it may need a bit of nurturing. It might grow and do well even if you ignored these things, but the chances of success are reduced.

Many of the methods are also of value in corporate turn-around situations, or in the due diligence process during acquisitions. How organisations currently tackle the task of the corporate appraisal - the process of identifying strengths and weaknesses - is amazingly variable. Rather than produce endless lists, I have written some of these into an imaginary situation. Books on marketing, finance and other functional areas of management will often cover methods of analysis that are relevant, but not positioned in the context of an overall appraisal. This book is an attempt to cover many important topics of capability management.

I am very thankful to Mr. Pranav Gupta, Director, Global India Publications Pvt Ltd, for his kind cooperation and support for this book.

Dr M S Saxena

Preface

The first is that for many organisations the task of assessing strengths and weaknesses has become an annual charade of little meaning, so much so that some organisations give little thought to this basic step in strategic thinking.

Corporate strengths and weaknesses do not of themselves make good strategies, but they are an essential foundation. If you want a tree to grow, you ensure that its roots are sound and that it is planted in a carefully prepared hole. Then it may need a bit of nurturing. It might grow and do well even if you ignored these things, but the chances of success are reduced.

Many of the methods are also of value in corporate turn-around situations, or in the due diligence process during acquisitions. How organisations currently, perform the task of the corporate appraisal – the process of identifying strengths and weaknesses – is amazingly variable. Rather than produce endless lists, I have written some of these into imaginary situation. Books on marketing, finance and other functional areas of management will often cover methods of analysis that are relevant, but not positioned in the context of an overall appraisal. This book is an attempt to cover many important topics of capability management.

I am very thankful to Mr. Pranav Gupta, Director, Global India Publications Pvt. Ltd. for his kind cooperation and support for this book.

Dr M S Saxena

Contents

	Preface	v
1.	Capability Management : An Introduction	1
2.	Capability Management Strategy	37
3.	Management and Leadership Capability	81
4.	The Purposes and Nature of the Appraisal	135
5.	HRM, Management Effectiveness, Culture and Structure	211
6.	Information Systems for Capability Management	237
7.	Industry Analysis	279
	Bibliography	305
	Index	309

Holistic management =

1

Capability Management
An Introduction

Capability management is a high-level integrative management function, with particular application in the context of defence. Capability management aims to balance economy in meeting current operational requirements, with the sustainable use of current capabilities, and the development of future capabilities, to meet the sometimes competing strategic and current operational objectives of an enterprise. Accordingly, effective capability management assists organisations to better understand, and effectively integrate, re-align and apply the total enterprise ability or capacity to achieve strategic and current operational objectives; and Develops and provides innovative solutions that focus on the holistic management of the defined array of interlinking functions and activities in the enterprise's strategic and current operational contexts. In military contexts, capabilities may also be analysed in terms of Force Structure and the Preparedness of elements or groupings within that Force Structure. Preparedness in turn may be analysed in terms of Readiness and Sustainability.

In both the military and commercial contexts, net-centric operations and related concepts are playing an increasingly important role in leading and driving business transformation, and contemporary capability management needs to have close regard of those factors. The level of interoperability, both technical and organisational/social, is a critical determinant of the net-centric capability that is able to be realised and employed.

Capability is the quality of being capable; to have the capacity or ability to do something, achieve specific effects or declared goals and objectives. Enterprises in essence consist of a portfolio or matrix of capabilities that are used in various combinations to achieve outcomes. Within that portfolio, a capability will be transient unless managed and maintained over time. Therefore, a typical capability lifecycle spans needs, requirements, acquisition, in-service and obsolescence/disposal phases.

While a highly developed management discipline within several national military organisations, the concepts, principles and practices of capability management are readily adaptable and effective for wide-ranging application in the strategy and operations of many other enterprises.

Definitions of Identified Capabilities Must Satisfy two Rules: Capability definitions must contain the required attributes with appropriate measures of effectiveness (e.g., time, distance, effect [including scale] and obstacles to overcome).

Capability definitions should be general and not influence a decision in favour of a particular means of implementation. The definition should be specific enough to evaluate alternative approaches to implement the capability.

Capabilities are organised around concepts of operations, because the CONOPS describe how a specified course of action is to be executed. The ability to execute the specified course of action depends on many factors and the relationship between those factors. Capabilities can be described as one or more sequences of activities, referred to as operational threads. The threads are composed of a set of activities that can be grouped to form the basis for a mission area architecture. The architecture then provides the structure for defining and understanding the many factors that impact the capability.

The Navy has also endorsed using architectures to understand and analyze capabilities and their associated requirements. The Navy performs this architecture analysis based on the <u>concept of MCPs</u>. The intent is to consider all of the factors that contribute to the desired mission capability as an integrated system. An MCP is defined as "a task-oriented bundle of CONOPS, processes, and organisation structures supported by networks, sensors, weapons, and systems, as well as personnel training and support services to sustain a core naval capability." The MCP and associated analysis then provide the basis for acquisition decisions.

CAPABILITY MANAGEMENT ISSUES

Due to the complexities of system-of-systems integration, interoperability, and the dynamic nature of operations, capability management is greatly assisted by <u>modelling and simulating</u> realistic strategic scenarios and contexts, in order to <u>inform business cases and decision-making</u>. Through those considerations and practices, the enterprise and its performance can be continuously assessed and projected into the future. Well executed capability management therefore clearly <u>informs strategic and operational decisions</u>, and <u>aids</u> in the <u>development</u> of diverse but well-considered <u>strategic and operational options</u>, so they are readily available off-the-shelf. This should also endow significant agility to an enterprise, providing enhanced <u>"contingency capital"</u> and <u>risk mitigation</u>.

Capability management therefore centres around:

- Strategic and operational appreciations and analyses.
- Capability conceptualisation, definition and development.
- Operations research and analysis.
- Context or scenario-based capability modelling and simulation.

4 | Capability Management

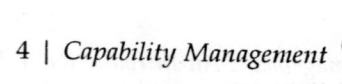

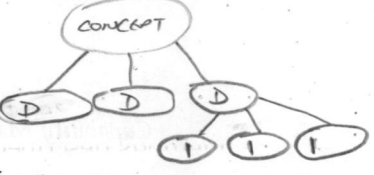

- Capability costing.
- Capital project business cases and management.
- Decision making and decision support.
- Capability assurance and performance management.

DOTLMPF

The interlinking functions and activities of the enterprise may be defined under several best-practice paradigms or frameworks, such as the Balanced Scorecard (BSC), or the US Department of Defense Architecture Framework (DoDAF).

Typically, capability is assessed and managed in several dimensions. The US military analyses its capabilities in the dimensions of "DOTLMPF", being:

- Doctrine
- Organisations
- Training
- Leader Development
- Material
- Personnel
- Facilities

[Handwritten notes: WE USE TEPIDOIL. EACH LETTER IS A DIMENSION OR INTEGRATIVE ELEMENT. TRAINING, EQUIPMENT, PERSONNEL, INFORMATION, CONCEPTS & DOCTRINE, ORGANISATION, INFRASTRUCTURE, LOGISTICS]

Corporate strengths and weaknesses do not of themselves make good strategies, but they are an essential foundation. If you want a tree to grow, you ensure that its roots are sound and that it is planted in a carefully prepared hole. Then it may need a bit of nurturing. It might grow and do well even if you ignored these things, but the chances of success are reduced.

Many of the methods described here are also of value in Corporate strengths and weaknesses do not of themselves make good strategies, but they are an essential foundation. If you want a tree to grow, you ensure that its roots are sound and that it is planted in a carefully prepared hole. Then it may need a bit of nurturing. It might grow and do well even if you ignored these things, but the chances of success are reduced.

[Margin note: Balanced Scorecard = Strategic planning & management system, aligns business activity to vision & strategy of the organisation, improves internal comms, monitor performance against goals.]

Capability Management: An Introduction | 5

Many of the methods described here are also of value in corporate turn-around situations, or in the due diligence process during acquisitions.

How organisations currently tackle the task of the corporate appraisal - the process of identifying strengths and weaknesses - is amazingly variable. Rather than produce endless lists, we have written some of these into an imaginary situation. To the best of our knowledge the Strategic Planning Society of the UK has never had the sort of meeting we describe here, nor do any of the people or companies exist. But the methods our characters discuss are very real.

All the assessments were made by the managers in the company, in a four-stage process:

1. Strengths and weaknesses are identified, defined and agreed in meetings of managers in one master list.
2. The planning team examines each item on the list in some detail, so that it can be more fully defined.
3. The carefully defined strengths and weaknesses are boiled down to a few pithy sentences in another meeting of the team.
4. Finally, it is sometimes found useful to rank them in order of importance.

LIFE CAPABILITY MANAGEMENT

Through Life Capability Management (Capability Management) translates the requirements of Defence policy into an approved programme that delivers the required capabilities, through-life, across all Defence Lines of Development (DLoDs).

Capability is the enduring ability to generate a desired operational outcome or effect, and is relative to the threat, physical environment and the contributions of coalition partners.

Capability is not a particular system or equipment. The adjacent figure shows the components of capability.

6 | Capability Management

Capability is delivered by Force Elements – Ships, Aircraft, Army formations, other Military Units and Force Enablers – combined into packages by Joint Force Commanders, tailored for particular operations or missions.

Each Force Element is delivered by either a single service, or by a joint organisation such as the Joint Helicopter Force, and requires the integration of the eight DLoDs. The purpose of Capability Management is to translate the requirements of Defence Policy into an approved programme that delivers the required capabilities Though-Life, across the DLoDs.

There are two integral parts: Management of Capability Change Planning; This identifies the changes required across all DLoDs to provide the right capabilities, at the right time within available resources. Management of Capability Delivery; Where Capability Change Planning identifies the need for a new or enhanced equipment requirement, a Programme Board may be formed. The Programme board will provide governance during the acquisition life cycle, and take full account of capability/industrial threats and opportunities to achieve coherence across all DLoDs.

Once In service the responsibility for the Management of Capability Delivery transfers from the Programme Board to an Availability Working Group led by the User.

SCOPE OF CAPABILITY MANAGEMENT

The Scope of Capability Management can be illustrated as a series of transitions from the analysis of Defence Policy through to the award of an Industrial Contract. At each transition, trades can be made which may affect the requirement through the performance, cost, and delivery timescale perspectives of a programme, across all DLoDs.

Defence Policy to Defence Planning Assumptions

Defence Policy is represented by a set of Defence Planning Assumptions (DPAs) which provide the envelope within which force structure and capability are resourced. MOD central staffs in D Pol Planning and DCDC / Force Development lead this activity which is largely outside the acquisition process.

Defence Planning Assumptions to Military Capabilities

The Defence Planning Assumptions are translated, through Concept Development, High Level Operational Analysis (HLOA) and Military Judgement, into a set of capabilities that are required in order to achieve the desired effects and campaign outcomes. This is a core activity for the Equipment Capability Customer (ECC), working with MOD central policy staff, and is a key part of Capability Planning.

Military Capabilities to Force Groupings

Each Military Capability can be delivered through different mixes of platforms, force elements and force enablers. This activity identifies the optimum balance of Force Groupings. This is a core activity for the ECC, led by Director Equipment Plan (DEP) and Directors Equipment Capability (DECs), supported by Capability Management Groups (CMG) and Capability Planning Groups.

Force Groupings to Lines of Development

To deliver the required capability, each Force Grouping needs to be integrated across all Defence Lines of Development (DLoDs) in a way that draws on opportunities offered by new technologies and is coherent with industrial capacity. This is the primary activity of ECC hosted Capability Planning Groups (CPG) which manage their force groupings usin pan DLoD Capability Management Plans (CMP). Each DLoD owner is responsible for ensuring coherency within their own DLoD area.

Line of Development to Project

Decisions made in the capability planning process may result in specific projects being initiated across one or more of the DLoDs. At this point the emphasis of Capability Management changes from one of planning, to one of delivery.

For capability changes that are predominantly equipment focused, a DEC acts as the Programme Sponsor, carrying out the duties of Senior Responsible Owner. The appropriate Integrated Project Team (IPT) will manage Equipment DLoD aspects of each project guided by relevant Defence Equipment and Support (DE&S) 2 Cluster Lead will guide the IPT.

Where projects are not equipment focused, then project leadership normally comes under the appropriate TLB. In some cases, where the capability planning process has identified the need for several pan DLoD projects to be initiated, a Programme board will be established to provide overall governance. For equipment-focused projects, the IPT is responsible for managing the contracts and commercial relationships with suppliers.

ROLES AND RESPONSIBILITIES IN CAPABILITY MANAGEMENT

Effective Capability Management demands a unity of purpose and shared ownership of capability decisions, whilst retaining clear responsibility for the delivery of business activities within each of the Defence Lines of Development (DLoDs). Key industrial considerations must be managed throughout the process, particularly where Defence Industrial Strategy, Long Term Partnering Arrangements, or significant sovereignty issues are involved.

Core Participants in the Capability Change Planning Process

The shared ownership of capability decisions is achieved through a 6-stage Capability Change Planning Process. The five core participants in the Process are known as the MOD Unified Customer and comprise of representatives from:

- The Equipment Capability Customer (ECC) (the Sponsor).
- The User.
- Science Innovation Technology (SIT).
- Defence Equipment and Support (DE&S).

Capability Management: An Introduction | 9

- The Central representative.
- The Development Concepts and Doctrine Centre (DCDC) and Industry can also provide support to the capability planning process at various times.

The Equipment Capability Customer

ECC acts as the Sponsor and DEC acts as the <u>Senior Responsible Owner</u> working to the direction set by DSG and the policy guidelines set by the PPSG.

The key roles and responsibilities of the Sponsor are:

- <u>To identify</u>, using DSG, the <u>capability required to meet the UK's defence objectives.</u>
- To <u>translate requirements into an approved programme</u> and <u>acts as sponsor of the capability until it is delivered into service.</u>
- Act as decider to provide new capability on behalf of the Department.
- Lead the Unified Customer team, advised and supported by the User and DE&S.
- Formulating and proposing the Equipement & Support (E&S) Plan to the Finance Director, for approval by the Defence Management Board (DMB) as part of the overall planning process.
- Generating Business Cases in response to new requirements. Supported by Capability Planning Groups (CPG).
- With ACDS RP running the Options process as part of the planning round.
- The delivery of an agreed and coherent combination of DLoDs to the User for integration at In Service Date (ISD).
- Seeking the agreement of the User to any decisions that impact upon his ability to declare ISD or to support and operate capability post ISD. This should

includ any support arrangements or commitments that would constrain the User's flexibility within Years 1 to 4 or which impact upon non-equipment LoDs.

The User

In the context of Through Life Capability Management the key roles and responsibilities of the User are:

- Informs and supports the planning of future capability.
- Participates in auditing and reporting the delivery of new capability.
- Informing capability requirements capture ensuring it meets the need and can be delivered at in service date.
- At Main Gate set the criteria for In Service Date.
- At Main Gate take on the assurance role confirming In Service Date criteria are met prior to declaration.
- Work with the Sponsor to ensure all risks and issues identified at Main Gate (or subsequently) are addressed to facilitate declaration of In Service Date.
- Assure, from User perspective, that the equipment solution and contributing DLoD can be integrated and supported through life.
- As a member of the CPG.
- Provide advice on trade offs and options.
- Provide evidence to support investment decision points.

Science Innovation Technology

SIT supplies Science and Technology officers, integrated within the ECC, on Capability Management and Planning Groups (CMG / CPGs).

Defence Source of Technology: DSG = MoD Chief Scientific Advisor to make the greatest possible use and technology for the defence and Security of UK.

In particular, the SIT representative:

- Works with Defence Science & Technology Laboratories (Dstl) Capability Advisors to provide scientific advice and underpinning knowledge and data in a timely manner.
- Assists CPGs to identify current or future capability needs or issues which can be addressed or informed by focused research.
- Articulates Research Goals and, through the relevant SIT Research Output, translates them into one or more Research Requirements which define the aim, desired outcome and milestones of the research activity.
- Assists CPGs in prioritising Research Requirements.
- Oversees appropriate research activities.
- Generates research and development plans which are coherent with capability plans and decision points.
- Identifies relationships with industry to develop key technologies jointly.

Defence Equipment and Support

The role of the DE&S is to acquire, deliver, support and sustain materiel for current and future operations that ultimately contributes to the generation of the User.

In the context of Through Life Capability Management the key roles and responsibilities of DE&S are:

- The commercial interface with industry for delivery of the E&S Plan; contracting for and assuring the delivery of equipment, services and support.
- Delivery of a coherent through-life output within and across project portfolios (in consultation with the User and Sponsor) to meet funded future capability requirements.

Capability Management

- The management of existing materiel assets to meet funded, current capability requirements defined by the User, outlined by agreed CSAs and TLMP.
- In conjunction with the User and Sponsor, ensure that common assumptions are used and that equipment support is coherent.

Provide a key input to the CPG [CAPABILITY PLANNING GROUP] process by:

- Informing on delivery.
- Advising on trade-off opportunities.
- Advising on industrial capacity.
- Providing advice on Commercial issues.
- Advising on opportunities for technology insertion.

The Central Representative

Within Head Office, it is the role of the Central Finance & Resource Planning Staff under the Finance Director to:

- Manage the overall Defence Corporate Programme and Planning process, balancing resources between TLB Plans and the ECC to meet defence priorities.
- Allocate resource control totals to TLBs and the ECC.
- Manage in-year expenditure at Departmental level.
- Sets Force Structures, Defence Planning Assumptions and Readiness Levels.

The Development Concepts and Doctrine Centre

The Development Concepts and Doctrine Centre (DCDC) provide additional support at various times. DCDC is the owner of the Concepts and Doctrine DLoD.

As sponsor of the "concepts to capability process", DCDC:

- Informs capability development in the ECC through PPSG endorsed Applied Concepts. In practice this is achieved through participation in CPGs.
- Provides authoritative policy direction on future military capabilities and the force structures required

to meet Defence Policy through the Future Capability Development chapter of Defence Strategic Guidance and participation in CMGs.
- Working with DEP, DCDC Force Development is responsible for ensuring that capability changes and trades are audited against Policy.
- Highlights changes that are not compliant to the JCB for further action.

Industry

Effective engagement with industry is a key principle of capability management, which is achieved at three levels:
- At the highest level, where MOD is defining its capability requirements in response to Defence Policy, the engagement is primarily with specialists who support the analysis function.
- Capability planning, where industry can provide an indication of:
  - Technical maturity.
  - Broad cost and programme data.
  - Industrial threats and opportunities arising from capacity, technology or other issues.
  - Export and international considerations.
  - Equipment and service delivery, normally subject to individual commercial arrangements between MOD and suppliers.

KEY PRINCIPLES OF CAPABILITY MANAGEMENT

The characteristics of highly effective Capability Management are:
- A top-down approach to the delivery of Military Capability, based on Defence Policy, tempered by tolerable risk.
- A rigorous proactive decision making process, taking a whole life, cross DLoD approach, which uses robust

trading techniques to optimise and balance demand and supply.

- Taking a Long Term View, building on extant capability, thus identifying opportunities and change drivers and understanding the impacts of today's decisions on the future.

- Continuous improvement in joint MOD and Industry performance in the delivery and availability of enduring Military Capability through improved relationships and behaviours and resilient, stable and coherent plans.

- Appropriate engagement as the MOD Unified Customer at all stages of the process, to inform the high level trade and participate actively in the other levels. Joint teams, joint approach, joint information.

- An approach that is capable of responding to changes and the changing environment.

THE CAPABILITY CHANGE PLANNING PROCESS

Capability Change Planning is a 6-stage process to produce a capability management plan. The Capability Change Planning Process requires the active involvement of all ECC staff, in particular Director Equipment Plan (DEP) and DECs, all DLoD stakeholders and the MOD Unified Customers members of the Capability Management Groups (CMGs) and Capability Planning Groups (CPGs). The output of the Capability Change Planning Process may be a series of endorsed changes to the current plan. The key planning documents used to enable this are:

- Capability Management Strategies (CMS) for each Capability Management Group (CMG).
- Capability Management Plans (CMP) for each Capability Planning Group (CPG).

Stage 1: Capability Definition

This stage develops a Capability Definition of the capability area for each Capability Management Group and Capability Planning Group. It also requires each DEC to establish and/or review Capability Planning Groups (CPGs) for their area. CPGs consist of those groups of stakeholders which are responsible for the coherent management of force groupings on an enduring basis and across multiple DLoDs.

Each DEC must identify dependencies on other CPGs and CMGs, including stakeholders for their area. This is a primary task of DEC strategy staff and DEP, in consultation with wider departmental stakeholders

Stage 2: Define Capability Goals for Area

This stage draws on Defence Planning Assumptions and other policy guidance and analysis, to develop a clear definition of the capability requirement in terms of one or more statements of capability need. The statements should be specific, measurable, solution independent characteristics for the capability area.

The capability characteristics are typically phrased in terms of broad performance characteristics required of one or more force groupings.

Capability goals are recorded at CMG and CPG levels within Capability Management Strategies and Capability Management Plans respectively.

This is a primary task of DEC strategy staff and DEP, in consultation with wider departmental stakeholders.

Stage 3: Baseline Review and Audit

This stage develops and validates a baseline assessment of the capability area across all DLoDs as currently planned.

This stage draws on the output of Stages 1 and 2, and presents the five perspectives relating to each CMG and CPG capability area:

- Capability
- R&T
- Industry
- Financial
- Commercial
- They may include current DLoD plans, and other known shortfalls, threats and opportunities.
- This is a primary task of DECs. It requires active engagement from all members of the MOD Unified Customer at CPG level.

This stage develops a baseline assessment across all Defence Lines of Development (DLoD) currently planned, and presents five perspectives relating to the Capability Area for each Capability Management Group (CMG) and Capability Planning Group (CPG).

The stage is necessary in order to indicate the existing risks from five perspectives for each CMG and CPG:

The Capability Perspective identifies critical capability shortfalls across all DLoDs within each CMG and CPG area.

The Research Perspective identifies how aligned the current research programme is with either individual, CPG wide or CMG wide Capability Goals derived in Stage 2.

The Industrial Perspective identifies how much impact each CMG and CPG planning area may have on their relevant industrial sectors. It also identifies how much impact key drivers and trends within industry may have on CMG and CPG planning areas.

The Financial Perspective identifies the key financial pressures relevant to CMG and CPG planning areas.

The Commercial Perspective identifies how constrained CMG and CPG planning aspirations may be by extant contractual commitments.

CMG and CPG virtual Team Sites record the outputs of this stage including:

The five perspectives relating to each CMG and CPG Capability Area.

A record of assumptions supporting each of the five perspectives, recorded in the Capability Planning Assumptions List (CPAL).

The Sponsor develops the five baseline perspectives with the active engagement of all members of the MOD Unified Customer at CPG level.

THE CAPABILITY PERSPECTIVE

The Capability Perspective measures the expected output of current plans and identifies surpluses and shortfalls in capability. The perspective is developed as a result of the Capability Audit.

The audit is intended to be quantitative rather than qualitative; objective rather than subjective. This means that Operational Analysis (OA) should be used wherever feasible including, where appropriate, the use of experimental or historical data.

The Capability Audit and the perspective that it develops determine if the UK's armed forces can fulfil their tasks based on the Equipment Procurement Plan (EPP) and Equipment Support Plan (ESP). The perspective informs decisions on any proposed changes to the EPP or ESP.

Although the perspective identifies areas where change may be needed it does not propose options for implementing the change.

The perspective identifies surpluses in capability as well as shortfalls and it is quantitative rather than qualitative, although some areas have not yet proved amenable to quantitative analysis.

It measures the expected output of the current plans and provides:

- Data to help the Joint Capability Board set strategic priorities.

18 | Capability Management

- Data to help the Directors of Equipment Capability compile their Capability Area Plans and Capability Shortfall Risk Registers.
- Input to the Equipment Capability Customer's Balanced Scorecard, the Defence Strategic Audit and the Defence Management Board's Quarterly Report.
- The context for Balance of Investment studies.
- The DEC Capability Audit submissions are synthesised by DEP into a consolidated Capability Audit report for consideration by the Joint Capabilities Board (JCB).
- The JCB reviews the Audit, provides direction and prioritisation for more detailed Capability Investigations, further Balance of Investment studies and the development of options to determine the changes required to the EP. Whilst taking account of the balance of capabilities and requirements across the Equipment Capability Customer as a whole.

THE COMMERCIAL PERSPECTIVE

The Commercial Perspective provides a view of the key commercial issues that Capability Management Groups (CMGs) and Capability Planning Groups (CPGs) should be aware of. This perspective enables CMGs and CPGs to develop an understanding of the Commercial environment that may impact their planning activities.

The Commercial perspective includes analysis of:

- Near term planned commercial commitments, and the impact they can have on decision making.
- How to exploit existing opportunities and levels of influence within the commercial perspective.
- The outputs of this perspective are two short reports hosted on relevant CMG and CPG Team Sites.

A description of the level of commercial commitment for the Capability Area, to include the Directors General of DE&S

Clusters, key companies, impending investment decisions and major decision support information for the CMG, including critical constraints and opportunities.

A graphical representation of the total Capital Defence Expenditure Limit (CDEL) and Resource Defence Expenditure Limit (RDEL) for the CMG showing committed funding versus uncommitted funding.

The Commercial Perspective is written by representatives from the Directors of Equipment Capability in concert with relevant Directors General of DE&S Clusters and Integrated Project Team staff.

DEVELOPING THE COMMERCIAL PERSPECTIVE

The Commercial Perspective at Capability Management Group (CMG) level is an analysis of the commercial opportunities and constraints facing the CMG.

Why the projects listed are of commercial interest to the CMG?

What innovative approaches can be or are being taken to existing and future programmes across the cluster that have commercial opportunities to achieve better Value for Money?

Are there new commercial opportunities that can be exploited to deliver better Value for Money?

How do existing commitments within the cluster constrain the CMG – if so how flexible are these?

Are there any decision points imminent that will constrain the CMG decision making – if so how flexible are these?

The Commercial Perspective report at the CMG level should be written by representatives from Director of Equipment Capability with relevant Director General (DG) cluster staff.

The Commercial Perspective at Capability Planning Group (CPG) level is an analysis of the commercial opportunities and constraints facing the CPG.

It includes reports that cover:
- The CPG Force Grouping Commercial Perspective
- The CPG Force Grouping Commercial Perspective for the Equipment Procurement Plan
- The CPG Force Grouping Commercial Perspective for the Equipment Support Plan.

CPG Force Grouping Commercial Perspective

Integrated Project Team (IPT) staff produce the Force Grouping Commercial Perspective which provides an analysis of the commercial opportunities and constraints for all programmes that are part of the Force Grouping managed by the CPG.

The analysis should include:
- Why the project listed is of commercial interest?
- A description of commercial commitment.
- Commentary on whether there are tensions in the supply chain.
- Assessment of whether there is flexibility in the contract.
- What commercial opportunities exist?
- What are the constraints in the contract?

CPG Force Grouping Commercial Perspective

A written description produced by IPT and Director General Commercial Staff of cross programme opportunities and planned commitment that the CPG should be aware of. This includes a graphical representation of the total expenditure limits - CDEL and RDEL - for the Equipment Procurement Plan (EPP), showing committed versus uncommitted.

The cross programme opportunities should include:
- A description of any opportunities for coherence across the programmes managed.

- What innovative approaches can be or are being taken to existing and future programmes that have commercial opportunities to achieve better Value for Money.
- A description of near term plans for commitment that may constrain CPG decision making. The commercial perspective for the Equipment Support Programme (ESP) should be compiled similarly to the Equipment Procurement Plan - this is primarily the responsibility of the IPT.

FINANCIAL PERSPECTIVE

The Sponsor completes this step in three parts in consultation with Integrated Project Teams:

- Key Financial Pressures
- Potential Capability Management Measures
- Potential Options.
- The data is collected from the "Feedback Form" from the 1* level Screenings for a Planning Round and through records of screening meetings and notes.

Analyse Outcomes of Screenings

This is done in four steps and recorded on appropriate data sheets:

- Identify the key financial pressures.
- Generate a list of potential Capability Management Measures.
- Generate a list of potential Options.
- Highlight areas where supporting data was not available.

From step 1, identify the key financial pressures on projects and programmes and the potential impact on capability outputs for years 1-10 and for future years for the following three categories of cost:

(New) Equipment – P9 Lines RDEL and CDEL (Re-costed programme or project requirements versus <PRYY> baseline funding).

Equipment Support Costs (New Equipment) – P10 Lines RDEL and CDEL (categorised by Upkeep, Update, Sustainability and Disposal).

Equipment Support Costs (In service Equipment) – Previously funded through the STP.

From step 1, compile a list of potential Capability Management Measures (CMM) to address the funding shortfalls identified for the Capability Planning Group to consider, and record this as suggested.

From step 1, compile a list of potential options being considered for Stage 2 of the planning round for the CPG to consider, and record this as suggested.

Highlight any areas where supporting data was not available for analysis and specify the reasons for this gap, and any key assumptions made in the absence of the data. Establish whether addressing this data gap is included in the Director Equipment Capability Action Plans.

PRESSURES THAT IMPACT CAPABILITY GOALS

Define the pressures that impact Capability Goals for a Capability Planning Group (CPG) from the point of view of the Equipment Procurement Plan (EPP) and the Equipment Support Plan (ESP) and create:

- A record of the key financial pressures in the EPP.
- A record of the key financial pressures in the ESP, including the totals.

When defining the key financial pressures in the EPP or the ESP for a particular Capability Planning Group, gather and record:

- *Project / Programme:* The name of the project or programme or Integrated Project Team (IPT).

- *Financial Variance:* The financial shortfall specified as an amount (£m) for the two expenditure limits (RDEL and CDEL), year by year, and the key factors driving the variance.

Impact of returning the programme to baseline. The impact on the programme, including the Capability Risk and relative Pain Level. Use the defined categories to record these.

Impact on the CPG's Capability Area and other CPGs. The impact of the projected financial shortfall on the outputs for the hosted CPG's Capability Area as well as other CPGs that are affected.

CPG Recommended Action. This might include the ability to fund using an Equipment Programme Measure (EPM), or to address in Stage 3 through a savings or enhancement Option.

GENERATE A CAPABILITY MANAGEMENT GROUP

To generate a Capability Management Group (CMG) view of the financial data:

- Request information - from other Directors of Equipment Capability - on any known financial pressures in other relevant projects or programmes in order to capture the remainder of the hosted Capability Planning Group (CPG) business.
- Incorporate key financial pressures identified by other contributing CPGs.
- Produce a narrative (for the CMG Team Site), summarising all the key financial pressures from all hosted and contributing CPGs and make clear whether the identified financial pressure emphasises an existing capability risk or shortfall or generates a new capability risk or shortfall.

Industrial Perspective Reports

Two short reports summarise the Industrial Perspective - at Capability Management Group (CMG) or Capability

Planning Group (CPG) levels. They are hosted on relevant CMG or CPG Team Sites:

- An Industrial Sector Overview.
- A SWOT analysis of the Industrial Sector.

This is an overview of the key issues highlighted by CPGs and Integrated Project Teams (IPTs) in scoping the industrial landscape. Director Equipment Capability (DEC) staff should complete this overview once inputs from IPTs (or Clusters) and CPGs have been received. Where it could affect a Capability Area, it is also necessary to have an understanding of the industrial landscape affecting supporting CPGs.

A strengths, weaknesses, opportunities and threats (SWOT) analysis provides a quick reference for the CMG. This example illustrates a basic SWOT analysis and extends to identifying overlapping initiatives, and innovative and alternative approaches.

Research Perspective

The Research Perspective captures a view of what the Research Programme will deliver to the respective Capability Planning Group (CPG) and how well it is aligned to their capability planning needs - if no further actions are taken.

It can also capture a view of any strategic or overarching research that more appropriately aligns to Capability Management Group (CMG) activity rather than individual CPGs.

This perspective is essential to ensure the Research Programme and Capability Planning are coherent – it identifies how aligned the current Research Programme is with either individual, CPG wide or CMG wide Capability Goals derived in Stage 2.

The outputs of the Research Perspective are recorded on the relevant CPG and CMG Team Sites and consist of:

- A CMG Level Research summary.
- A CPG Level Research summary.

Shortfall and Opportunity Analysis

The Shortfall and Opportunity Analysis stage develops a clear understanding of risk-based capability priorities and opportunities.

It draws on the previous stages, together with other scenario based operational analysis, Balance of Investment (BOI) studies and military judgement. These priorities and opportunities include an assessment of the level of tolerable operational risk. This is a primary task of DECs, supported by the CPG members. Shortfall and Opportunity Analysis provides an audit trail and documents decisions made about what to take forward and what to dismiss. This audit trail provides an invaluable context for the current Planning Round, and those conducting subsequent Planning Rounds.

The outputs of Shortfall and Opportunity Analysis are decisions:

- To raise Options immediately; or
- To conduct Capability Investigations, which may result in raising Options; or
- To take No Further Action but to record the reasons.

The stage involves collaborative working between related Capability Management Groups (CMGs) and Capability Planning Groups (CPGs) to identify shortfalls and opportunities associated with each of the five perspectives.

Capability (pan-DLoD). Measure capability shortfalls and surpluses against current Direction and Guidance and prioritise for action accordingly. 'Red' and 'blue' areas in the Red-Amber-Green-Blue (RAGB) assessment for the Capability Audit identify shortfalls and surpluses. Some capability shortfalls will not merit immediate attention and therefore represent 'tolerable risk' in the current Planning Round - record these as such in the record of decisions and assumptions. Quantifying tolerable operational risk is a complex task and requires Military Judgement, significant User input and High Level Operation Analysis (HLOA) support.

Refer unresolved issues that are beyond the remit of the CPG / CMG up to the governance level above.

Financial & Commercial. Look at the availability of expenditure limits - RDEL and CDEL - year on year to identify shortfalls and opportunities by reshaping the Plan. The issued Direction and Guidance must be taken into account. It is possible that areas of strategic importance will attract new investment, whereas less important areas may have to rebalance their plan within previously allocated resource levels and CPGs / CMGs should plan Options accordingly. Consider the financial and commercial perspectives together, as the level of commitment year on year will help to identify the degree of planning flexibility available in any given year.

Industrial: The industrial perspective seeks to establish a mutually supporting relationship between the Defence Industrial Strategy (DIS) and the CMG and CPG Capability Areas. What does the plan do for DIS and what does DIS do for the plan? Are there any shortfalls and opportunities within industry – is there a minimum throughput required in sovereign industry? Have industry suggested any innovative solutions?

Research: Timely research will underpin the Capability Management Plan, especially in the later years where questions, as of yet unanswerable, will inform decisions. Review the available research in order to remove gaps - where affordable - and to assure the timely delivery of enabling work.

Capability Investigations

Capability Investigations are undertaken to identify generic options across all DLoDs, which could resolve capability shortfalls and exploit opportunities. Down-selection to a leading option and key alternatives is based on capability, affordability and, where appropriate, industrial considerations. Capability Planning Groups, Capability Management Groups, or the JCB may initiate Capability Investigations. In some instances, Capability Investigations may form the basis of a concept phase for a new equipment project. The Requirements and Acceptance process captures, analyses and tests the documented statement of the User's needs. Capability Investigations should be conducted with the best experts selected from across Defence and Industry as required.

THE CAPABILITY INVESTIGATION (CI) FILE

A Capability Investigation (CI) File is a virtual folder on the relevant Capability Management Group (CMG) or Capability Planning Group (CPG) virtual Team Site.

A Capability Investigation (CI) File: Provides an appropriate level of rigor, project management discipline, and documentation to a CI. Sets out the evidence and conclusions reached, and provides a record of the decisions made with their context. Enables audit and scrutiny, and could form the basis for future business cases. Allows third parties to review the work undertaken and safeguards against change of personnel. Provides a formal framework that stimulates thinking and drives a structured approach to CIs.

Saving all CI documentation, working papers, analysis and conclusions in the CI folder on the Team Site ensures:

- Shared access to CI information.
- Sponsor visibility of CI progress.
- Consistent structure and approach to CI work.
- An audit trail exists for decisions.
- Safe retention of CI data.

A CI File Comprises:

- Mobilisation, Governance and Control.
- The Conclusion.
- The Capability Investigation Data and Working Papers.
- Finance.
- Decisions, Assumptions and Provenance.

Endorse the CMP

This stage covers the prioritisation and resource allocation that allows the production of an endorsed CMP, which is affordable, stable, agile and realistic.

Decision Conferencing (using the Equity Software tool) helps to choose the best range of Options that maximise capability within financial limits.

During the biennial Planning Round, Options are drafted which provide opportunities for the Equipment Capability Customer (ECC) to rebalance the Equipment Procurement Plans (EPP) and Equipment Support Plans (ESP).

Decision Conferencing is necessary to identify and evaluate the savings Options to be "bought back" and the enhancement Options to activate, in order to return the programme to budget. Decision Conferencing provides clear advantages over a less structured informal approach:

- It achieves buy-in across a wide range of stakeholders (within the MOD unified customer).
- It provides a clear audit trail that:
- Captures all decisions.
- Records the reasoning behind scores.
- Provides robustness to subsequent challenge from the wider MOD.
- Provides a firm foundation for submission to HM Treasury.
- It provides the Joint Capability Board (JCB) with transparency of all Options across the whole of the ECC.

As a result of Stage 2 of the Planning Round it is assumed that all Options / Capability Management Measures are taken to move the programme below the control total baseline.

Decision Conferencing identifies:
- The savings Options that can be "bought back".
- The enhancement Options to be activated to return the programme to budget.

IMPORTANT TO DECISION CONFERENCING

- Decision Conferencing is a method of facilitation and so relies on strong facilitation skills to achieve an effective and efficient process.
- Decision Conferencing scores Options against criteria but does not challenge the criteria, so the criteria used for scoring benefits should be considered carefully.

Role of the Equity tool

The Equity tool supports the whole Decision Conferencing process.

The benefit criteria (three in the case of PR08), along with cost and descriptions for all relevant Options, are loaded into the system prior to the Decision Conferences by the Decision Conferencing "analyst".

During the Decision Conferences:
- The benefits of all individual Options are scored against the criteria and recorded in Equity.
- The Equity software, using economic theory, compares the benefits of all the Options against their respective costs giving a range of Value for Money indicators.
- The range of Options are then plotted on a graph that shows the best portfolio of Options for a given level of available financial resource.
- Numerous iterations of the prioritised "Order of Buy" (OOB) can be run during Decision Conferencing using Equity with the final output being a consensus decision on the stack of Options to be taken forward to the next level in the process.

Prioritising Options

A four stage approach for prioritising Options applies for PR08, with each stage focussing on a progressively higher level:

- At Capability Planning Group (CPG) level.
- Across CPGs to the Capability Management Group level.
- Across CMGs.
- At extended JCB level.

For each of the four levels an OOB is agreed, culminating in a proposal - including alternatives - being presented to the Policy Programme Steering Group (PPSG) and Defence Management Board (DMB).

THE CAPABILITY DELIVERY PROCESS

The next stage of Capability Management is concerned with Capability Delivery through the establishment of a pan-DLoD Programme Board, led by the Sponsor as SRO. This provides governance over the delivery of a programme up to the In Service Date, where responsibility is transferred to the User.

Capability Delivery takes the recommended option(s) and establishes the strategies and programme plans to enable capability delivery, describing how the cross DLoD option(s) will be delivered.

These define how the associated portfolio of cross DLoD change programmes and projects are managed. In the case of the Equipment and Support DLoDs this may drive changes to the supporting Through Life Management Plans (TLMP) or lead to a new project commencing.

The focus of these plans, which is a primary task of a Programme Board, is:

- Defining new project and programme boundaries and changes needed to existing projects and programmes across all DLoDs.

Capability Management: An Introduction | 31

- Identifying important internal dependencies between the plans and links to external plans.
- Managing top-level risks, issues and assumptions.

GOVERNANCE

The Governance of Capability Change Planning is achieved at 3 levels:

- The Joint Capabilities Board (JCB).
- The Directors of Equipment Capability (DECs) supported by Capability Management Groups (CMG).
- The Capability Planning Groups (CPG).

Joint Capabilities Board

The JCB is chaired by Deputy Chief of Defence Staff (Equipment Capability) (DCDS (EC)). The activities of the JCB are described in the Equipment Capability Customer section of the Acquisition Operating Framework (AOF).

The JCB members are:

- The Capability Managers
- Director General Equipment (DGE)
- Director General Science and Technology (DG(S&T)) - based in the Chief Scientific Advisor's (CSA) area.
- Key stakeholders - through the forum of the Extended JCB and Enhanced JCB - also support the JCB.

Directors of Equipment Capability

A Director of Equipment Capability (DEC) manages one or more Capability Areas on behalf of the JCB. Each DEC, supported by a stakeholder group - the Capability Management Group (CMG).

The CMG:

- Works with Director Equipment Plan (DEP) and Development Concepts and Doctrine Centre (DCDC)

/ Force Development to set capability priorities within its own area through a Capability Management Strategy.

- Details prioritised, risk-based capability opportunities and shortfalls and its strategy for exploiting or resolving them.
- Identifies and places capability goals on CPGs within and, where necessary, outside its own capability area.
- Conducts trades between CPGs within its own capability area.
- Commissions capability investigations.

Capability Planning Groups

Typically 2-3 CPGs represent each DEC, each addressing the capability delivered by a coherent force grouping on an enduring basis and across multiple DLoDs.

Led by the ECC, the CPG:

- Has members representing the User, DE&S, Central Representative, and Science Innovation Technology (SIT).
- Interprets the capability goals derived by the relevant DECs into efficient equipment and support plans that are coherent across lines of development.
- Records the status of the capability delivered by the CPG over time in a CMP, supported by the detail contained in the TLMP for each in-service and future equipment project, maintained by the relevant IPT.
- Reacts to changes in capability provision resulting from shortfalls across the DLoDs, threat change, policy direction or financial pressures.
- Considers and develops the best cross-DLoD solutions for Defence to meet these changes, identifying and exploiting opportunities as appropriate.

- Ensures industrial opportunities, threats and constraints are effectively incorporated into capability planning.
- Recommends or conducts trades within its own area, including preparation of Equipment Programme Measures (EPMs) and Options.
- Understands linkages and dependencies between DEC and CPG areas.
- Commissions Capability Investigations.

Programme Boards

The CPG establishes Programme Boards for portfolios of one or more pan DLoD projects, through which the Senior Responsible Owner (SRO) function is discharged.

The Programme Board:

- Manages the progress of individual or portfolios of projects through the acquisition cycle.
- Oversees requirement definition, the generation of Business Cases and acceptance in to service.

Capability Investigation

The JCB, DEC, or CPGs may initiate a Capability Investigation, supported by research and analysis.

A Capability Investigation:

- Focuses on a particular aspect of the capability programme.
- Explores opportunities and develop better strategies (e.g. moving towards an incremental acquisition approach).
- Responds to specific policy direction.

Other DLoD Governance Arrangements

Other governance arrangements for individual DLoDs include:

- *Personnel & Training:* Individual Service and Joint policies.
- *Concepts & Doctrine:* The 7-Step Concept to Capability process (owned by Development Concepts and Doctrine Centre).
- *Infrastructure:* TLBs through the Non-Equipment Investment Plan, managed by RP (Centre).

In addition to the formal DLoDs governance arrangements, implementation of the Defence Industrial Strategy is achieved through DE&S 2 Cluster Strategies.

CAPABILITY INTEGRATION

Capability Integration is the means by which Equipment Capability is made into useable Military Capability by the combined activity of all Defence Lines of Development (DLoD).

It involves planning the DLoD activities to meet the required level of Capability Integration, this may be at the lowest level within a platform to the highest level across international boundaries.

It is a critical part of meeting the User expectations and achieving the benefits identified within an individual project and programme business cases.

Responsibility for Capability Integration

The Sponsor has overall accountability for the delivery of Military Capability and will chair the relevant Programme or Portfolio Board.

The User takes the lead on Capability Integration. DE&S has responsibility for management of the equipment and logistics lines of development.

Capability Integration achieved

Capability Integration is achieved by identifying, planning and implementing the requirements for other DLoDs to achieve the necessary change in Military Capability.

The requirement for activity in the non-equipment DLoDs will be captured within the Capability Integration Products:

- project or programme Concept of Employment (CONEMP),
- or, post Main Gate, its Concept of Use (CONUSE).

These documents provide the context to support the User Requirement Document. Capability Integration activity should feature as part of the project and/or programme Through Life Management Plan (TLMP) and may be documented within a subordinate Capability Integration Plan.

All test evaluation and acceptance activity in each of the DLoDs must be captured within the project and/or programme integrated test evaluation and acceptance (ITEA) plan.

Levels of Capability Integration

Capability is integrated at different levels. In addition to activity at the project and platform level, there is a need to address the requirement for integration within and across environmental (Sea, Land and Air), Service and national boundaries.

The levels of integration set out below align with those in the Army User Handbook. They are intended to assist a structured approach to the management of often complex Capability Integration activity and to provide a common frame of reference across the MOD Unified Customer.

Capability Integration in Acquisition

A key stakeholder group should be established as early as possible to identify the full range of cross-Defence Lines of Development (DLOD) factors and constraints, inform the Concept phase work and selection of solution options to be pursued in Assessment phase.

As an integral member of both the relevant Capability Planning Group and the specific Programme Board, the Designated User will provide advice on the requirement priorities and co-ordinate the production of the CONEMP to support both Initial and Main Gates. Post Main Gate and with the solution defined, the Designated User will develop the CONUSE, drawing from the CONEMP and associated applied concept.

The coordinated input from all DLODs supports project acceptance through the development of an Integrated Test Evaluation Acceptance (ITEA) Plan.

To co-ordinate the activities of the CIWG, it may be appropriate to employ a Capability Integration Plan and a supporting Integrated Analysis and Experimentation Campaign Plan (IAECP); where employed these documents form part of the Through Life Management Plan (TLMP).

The Capability Integration Plan (CIP) does not have primacy over documents such as the IPT Project Responsibility Matrix (PRM), TLMP, or ITEAP, nor does it absolve either Sponsor or the IPT from their own responsibilities in respect of delivering and maintaining equipment capability and other aspects delivered by the contractor.

> apply existing concepts to CONEMP, for instance - TAPS or LAFS

2
Capability Management Strategy

A Capability Management Strategy (CMS) expresses how a Capability Management Group (CMG) develops its defined Capability Area in line with the Joint Capability Board's (JCB) stated direction and guidance, taking account of all Defence Lines of Development.

A CMG uses a CMS to issue direction, guidance and tasks that govern Capability Planning Groups (CPGs) in planning and delivering capabilities on behalf of the CMG. It guides and expresses the business and intent of a CMG in a standard and defined format.

The sum of all Capability Management Strategies within the Equipment Capability Customer (ECC) equates to the strategy of the Joint Capabilities Board and each CMS assures the JCB that its direction and guidance has been interpreted appropriately.

STRUCTURE FOR CAPABILITY MANAGEMENT STRATEGIES

The standard structure of a CMS ensures it is readily understood by:

- Members of the JCB.
- Stakeholders who attend multiple CMGs.

38 | Capability Management

- CPGs tasked to deliver a discreet output on behalf of the CMG.

Capability Management Plan

A Capability Management Plan (CMP) expresses how a Capability Planning Group (CPG) sets the strategic conditions for success within the group's defined Capability Area.

The plan must take into account:

- The direction provided from Capability Management Groups (CMG).
- The results of the analysis conducted during Through Life Capability Management (TLCM) Stages 1-4.
- Key recommendations from Capability Investigations (Stage 5).

A CMP is necessary in order to establish a single authoritative source of information that defines and guides the activities of a CPG in an auditable, transparent and consistent manner.

Virtual Team

Through Life Capability Management (TLCM) relies on the effective working of Capability Management Groups (CMGs) and Capability Planning Groups (GPGs). These groups are virtual teams with members from different MOD organisations.

A virtual team is made up from members of different MOD organisations who are located at various geographical sites. Most CMG and CPG work should be undertaken by their virtual teams out of committee with meetings only held when necessary.

Guidance on virtual environments is necessary to promote good working practices in support of virtual team working. Guidance on making Virtual Teams work is available which includes the behaviours needed to support TLCM.

The outcome of effective virtual team working is informed and efficient decision making. For this, the team needs to have access to relevant information and individual members need to be empowered to make decisions.

For effective virtual team working:
- Exploit team skills.
- Hold the team together.
- Use technology to simulate reality.

Recording Assumptions

Assumptions inform current and future stakeholders about the context for decisions. Every decision made in Capability Management Planning will be underpinned by a number of assumptions and these must be captured and supported by rigorous data where possible.

Capture pertinent assumptions in a Capability Planning Assumptions List (CPAL) and store the CPAL and decision log on the appropriate Capability Management Group (CMG) or Capability Planning Group (CPG) Team Site with restricted editing rights.

Nominate a CPAL manager for each CMG and CPG to drive the collection of assumptions and update the CPAL.

Construct a CPAL for each CMG and CPG and include assumptions based on:
- Policy, threat and finance.
- The capability perspective - including all Defence Lines of Development.
- The other 4 perspectives: financial, commercial, research and industrial.
- The interdependencies between CMGs and CPGs.

Assign an 'owner' for each assumption who is responsible for ensuring the ongoing validity of the assumption and for amending the CPAL to reflect any changes. When a Programme Board initiates a Through Life Management Plan, the CPAL manager is responsible for transferring all relevant

40 | *Capability Management*

assumptions to the Programme Board Master Data Assumption List (MDAL).

OPTIONS

An <u>Option can be a measure</u> - or set of measures - designed to enhance capability or save cost against the equipment or equipment support programme, and will have an impact on defence final outputs:

- <u>Enhancement Options</u> are designed to address a capability shortfall or exploit an opportunity to enhance capability.
- <u>Savings Options</u> are designed to remove cost or address an overprovision.
- There are examples of <u>composite Options</u> which have both enhancement and savings aspects.

Requirement to Write an Option

The Biennial Financial Planning Round places pressure on the Equipment Capability Customer (ECC):

To restore both the equipment and equipment support programme back to baseline ('<u>control total</u>').

To build in any new capability requirements from changes in Defence Planning Assumptions.

Savings Options and enhancement Options help to resolve this pressure.

Within Through Life Capability Manangement, Capability Investigations are used to identify potential Options to resolve capability shortfalls as well as exploit opportunities. Shortfalls are normally identified through a Capability Audit or Balance of Investment (BOI) study.

<u>A well worded Impact statement (IS) is essential to allow an Option to be considered properly.</u>

All Impact Statements <u>must be objective</u>, <u>clear</u> and <u>concise</u>, and be written in a manner appropriate for Ministers with all abbreviations spelt out.

[margin note: Now ABC – Annual Budget Cycle.]

QRPC – Quarterly Review Programme Costs.
QPRR – Quarterly Period Risk Review.

There is an 800 character limit and all Impact Statements are to start 'This Option would...'

The points to consider in the Statement include:

- Implications of the Option in the wider context of Defence Final Outputs.
- Implications across all Defence Lines of Development (DLoD).
- Implications for Industry and the Defence Industrial Strategy.
- Balance of Investment considerations.
- Absolutely compelling requirements – such as a legal responsibility to carry out a course of action.
- Options are raised using a spreadsheet pro-forma, completed by Director Equipment Capabilities (DEC) - or by Resource and Plans (RP) for S08 Options - in consultation with Capability Planning Group (CPG) members.
- Completing a pro-forma for an Option requires a clear understanding of the key underlying assumptions. These should be clearly documented within the pro-forma and all DLoDs must be reflected.

The following are attributes of a good Option:

- The Option focuses on the capability implications of the Option, that is, outcome not input.
- The Option clearly demonstrates an integrated and unified approach across:
- Capability Planning Groups within Capability Management Groups.
- Separate Capability Management Groups.
- All DLoDs – with documented evidence of stakeholder engagement and agreement.

The Option is written in a manner which clearly considers all 5 aspects of TLCM Stage 3:

- Capability
- Research and Development (R&D)
- Industrial
- Commercial
- Financial.

The Option clearly displays positive open language throughout. All descriptions contained within the Option are comprehensive, understandable and clear.

STRATEGIC LAYER

The Strategic layer is an ideal source for new users, providing an overview of how our business operates, and a reminder to all of us of what the 'big picture' looks like and where we fit in to it.

The Strategic layer:

- Defines Acquisition and the Acquisition community.
- Outlines how Acquisition works.
- Explains how Acquisition contributes to the Defence Vision.
- . Explains the context for the current improvements in Defence Acquisition.
- Explains the key themes that will guide further improvements.

ACQUISITION

Acquisition translates industrial capacity into effective military capability.

Acquisition is defined as:

"The activities of setting and managing requirements, negotiating and managing contracts, project and technology management, support and termination or disposal based on a through life approach to acquiring military capability."

The acquisition community is large and diverse, and is supported by Other Government Departments.

The acquisition community includes:
- The Sponsor Organisation (DCDS(EC)).
- The User who generates the Force elements.
- Project Teams who contract for equipment, infrastructure and services.
- Finance and Planning teams.
- Research and Development teams.
- Commercial teams.
- Technical Support and Challenge teams.
- All of the teams dedicated to supporting acquisition people and activities.
- All companies providing infrastructure, equipment and services to Defence.

THE DEFENCE VISION AND VALUES FOR ACQUISITION

The Defence Vision states the key principles which provide the basis of the Department's work:

We achieve this vision by working together on our core task to produce battle-winning people and equipment that are:
- Fit for the challenge of today.
- Ready for the tasks of tomorrow.
- Capable of building for the future.

We will base our future direction on:
- Providing strategy that matches new threats and instabilities.
- Maintaining flexible force structures.
- Reaching out into the wider world.
- Leading a high performing organisation.
- Investing in our people.

IMPROVE ACQUISITION

The future operational environment is highly unpredictable with new and more rapidly changing threats. Consequently, we need to be more agile and flexible in the way we deliver future military capability.

The pace of technological advance is increasing, yet new platforms and equipment will remain in service for longer periods. Consequently, we need to plan for, and enable, more frequent technology upgrades.

Reacting to the changes outlined will place a higher premium not only on our individual skills but also on our ability to work as a defence team. Consequently, we need to invest in the professional skills of our people, as well as make changes in delegations and rewards and recognition for meeting performance objectives and taking tough, risk-based decisions.

THEMES FOR IMPROVEMENT

The ultimate goal for change is to provide battle-winning capability for Defence and value for money for the taxpayer. To achieve this goal four themes have been established to describe how we continue to develop and strengthen our acquisition performance under the DACP and DIS.

The four themes are:

- Removing barriers to a collective ownership of acquisition and to a truly through-life approach. The key enablers are:
    - MOD Unified Customer (ECC, User, Defence Equipment and Support, Science Innovation and Technology, The Centre Representative.
    - Defence Equipment and Support (DE&S).
    - Planning Equipment and Support over the long term.
    - A more agile Research and Development programme that supports technology pull through.

- Better decision making based on a more comprehensive approach to Capability Management. The key enablers are:
  - A unified Capability Change Planning process.
  - A stronger focus on through-life management of costs across all DLoDs.
  - Closer involvement of the User.
- Developing a more effective relationship with Industry. The key enablers, delivered through the Defence Commercial Function (DCF) are:
  - Commercial management of our portfolio of projects.
  - Building and maintaining strategic relations with suppliers.
  - Applying consistent commercial approaches matched to the market.
  - Developing e-business capability.
  - Evolving the DIS.
- Creating the environment for high performing people and teams to thrive. The key enablers are:
  - More sustained and structured investment in skills development.
  - Improved reward and recognition.
  - Career development in acquisition.
  - Consistent constructive behaviours (DvfA).

DEVELOPING THROUGH LIFE CAPABILITY MANAGEMENT

Through Life Capability Management includes capability planning and capability delivery. The MOD's approach to capability delivery is being developed, recognising that complex changes in capability require proactive programme management.

These programmes will be overseen by programme boards chaired at a senior level, managing the delivery of a set of interdependent projects, and ensuring we remain focused on the required outcome and military benefits.

Appropriate Acquisition Approaches (A3) will increase the agility in acquisition through the increased use of incremental capability enhancements and modified off-the-shelf (MOTS)/ commercial off-the-shelf (COTS) solutions. This increased agility will improve our responsiveness to changing requirements and capability needs.

Earlier acquisition strategy selection lays the foundation for good decision making through life. The Acquisition Strategy Development Guide will assist in selecting the most appropriate acquisition strategy.

The 'Fit for Business' programme will transform the commercial function across the MOD. It will deliver a commercial function with the right people, skills, policies and tools to provide innovative, flexible solutions to the Front Line through life. To achieve this, professionalism and skills in the Defence Commercial community are being developed and the commercial guidance and tools across MOD are being improved and simplified.

The 'Fit for Business' programme embeds commercial considerations across all aspects of acquisition from policy making, through capability planning, to delivery.

It will deliver a commercial function with the right people, skills, policies and tools to provide innovative, flexible solutions to the Front Line through life. To achieve this, professionalism and skills in the Defence Commercial community are being developed and the commercial guidance and tools across MOD are being improved and simplified.

The 'Fit for Business' programme embeds commercial considerations across all aspects of acquisition from policy making, through capability planning, to delivery.

DEPARTMENTAL PLANNING

Departmental Planning aims to deliver a balanced and coherent Defence Programme within the budget allocated to the MOD by HM Treasury:

- The MOD planning staffs generate Resource Control Totals (RCTs) for the User and ECC, and programme Operating Costs for DE&S.
- The ECC programmes the costs of new equipment and associated support in years 1-10 and for supporting in-service equipment in years 5-10.
- The User programmes the costs of supporting in-service equipment in years 1-4.
- The 10-year Equipment and Support (E&S) Plan brings these component parts together as a single programme.
- The E&S Plan is based on a single data set held at Integrated Project Team (IPT) level, used as required to support decision making across the Acquisition Community.

Through Life Capability Management

Through Life Capability Management (Capability Management) translates the requirements of Defence policy into an approved programme that delivers the required capabilities, through-life, across all Defence Lines of Development (DLoDs).

Capability Management provides a new approach to the way in which the Unified Customer:

- Conducts Capability Management planning activities to deliver new programmes.
- Provides governance for the delivery of new programmes.

Key elements of a Capability Management approach are:

- Examining a wider range of options that consider:
  - New equipment.
  - Upgrade of in-service equipment.
  - Opportunities across all DLoDs.

- Taking a longer term view of capability in the context of:
  - Defence policy.
  - Industrial strategy.
  - Research and development opportunities.
  - Commercial constraints and opportunities.
  - Financial pressures.

There are two integral parts of Capability Management:
- Capability Change Planning
- Capability Delivery

Capability Change Planning

Capability Change Planning identifies the changes required across all DLoDs to provide required future military capability, at the right time and within resource constraints.

The ECC leads the Capability Change Planning process, responding to central policy guidance and resource controls.

The ECC develops options to change military capability in response to:
- Changing threat.
- Capability excess or shortfall.
- Policy priorities.
- Resource constraints.
- Out of service or obsolescence events.
- Industrial constraint or opportunity.

The Directors of Equipment Capability (DECs) manage this effort through a Capability Management Group (CMG). The CMG examines trades across their area of responsibility and manages important cross-DEC opportunities and constraints. Beneath the DECs, Capability Planning Groups (CPG) bring the five Unified Customer stakeholders together to manage a particular capability area as subject matter experts.

The output of the Capability Change Planning process is an endorsed option that changes the current plan.

Capability Delivery

Capability Delivery transforms the pan-DLoDs Capability Change Plans into the required capabilities at the Front Line. The endorsed option may lead to the establishment of a Programme Board, providing the pan-DLoDs governance over the delivery of the change programme up to acceptance by the User at In Service Date.

Once a system or equipment is in service, the Capability Delivery aspects of Capability Management are managed through an Availability Working Group, led by the User up to Disposal.

THE MOD UNIFIED CUSTOMER

The primary role of the MOD Unified Customer is to translate industrial capacity into effective military capability, joining equipment and support.

The Unified Customer brings together five principal participants to share ownership of capability-based decisions.

Principal Participants

The five principal participants within the Unified Customer are:

- The Equipment Capability Customer (ECC) – the Sponsor for the Unified Customer.
- The User.
- Defence Equipment & Support.
- Science Innovation Technology.
- The Central Representatives (drawn from MOD Head Office).

Role of Research and Development

Research and Development (R&D) are key enabling functions throughout Acquisition. Much of R&D is

50 | Capability Management

fundamentally creative and has the important purpose of expanding the knowledge and range of options available to Acquisition and more widely to Defence.

R&D includes:

- Horizon scanning and technology watch to identify important emerging technologies.
- Exploration of promising technologies for Defence.
- Invention of new technologies and approaches.
- Nurturing technical skills and expertise within the supply base.
- Development of data sets and models to support planning and policy decision making, including strategic technologies and advice to Ministers.

Research Outputs

Research within MOD is undertaken and delivered in three new outputs:

- Enabling Research Output:
  - Provides access to high quality scientific and technical advice across all DLoDs.
- Capability Planning and Management:
  - Generates capability options and trade space to support Capability Change Planning.
- Technology Development Output:
  - Develops and matures technology options than can be exploited by DE&S projects.

The rationalisation of Research Outputs will enable a more progressive and responsive transfer of Research into technology development and exploitation throughout acquisition.

There are a number of tools available to assist in delivering Research Outputs, one of which is Modeling, Simulation and Synthetic Environments MS&SE.

Capability Management Strategy | 51

Through Life Management (TLM) is the philosophy that brings together the behaviours, systems, processes and tools to deliver and manage projects through the acquisition lifecycle.

The approach to TLM has a number of easily identifiable characteristics when applied to a project:

- Whole life outlook
- Whole life system outlook
- Whole Life Costs
- Involvement of Stakeholders
- Through Life Management Plan
- Better informed decision making
- IPT and stakeholder processes

The application of TLM improves the management of projects and programmes within the MOD by forcing individuals and teams to consider the long term implications and requirements of the capabilities they were procuring to support the Front Line.

Integrated Project Teams must use the Through Life Management Plan (TLMP) as the primary means to effect Project and Programme Management (PPM) across all DLoDs as the project develops.

The essential elements of an effective TLMP are:

- TLMP Executive Summary.
- Defined Requirements.
- Realistic plans and schedules.
- Realistic Whole Life Costs across all DLoDs.
- Management Tools - including Risk Register and Earned Value Management (EVM).
- Management Strategies.

Through Life Management (TLM) remains at the heart of managing project and programme delivery throughout the life cycle and across all Defence Lines of Development (DLoDs).

THE ACQUISITION LIFE CYCLE

The acquisition life cycle remains the key roadmap for delivering projects effectively and efficiently on a through life basis.

The typical acquisition life cycles are:

- Traditional Sequential Acquisition (e.g. CADMID, CADMIT)
- Incremental Acquisition
- Evolutionary Acquisition
- Hybrid Acquisition

The Traditional Sequential approach is the most common. Future updates or upgrades require separate acquisitions as the complete response to a requirement is planned to be achieved at the point of Full Operating Capability.

An incremental approach delivers systems against requirements step-by-step. A series of capability enhancements are planned to enhance an initial level of capability.

An evolutionary approach to acquisition enables experiences of the development and operation of a previous version of a system, advances in technology and emergent requirements to inform the development of subsequent versions.

A 'hybrid' approach may be feasible, employing a combination of approaches. For example, it maybe decided that a Traditional Sequential approach is appropriate for the base platform, but that an evolutionary approach is more applicable to the acquisition of certain sub-elements.

Selection of the most appropriate acquisition lifecycle strategy is a key factor to determining the long term success of a military capability and providing the required capability to the user when it is needed.

Project Initiation

The ECC applies TLCM principles to translate Defence Policy into an approved programme and initiates new projects based on:

Capability Management Strategy | 53

- An approved equipment solution defined in the CMP.
- A Single Statement of User Need and candidate Key User Requirements (KURs).
- An allocated resource defined in the Equipment and Support (E&S) Plan.
- Established requirements with the User and relevant non-equipment DLoD owners.
- Programmed non E&S activities.

Following project initiation, the relevant DE&S 2 Cluster Director General (DG) or equivalent Project Board for non-equipment project owners becomes accountable for project delivery assurance.

Decision Points

The early stages of a project Lifecycle contains two major decision points as defined in the Approvals and Scrutiny process – Initial Gate and Main Gate.

Sponsors and project teams are required to develop a Business Case at both of these stages justifying the project proceeding to the next stage. Prior to approval no manufacture or service contracts can be signed.

The Early Decision Point

Initial Gate remains the first approval point in the life cycle, which occurs before any assessment work is undertaken and is considered to be a relatively 'low hurdle'.

Projects will return to the appropriate Approval Authority if agreed targets are breached.

The Key Decision Point

Main Gate occurs after the assessment work has been undertaken and is the major decision point at which the solution and 'not to exceed figures' are approved.

Main Gate approval:
- Remains the key investment decision point for Projects, where the risks to successful delivery (e.g. financial, technical, industrial, Defence Lines of Development (DLoDs)) are considered against the benefit of the proposed solution in meeting an endorsed Defence requirement.
- Sets targets against which the acquisition performance of the project is assessed and contains defined trade boundaries for the project – targets are only established at Main Gate, when all the risks are sufficiently understood.
- Considers Whole Life Costs across all DLoDs – crucially, it addresses the support solution as well as the equipment procurement.
- Will require an assurance by the User (generally the Front Line Command) that the proposal can be integrated across DLoDs and with existing systems to deliver an effective military capability from In Service Date.

The Approving Authorities will increasingly expect to see at the Decision Points that a wider range of Acquisition Lifecycle Strategies e.g. incremental, partnership, have been considered.

Acceptance

The Integrated Test, Evaluation and Acceptance Plan (ITEAP) remains the foundation for defining and managing delivery of the overall military capability established for the project.

In terms of the ITEAP and Acceptance Criteria:
- The Requirement Manager remains accountable for this work.
- The DEC (ECC) remains responsible for gathering evidence for acceptance across all DLoDs, and for

accepting equipment solutions against the endorsed requirements.
- The User remains responsible for declaring In Service Date (ISD) against the agreed criteria based on a formal recommendation by the DEC.

The transfer of programming responsibility from the Equipment Capability Customer (ECC) to the User must be seamless. This requires consideration of the E&S project as a singular, through-life activity with full visibility and shared ownership by both the User and the ECC as the 10-year planning period passes.

The single project data set and Through Life Management Plans (TLMP) are used to support the DE&S Chiefs of Materiel (CofMs) in their role to translate capability needs identified by the ECC into the operational readiness and sustainability needs of the User.

The Assistant Chief of Defence Staff (Logistics Operations) – ACDS(Log Ops) - continues to provide logistics input to Defence commitments planning.

The Director General Supply Chain continues to be responsible for optimising the performance of the Defence Supply Chain, ensuring that it is aligned to User priorities and delivers Military effectiveness and logistics efficiency.

The User retains access to those directly responsible within the DE&S for commodity provision, services and logistic supply chain management.

DISPOSAL

Disposal may be the final element of the acquisition lifecycle but the implications of the disposal of MOD assets must be considered at all stages in the acquisition lifecycle.

Advice and guidance given at the Concept stage and included in Through Life Management Plans (TLMP) will assist design and development planning, so as to avoid for example the problems of hazardous waste, or in the

56 | Capability Management

identification and management of such hazards in the current environmentally aware climate.

The Disposals Services Authority (DSA) is responsible for all aspects of disposals policy and activity undertaken by the MOD. The DSA is the MOD's primary disposal service provider managing the current Marketing Agreement Contracts.

The DSA is responsible for the Government-to-Government sales, auctions, tender and private treaty sales of surplus equipment and material declared to them for disposal.

Projects must take the elements detailed below into account in their disposal plans:

- Re-deployment (can the equipment be used for training/instructional use, as a Heritage asset for transfer to Service museum, for spares recovery or as a Gate Guardian).
- Reclamation, recycling, re-manufacture, buy-back and part exchange (i.e. is there a possible alternative use as opposed to disposal?).
- Sale(the Project Team may know of potential customers that could be advised to the DSA).
- Waste disposal and disposal of recovered material by sale or scrap.
- Disposal at cost to MOD (we may have to pay for some materials to be disposed of and any such cost must be identified and funded).
- Influence equipment design throughout its maturity to reduce disposal costs.

PERFORMANCE MANAGEMENT

The purpose of Acquisition performance management is to support the overall vision of providing battle-winning capability for Defence and Value for Money for the Taxpayer.

Performance is assessed via the Acquisition Performance Framework with the following four perspectives:

1. *Output:* Our capability is highly responsive to operations and Departmental objectives and is underpinned by more realistic and flexible capability planning.
2. *People:* Our people have the 'skill and will' to deliver, are employed to best effect, are encouraged to develop and improve and demonstrate our core values and behaviours.
3. *Process:* Our through life acquisition processes are agile, efficient, consistently applied and continuously improving.
4. *Industry:* Our relationship with industry is transformed and we build a reputation for delivery.

The purpose of this framework is to provide a set of performance metrics which are intended to allow management to address systemic acquisition issues and focus on the implementation of Through Life Capability Management. These higher level metrics are aimed at the overall system and complement those being used to monitor constituent parts of the Acquisition System.

Performance metrics from a range of stakeholders across the Acquisition System are collated and are reported to the Defence Acquisition Change Programme (DACP) Acquisition Group, chaired by PUS, on a quarterly basis. This performance management regime is continually developing, to reflect improvements in the acquisition system.

The Importance of MOD's Relationship With industry

An effective and efficient relationship with Industry is essential throughout acquisition as highlighted in the Defence Industrial Strategy. The Defence Commercial Director (DCD) provides the framework for commercial operations across MOD.

The DCD supports Acquisition by:

- Applying Portfolio Management to ensure decisions are:
  - Fully informed by industry strategy and commercial relationships as well as cost (both equipment and support).
  - Joined-up across MOD.
- Developing and maintaining effective strategic relations with industry that are:
  - Focused, appropriately formed by scale and consistent at all levels.
- Applying standard Commercial Approaches that are:
  - Open, robust and consistent and deliver through life capability at best long-term value for money.
- Applying a standard Procurement Process:
  - A common framework for procurement across MOD.
- Ensuring e-business capability to enable:
  - Increased efficiency
  - Closer and more flexible working with industry
- Evolving the DIS and ensuring it remains relevant to changing business needs of MOD and Industry.

The Importance of High Performing People and Teams

It is through our Acquisition People and teams that we will:

- Embed a through life approach to acquisition.
- Achieve a better and more open relationship with industry.
- Improve our ability to deliver military capability.
- Give the taxpayer better value for money.

Previous reforms in acquisition have focused on changes to organisation and process but have lacked sufficiently sustained commitment to develop the required behaviours, culture and professionalism among our staff.

Behavioural and Cultural Change

We have recognised that behaviour and culture are central to creating a high performing acquisition organisation, as is having skilled and professional staff where and when they are needed by the acquisition business. We also recognise that Human Resources (HR) processes are important in ensuring that staff are better motivated, rewarded and recognised for demonstrating improved acquisition performance.

The MOD is investing in behavioural change and the recruitment or development of staff with the professional skills necessary for acquisition roles. The MOD is making changes to HR processes or delegations to ensure the acquisition business is able to deliver the improved capability required by our Armed Forces.

People in acquisition must demonstrate the Defence Values for Acquisition and they will be accountable for the difficult decisions they make, but they will be rewarded appropriately.

Development of Skills

The acquisition community is large, and the range and depth of skills and knowledge needed is diverse. People working in acquisition will be encouraged to develop a range of skills through increased practical experience and professional qualifications.

Increasing skills will facilitate flexible resourcing and enable the deployment of our people to best effect. Flexible resourcing is being piloted in the DE&S to enable us to allocate scarce and valuable resources to the right team at the right time.

SUSTAINABLE DEVELOPMENT

MOD is fully committed to supporting the UK Government Sustainable Development (SD) Strategy. All MOD programmes and projects must consider the environmental, social and economic effects of their operations as set out in JSP 418 - the Sustainable Development and Environmental Manual.

The MOD published its Sustainable Development Action Plan which commits the Department to:

- Embedding SD principles into our relationships with suppliers.
- Ensuring all new contracts meet the Government's minimum environmental standards.
- Reflect SD principles in the DIS.
- Agree a 4 year MOD / Industry action plan on sustainable development.
- Meeting the Government estates sustainable operations targets on:
  — Reducing carbon emissions
  — Reducing waste
  — Reducing water consumption
  — Increasing energy efficiency

DCD is the MOD sustainable procurement champion and chairs the Sustainable Procurement (SP) Board with representatives from DE&S, DE and Directorate Safety & Claims (DS&C).

ACQUISITION ASSURANCE

Internal audit assesses risk, with the Defence Audit Committee (DAC) assessing the overall Departmental risk.

The DAC audits Departmental acquisition-wide risks. The DAC findings are also considered and addressed by individual acquisition organisations.

Assurance of projects and programmes is also undertaken via Acquisition organisations' own processes, for example DE&S' Director General Business Review of projects. The major projects and programmes are scrutinised separately by the IAB.

External Assurance

The National Audit Office (NAO) provides external assurance for acquisition, directed by Parliament. The NAO also publishes the annual Major Projects Report (MPR).

To improve the utility of the MPR, the Department, in conjunction with NAO, is developing the report to ensure it is aligned with the evolving pan-acquisition performance regime.

Other Parliamentary procedures that examine acquisition are:

- Parliamentary Questions.
- House of Commons Defence Committee.
- Public Accounts Committee.

The Office of Government Commerce (OGC) also provides assurance at the programme and project level through OGC Gateway Reviews.

LEARNING FROM EXPERIENCE

Learning from Experience (LFE) is a through life process which enables Organisational Learning by:

- Replicating successes.
- Avoiding mistakes.
- Publicising and promoting good practice.
- Keeping policy, processes and guidance up to date and reflecting good practice.

Learning From Experience is closely linked to but is distinct from Project Evaluation (formerly known as Post Project Evaluation). LFE facilitates organisational learning whilst project evaluation assesses how the outcome of a project accords with the initial investment appraisal.

The Defence Industrial Strategy (DIS) identifies LFE as one of the key drivers of the business – "Central to this strategy is the [Organisations'] ability to transform the knowledge necessary for optimised decision making."

DIS also states that the knowledge within the Organisation should - "be managed, shared and re-used across applications, enterprise and community boundaries much more easily."

LFE is recognised as a key business process, ensuring that the project planning process takes account of LFE throughout the project lifecycle. The application of LFE will aid in anticipating risks, issues and will also increase the probability of future success.

DEFENCE LINES OF DEVELOPMENT

The Defence Lines of Development (DLoDs) are described below.

Training

The provision of the means to practise, develop and validate, within constraints, the practical application of a common military doctrine to deliver a military capability.

Equipment

The provision of military platforms, systems and weapons, (expendable and non-expendable, including updates to legacy systems) needed to outfit/equip an individual, group or organisation.

Personnel

The timely provision of sufficient, capable and motivated personnel to deliver Defence outputs, now and in the future.

Information

The provision of a coherent development of data, information and knowledge requirements for capabilities and all processes designed to gather and handle data, information and knowledge. Data is defined as raw facts, without inherent meaning, used by humans and systems. Information is defined as data placed in context. Knowledge is Information applied to a particular situation.

Concepts and Doctrine

A Concept is an expression of the capabilities that are likely to be used to accomplish an activity in the future. Doctrine is an expression of the principles by which military forces guide their actions and is a codification of how activity is conducted today. It is authoritative, but requires judgement in application.

Organisation

Relates to the operational and non-operational organisational relationships of people. It typically includes military force structures, MOD civilian organisational structures and Defence contractors providing support.

Infrastructure

The acquisition, development, management and disposal of all fixed, permanent buildings and structures, land, utilities and facility management services (both Hard & Soft facility management (FM)) in support of Defence capabilities. It includes estate development and structures that support military and civilian personnel.

Logistics

The science of planning and carrying out the operational movement and maintenance of forces. In its most comprehensive sense, it relates to the aspects of military operations which deal with; the design and development, acquisition, storage, transport, distribution, maintenance, evacuation and disposition of materiel; the transport of personnel; the acquisition, construction, maintenance, operation, and disposition of facilities; the acquisition or furnishing of services, medical and health service support.

Interoperability (Overarching Theme)

In addition to the DLoDs, Interoperability is included as an overarching theme that must be considered when any DLoDis being addressed.

The ability of UK Forces and, when appropriate, forces of partner and other nations to train, exercise and operate effectively together in the execution of assigned missions and tasks.

In the context of DLoDs, Interoperability also covers interaction between Services, UK Defence capabilities, Other Government Departments and the civil aspects of interoperability, including compatibility with Civil Regulations.

Interoperability is used in the literal sense and is not a compromise lying somewhere between integration and de-confliction.

THE AOF OPERATIONAL LAYER

The AOF has three layers, each serving a specific purpose with varying degrees of detail.

The Operational layer provides detail on:

- Our organisational structure, roles and responsibilities.
- How we manage and develop our people.
- The information, guidance and instruction that sets out how we conduct acquisition business.

The Operational layer is an important resource for the acquisition community. Its purpose is to provide a 'check list' of key principles and processes, including those that are mandated, across the major elements of acquisition business.

ACQUISITION ORGANISATION

The Head Office is responsible for:

- Leading the Defence contribution to the development of the Government's foreign and security policy and wider government objectives.
- Translating government objectives into departmental policy.

- Planning of defence capability needed to deliver departmental policy.

Head Office has four main roles:

- Advising Government on Defence by:
  - Advising Ministers (and other government departments) on the Defence contribution to Government policy.
  - Supporting Ministers in discharging their Parliamentary accountability for the Armed Forces and the Ministry of Defence.
- Making Policy and setting Departmental Strategy by defining:
  - Defence policy, in particular the military capability and other Defence objectives which meet the Government's policy aims and match the resources available for defence.
  - Policy for the management of the Armed Forces in order to maximise their fighting effectiveness, efficiency and morale.
  - Strategic direction of military operations.
- Planning and resource allocation by:
  - Translating Defence objectives into a departmental programme matching available resources to Top Level Budgets (TLBs) and Agencies.
- Management of Defence by:
  - Managing delivery of planned objectives by monitoring performance and expenditure of TLBs and Agencies.
  - Highest level management of military activity including the operation of crisis management support to Government.
  - Defining the corporate framework for Defence that:

- Meets legislative requirements, including those as an employer.
- Drives continuous improvement by setting and upholding defence-wide standards and processes.

THE STRUCTURE OF HEAD OFFICE

The Head Office is organised into a number of key areas:

- *Director General Strategy (DG Strategy):* Responsible for leading the Defence contribution to cross-Whitehall strategic planning, supporting the Defence Board in its development of strategic guidance and its delivery of the Defence corporate strategy. Leading the process of producing a Defence programme for agreement and Defence Spending Review negotiations including cross cutting Public Service Agreements.
- *The Director General Security Policy (DG Sec Pol):* Responsible for the formulation of strategic defence and security policy, both long and short-term.
- *The Deputy Chief of the Defence Staff (Commitments) (DCDS(C)):* Responsible for planning the actual or potential commitment of British forces to crises, operations and exercises. DCDS(C) and DG Sec Pol effectively work together leading the Policy and Commitments staff.
- *Finance Director:* Responsible for all aspects of the MOD's financial management, including Resource Accounting and Budgeting (RAB), cost control and matters of Parliamentary financial accountability and propriety.
- *Deputy Chief of Defence Staff (Equipment Capabilities) (DCDS(EC)):* Responsible for constructing a balanced, coherent Equipment and Support Plan and seeking approval for individual equipment projects.

- *Science and Technology Director:* Supports the Chief Scientific Adviser and provides scientific advice, including technical scrutiny of equipment projects.
- *Deputy Chief of Defence Staff (Personnel):* The principal adviser on Service personnel policy and reserve forces matters, including training.
- *Personnel Director:* Heads the corporate services and civilian personnel area.
- *Defence Commercial Director:* Leads on shaping the MOD's relationship with industry and future strategic commercial relationships, playing vital role in implementing Defence Industrial Strategy

Equipment Capability Customer

The role of DCDS(EC) is to decide what capabilities our forces need and work alongside the supplier (the DE&S) to deliver the requisite equipment or systems.

DCDS(EC) chairs a Joint Capabilities Board, which makes high-level balance of investment decisions within and across the organisation's three capability areas.

The three capability areas are:
- Battlefield Manoeuvre
- Information Superiority
- Precision Attack

Policy and Commitments

The Policy and Commitments staff, under DCDS(C) and the Policy Director, are responsible for:
- Formulating national defence and international security policy.
- Providing strategic operational advice to Ministers.
- Managing bi-lateral defence relations and defence diplomacy.

- Formulating campaign plans and strategic military directions for operations.

The Governance of Head Office

The Defence Council is the senior Departmental committee.

The Defence Council is chaired by the Secretary of State and comprises:

- The other Ministers.
- The Permanent Under Secretary.
- The Chief of Defence Staff.
- Senior Service officers and senior officials who head the Armed Forces.
- MOD's major corporate functions.

It provides the formal legal basis for the conduct of defence in the UK through a range of powers vested in it by statute and Letters Patent.

The Permanent Under Secretary chairs the Defence Management Board (DMB) which is the highest non-ministerial committee in the MOD. The DMB is the main corporate board of the MOD, providing senior level leadership and strategic management of Defence. Its role is to deliver the Defence Aim set out in the Public Service Agreement and it owns the Defence Vision.

The DMB is made up of:

- The non-Ministerial members of the Defence Council.
- The Finance Director.
- External, independent non-executive members.

A number of key corporate Head Office committees support the Board, in particular:

- *Investment Approvals Board:* Responsible for the approval of all investment projects.

- *Defence Audit Committee:* Responsible for ensuring corporate governance requirements are met, advising on the adequacy of internal controls and effective risk management.
- *Policy and Programmes Steering Group:* Provides guidance to the Defence Management Board on major balance of investment issues, the capability implications of significant changes in resources or policy and identifies coherent capability and policy options for consideration in the planning process.
- *Defence Estates Committee:* oversees the development and implementation of policy for Defence Estates.
- *Chiefs of Staff Committee:* Chaired by the Chief of Defence Staff, it is the main forum in which the collective military advice of the Chiefs is obtained on operational issues.

EQUIPMENT CAPABILITY CUSTOMER

Purpose and Role

The Equipment Capability Customer (ECC) is responsible for leading the Capability Change Planning Process and for identifying the equipment and support requirements to optimise the UK's Defence capability within allocated resources. In doing so, the ECC acts as the Sponsor for new and enhanced equipment and support programmes.

In order to fulfil its strategic purpose the ECC discharges the following roles.

Capability Change Planning

The ECC:
- Identifies the capability required to meet the UK's Defence objectives, working to the direction set by Defence Planning Assumptions, Defence Industrial Strategy and the Policy and Programmes Steering Group (PPSG).

- Directs the decision support activities necessary to underpin capability change planning (e.g. Capability Management Strategy, Capability Audit, supporting research and operational analysis).
- Sets prioritised goals for the underpinning Research Programme and uses Science and Technology (S&T) input as an integral part of capability change planning.
- Ensures industrial opportunities, threats and constraints are effectively incorporated into capability change planning.

Programming

The ECC:

- Operates as the decider in providing new equipment and equipment support on behalf of MOD, leading the MOD unified customer team, advised and supported by the User and Defence Equipment and Support (DE&S).
- Produces an ECC Plan, comprising new equipment and upgrades and their support (including initial spares) over years 1-10, and support to all in-service equipment over years 5-10, noting that:
    - Support funding comprises equipment upkeep, update, sustainability and disposal costs.
    - DEC CCII will additionally programme years 1-4 for in-service equipment delivered by DCSA IPTs which support multiple customers.

Delivering Programmes

The ECC:

- Provides Directors Equipment Capability (DECs) to act as Programme Sponsors of new and enhanced equipment programmes, carrying out the duties of

Senior Responsible Owner (SRO) until the delivery of an agreed and coherent combination of Defence Lines of Development (DLoDs) to the User for integration at In-Service Date (ISD).
- The Joint Capabilities Board (JCB) leads the ECC.
- The JCB provides strategic leadership and direction in order to deliver a balanced, coherent and affordable ECC Plan to meet MOD policy requirements.

Beneath the JCB, DECs are responsible for discrete capability areas and define capability requirements, identifying equipment-based options that are coherent across all DLoDs. The DECs ensure that capability change planning is effectively conducted.

There are four other key 1 star areas within the ECC:
- Director Equipment Plan.
- Director of Capability and Resource Scrutiny.
- Director of Analysis, Experimentation and Simulation.
- Director Concepts and Technology.

The ten core functions of a Director of Equipment Capability are:
- Capability Planning.
- Capability Investigations.
- Programming.
- Programme Management.
- Team Management and Development.
- Administration.
- Communication and Stakeholder Engagement.
- Research.
- Requirements Management.
- Sector Leadership.

GOVERNANCE OF THE EQUIPMENT CAPABILITY CUSTOMER

The Deputy Chief of Defence Staff (Equipment Capability) (DCDS (EC)) chairs the Joint Capabilities Board (JCB) which delivers the governance of ECC activities.

The JCB is supported by:

- Three Capability Managers:
  - Precision Attack
  - Battlefield Manoeuvre
  - Information Superiority.
- Director General Equipment (DGE)
- Director General Science and Technology (DG(S&T)).

The JCB formally interacts with the wider Defence community through the forum of the Extended JCB and Enhanced JCB.

Functions of the Joint Capabilities Board:

- Produces a Capability Change Plan to manage the high-level delivery of capability.
- Provides direction and guidance to DECs, derived from Defence Planning Assumptions and Future Capabilities Requirements, on the formulation of the ECC Plan.
- Identifies linkages and dependencies between DEC Capability Areas and makes cross-DEC Balance of Investment (BoI) decisions.
- Allocates the resources required (including manpower, skills and finance) to enable the organisation to deliver its key objectives.
- Manages ECC performance, particularly the delivery of key objectives and targets.
- Provides the ECC's corporate focus for communication with external stakeholders including,

specifically, the DE&S, Industry and the User and SIT communities.

JCB Membership

At certain decision / intervention points through the Department's Planning process, the JCB will invite additional non-executive members, to represent their organisations at an ECC board meeting.

Meeting Types

The JCBf is DCDS (EC)'s formal monthly Board meeting where matters affecting the ECC at the strategic level are considered i.e.:

- Through life capability management.
- The delivery of the ECC's outputs.

The agenda will generally be structured around the JCB's strategic objectives:

- Effective planning and investment.
- Identifying and managing risk.
- Stakeholder engagement.
- Effective leadership.

The JCB's Campaign Plan review will form a standing agenda item whilst all other agenda items must be supported with a clear objective.

A 6 month forward programme covering all JCBf meetings will be maintained on the ECC Portal.

The records of decisions from JCBfmeetings will be published to DECs and available to all staff through the ECC Portal.

JCB (Informal)

- The JCBi allows the JCB to meet weekly, but on a less formal basis.

- The JCBi will monitor performance and receive much of the routine briefing / input associated with delivering the ECC's key outputs.
- At each JCBi one DEC will attend part of the meeting to discuss matters affecting his Capability Area / CMG / CPGs. This ensures that the JCB sees each DEC on a quarterly basis.
- A 3 month forward programme covering JCBi meetings will be maintained on the ECC Portal.
- A record of decisions and action grid will be maintained for all JCBi meetings.

JCB (Out of Committee)

The JCBo reduces the amount of committee time spent on reviewing non-contentious routine business and is an on-going activity.

DCDS (EC)-AMA maintains a tracking grid to record all documents on JCB circulation and members comments. Documents will be considered at the next JCBi if out of committee comments deem it necessary.

Out of Committee (OOC) documents must be forwarded to DCDS (EC)-AMA for distribution to JCB members. Each request must be endorsed at Director level and explicitly state:

- Desired response date (2 weeks is considered the norm).
- What previous groups have considered the document / circulation completed.

The Enhanced JCB

The EJCB brings together the key components of the MOD Unified Customer to enable collegiate strategic decision-making regarding the Equipment and Support Plan (E&SP), Industrial engagement and delivery of capability to the front line.

The EJCB will meet at key decision points during the planning round, DEP staff will lead on the preparation of the agenda / pre-briefing for planning round items.

Membership:
- JCB (Sponsor)
- 3 x DE&S CofM (Supplier)
- 3 x FLC + PJHQ (User)
- 3 x Assistant Chiefs (User)
- ACDS(RP)
- DG(RP)

The XJCB briefs and informs the wider Defence stakeholder environment on strategic issues regarding the E&SP, including savings and enhancement measures.

Membership: The XJCB includes a wide range of stakeholders from across "Defence".

PERFORMANCE MANAGEMENT

As a result of the Defence Acquisition Change Programme, new targets have been developed for managing acquisition performance.

The ECC is responsible for reporting against an element of the Defence Acquisition Performance Framework 'Output' perspective, which is based on the effectiveness of capability change planning and the balance between stability and agility in the equipment programme.

DEFENCE EQUIPMENT AND SUPPORT

The mission of Defence Equipment and Support (DE&S) is to equip and support our Armed Forces for operations now and in the future.

Role of DE&S

In order to fulfil its mission, DE&S needs to perform the following roles:
- The timely and reliable provision of operational logistics and equipment support.

- The commercially astute and cost-effective management of a portfolio of complex projects and the associated support network, on the basis of accurate forecasts and a through-life approach.
- Management of the commercial interface with the defence industrial supply chain, end-to-end.
- Effective financial management.
- Technology insertion to facilitate innovation and reduce risk, through-life.
- Safety, environmental and technical assurance.
- Workforce management, including skills identification, development and retention, people performance management and staff deployment.

DE&S is a key member of the MOD Unified Customer.

DE&S takes funded capability requirements from the Equipment Capability Customer (ECC) and delivers equipment, services and support to the User.

STRUCTURE OF DEFENCE EQUIPMENT AND SUPPORT

The DE&S business model is based on the following three tasks:

- Delivering and supporting the equipment-based component of capability, now and through-life.
- Managing key relationships with the Equipment Capability Customer (ECC), User, others in Government and with our Industry partners.
- Managing the business as effectively as possible.

These tasks are reflected by three business areas headed by:

- Chief Operating Officer (COO)
- Chiefs of Materiel (CofM)
- Chief of Corporate Services (CCS).

Chief Operating Officer

The Chief Operating Officer is responsible for delivering and supporting the equipment-based component of capability through life, driving project performance and through this, the performance of the industrial supply chain.

DE&S brings Integrated Project Teams (IPTLs) together in clusters, to best exploit technological developments and industrial capacity in accordance with sector strategies.

The COO ensures that strong links to the research programme are maintained to ensure rapid pull-through of technology into both new and current assets, in line with the overall Capability Management process.

Chiefs of Materiel

The Chiefs of Materiel are responsible for managing key relationships with the ECC and User working at the strategic level to ensure the operational readiness and sustainability needs of the User are satisfied.

The CofMs ensure an ethos of support to operations to the User is in place throughout all DE&S activity.

Chief of Corporate Services

The Chief of Corporate Services is responsible for managing the business as effectively as possible and setting policy in key corporate functional areas.

The CCS ensures the delivery of the essential corporate services:

- Commercial
- Human Resources
- Safety & Engineering.

The CCS drives the development of professional skills in these key disciplines.

The CCS also develops DE&S's strategic relationship with MOD Head Office.

KEY PROCESSES AND STANDING INSTRUCTIONS FOR DEFENCE EQUIPMENT AND SUPPORT

The DE&S delivers its outputs by implementing several key processes, including:

- Through Life Management
- Project and Programme Management
- Logistics
- Technology Management
- Engineering
- Safety
- Finance
- Commercial
- Human Resources
- Approvals.

Through Life Management

Through Life Management (TLM) is at the heart of DE&S's ability to deliver equipment and support to the User. The TLM methodology helps DE&S to manage the acquisition of new equipment, upgrades and support through its life until it is finally disposed.

The DE&S Through Life Investment Assurance Framework is in place to provide the DE&S Main Board with confidence in the investments that DE&S is responsible for delivering, and to support DGs and IPTs in that delivery.

The Assurance is provided through a single-point assuror for each DE&S Functional Assurance area: Finance, Commercial, HR, S&E, JSC and IS.

It is a through life activity based on early engagement, and the agreement of a tailored assurance plan between functional experts and project staff".

Project and Programme Management

All projects in the DE&S must adhere to, and follow recognised good practice in Project and Programme Management (PPM), fully embracing the concept of Through Life Management.

The Through Life Management Plan (TLMP) lies at the heart of all projects and is the tool through which all projects are managed.

Logistics

Logistics plays a major role in the provision of support and the MOD has a pan-Departmental Logistics Process, which is owned by CDM and managed by Assistant Chief of the Defence Staff (Logistics Operations) (ACDS(Log Ops)).

Technology Management

Technology Management, from the development of new research into usable systems, to the insertion of new technology into existing platforms is an important facet of TLM.

DE&S has a strong relationship with the Science Innovation Technology (SIT) Top Level Budget (TLB), helping to steer the MOD's research programme and exploit innovative ideas to enhance our Armed Force's capabilities.

Engineering

Defence equipments and the services that support them are technically complex and are required to integrate together in a multitude of ways – from communications to weapon systems. DE&S must excel in Engineering and a wide range of other technical disciplines to ensure what DE&S procures is fit for purpose.

DG Safety and Engineering is the primary source of technical advice and assurance to the organisation.

Safety

Ensuring the equipment and services DE&S provides to the User are safe, is a fundamental responsibility of the organisation. The aim is to ensure that the risk to the workforce and third parties is as low as reasonably practical.

DE&S has a clear Safety framework that defines how safety should be managed and how equipment should be shown to be safe through rigorous assurance.

Finance

The DE&S Finance process is focused on:

- supporting sound financial decisions.
- providing the organisation with accurate corporate financial data.
- ensuring money is being spent and committed appropriately.

Commercial

DE&S strives to be a commercially astute organisation which means teams require access to high quality commercial support, both in terms of skilled people and a comprehensive set of commercial guidance and tools.

DE&S Commercial processes are driven by the policies defined by the Defence Commercial Director, as head of the Defence Commercial Function.

Human Resources

Human Resources (HR) in DE&S supports the organisation by defining the overall skills development process for staff and developing means of providing a flexible workforce that can be deployed to meet challenges quickly.

HR also ensures there are suitable tools available to manage staff performance, which in turn helps drive DE&S's performance.

3

Management and Leadership Capability

Our current ideas about the nature of management and leadership have evolved through several decades. New ideas, such as emotional intelligence, tend to add themselves to older ideas, such as planning and organising. The debate about management versus leadership will no doubt continue, but has probably served its purpose. Suffice it to say that the aspects of management concerned with giving people direction and motivating them are now seen as very crucial.

There has been significant research into attributes of managers who are 'high performers.' However, different researchers have approached this task in different terms. Some have looked at tasks/ activities, some at skills/ behaviours and some personal qualities. Research has usually been focused on improving selection, so has not told us much about the relationship between capability and management development. 'Competence' frameworks are used in many organisations as summaries of descriptions of desired management behaviours, often including activities and personal qualities as well.

National Management Standards have been in existence for a decade, and have been amended several times over that period; mainly reflecting informed opinion about management and leadership rather than rigorous research. Major employers continue to use their own competence frameworks, even in the public sector, although the National Standards are widely used to accredited vocational management education.

Many of our ideas about management and leadership capability come from work on senior managers, and may not apply so well to junior and middle managers. There are also limitations to the evidence base in terms of nationality, gender (mostly male) and race (mostly white).

TRENDS IN MANAGEMENT AND LEADERSHIP DEVELOPMENT

Management and leadership development is provided by a complex mix of further and higher education, and formal and informal training provided by employers. Arange of other suppliers (large and small training companies and management consultancies, professional bodies etc) play into both the education and employer sectors. Nearly 100,000 qualifications in management and business are awarded each year, including about 19,000 first degrees and 10,000 MBAs. There is large raft of varied vocational qualifications - NVQs, certificates, diplomas etc. awarded in both further and higher education.

Management training in employing organisations has been growing slowly from a low base. Work-based learning approaches (coaching, project work etc.) are popular with HR professionals and with individuals, but they are often difficult to support and we have no reliable estimates of the volume of such development activity. The more exciting and innovative approaches to management and leadership development tend to be offered only to small populations - senior managers or those on high potential development programmes.

CHANGING IDEAS ABOUT MANAGEMENT AND LEADERSHIP

The present debate about 'management' and 'leadership' is not new. There is a long history of research into what management is, what managers do, and what managers need to have in order to do their jobs well. 'Leadership' has been of interest at different times and in different ways. It may help to start by highlighting some of the key ideas about management and leadership that colour our current views on management and leadership capability.

Some of these ideas are based on empirical research, but some are simply making sense of what people perceive to be the changing nature of the managerial or leadership task:

- Work by Mintzberg showed that management work as actually carried out is not an orderly and pre-planned process, and that managers actually spend their time in a fragmented and responsive way. The idea of the manager as 'fixer', problem-solver, and fire fighter is very prevalent.
- Bass talked of transformational leadership, as characterised by vision, optimism, integrity, intellectual challenge and consideration for individuals. Kets de Vries writes of the charismatic versus the architectural leader, and Shamir of the differences between the 'nearby' and the 'distant' leader. Alimo-Metcalfe and Alban-Metcalfe have examined the idea of transformational leadership in relation to the public sector, covering the elements of innovation, culture and people.
- Argyris has examined the notion of empowerment in relation to leadership and the tension between extracting compliance from the workforce as opposed to raising their internal commitment, especially during change.
- Strebel has also highlighted the link between leadership and change and the delicate balance to be struck between top-down and bottom-up approaches to achieving change.

- Hiltrop points to the self-reliance and resilience needed by leaders, linked with the recently fashionable idea of 'emotional intelligence'.
- 'Learning to learn' is seen as an increasingly important meta-skill for managers. Antonacopoulou and Bento take the idea of learning much further in placing the idea of learning at the heart of leadership:
  - 'Leadership is not taught and leadership is not learned. Leadership is learning.', a thought previously also applied to management by Burgoyne.
- Many other studies have looked at specific skills needed by senior managers. They include the ability to see the 'big picture' and deal with relationships and the ability to work across boundaries. The more complex the situation, for example in mergers or business alliances the more a capacity to deal with personal relationships is necessary to enable progress towards achieving the strategic business vision.
- Mabey and Thomson highlighted some management skills in high demand:
  - managing people, leadership, team working and customer focus. Within leadership
  - they picked out motivation and teamwork followed by strategic vision and delivering results.
  - We see all these ideas, and more besides, in the current discussion of managerial skills. It is fairly unclear which of all these skills have been shown to link with performance, and which just seem sensible ideas.
- A recent telephone survey of Business Schools conducted by the Institute for Employment Studies asked about the people management and leadership skills which individual managers attending Business

Schools were highlighting as their own learning needs. The list included: giving negative feedback; dealing with the tension between 'hard' and 'soft' management styles, delegating well when under pressure; and dealing with conflict and politics. It is interesting to note that Business Schools were unsure as to whether they followed genuine changes in the demands on managers, or whether they themselves 'led' shifts in thinking by finding new angles for training programmes. Some older empirical work by psychologists has attempted to discover which features differentiate managers who perform well, so as to identify capabilities which link with performance. These studies have looked for features of different kinds and used different methods.

So the definition of what managers and leaders need can be expressed in terms of management tasks; management or leadership skills or behaviours; or in terms of personal qualities. It is important to think about these different ways of expressing management and leadership capability when seeking to use any of the frameworks on offer. Beech is in favour of unpicking tasks, personal attributes and skills in order to clarify the objectives, design and measurement of management and leadership development. The knowledge that managers also need to have has been rather neglected in this field of work, although organisations see this as one important critical outcome of career experience and, of course, it is largely what Business Schools have taught.

LEADERSHIP AND MANAGEMENT

The term 'leadership' causes considerable confusion. Some people assume leaders are those near the top of organisations and therefore define leadership in such terms, often emphasizing strategy and vision. Others use the term 'leadership' to describe the more transformational aspects of management at any level, especially the motivation of employees and the management of change. So in English, the idea of 'leadership' embodies both the heroic leader at the top and the brave foot soldier - a pretty confusing mix. Management on the other hand, appears a more mundane and formal affair, the dictionary definition including words like 'direct', 'control' and 'resources.' Some writers seem to take it as given that leadership and management are distinct.

For example, Boyatzis sees management concerned with competitive advantage, predictable results, and solving problems. He sees leadership as concerned with mission, purpose, change, excitement, and inspiration. Others feel that management and leadership are 'inseparably interwoven in life at work'. This debate about whether leadership is different from management has probably now served its purpose - to recognise that managers need to provide direction and motivate people as well as organise work.

COMPETENCIES AND FRAMEWORKS

Boyatzis and others took up ideas about managerial work in the study of 'management competency.' Derivatives of the work of Boyatzis and McClelland are widely used.

Competence Frameworks Used by Employers

Both the idea of management competencies, and their arrangement in frameworks, has roved very attractive to major employers as part of their approach to HRM. In translation to use, the idea of 'competency' as a personal attribute became muddled with 'competence' as skills to do a job. However, even though the two spellings and a variety of meanings persisted, by the late 1980s many large employers had developed competence frameworks and were using them in a variety of HR applications.

National Management Standards and General Frameworks

The ideas of management competence were adopted at national level in the MCI: Management Standards, in the 1990s. These were offered as a tool for employers, but also as a framework for structuring management and leadership development in the education sector i.e. for the accreditation of vocational qualifications. The standards were first accredited as the basis for qualifications in 1991, and a revised set similarly accredited in 1997. The original Standards were a complex framework, taking a largely task-based view of management broken down into managing operations, managing finance, managing people, managing information. Each of these main groups was broken down into units of competence and further into elements of competence. For each element, performance criteria and range indicators were produced, for use in assessment. These early Standards were also differentiated for various levels of management - supervisory, first line, middle, and senior management.

Versions of competence frameworks are used across large areas of the public sector, for example the Senior Civil Service and the leadership of the NHS. Employers have struggled with earlier versions of the National Standards and how to use them alongside their own competence frameworks. The complexity of accrediting tailored management learning against the Standards has made such accreditation problematic for employers. This is one of the issues being addressed in the shortly to be released revision of the standards.

Issues in Relation to Management Skills and Competencies

- Although many skill frameworks used by employers are based on some analysis of good performers, the approach to National Standards has been that of informed opinion. So although national approaches to management and leadership rest on a kind of consensus, we cannot be sure that the resulting definition of capability captures the essence of high performing managers. We also do not know which competencies can be significantly improved by training, or what kind of training may achieve this.
- Organisations behave as though they value knowledge as well as skills, especially knowledge

gained through career experience of functions, industries, recurring situations etc. Approaches to capability have tended to by-pass knowledge and its relationship with performance.

- Psychological research on management and leadership capability has mostly focused on selection or performance management. Using competence-based management development is perceived as effective, but tends to come later than other uses and presents several significant challenges. One is that we really do not know which competencies can be improved by training. Although it is a common belief that all competencies can be learnt – and that advances in learning methodologies make this more so – there is evidence based argument that some characteristics, particularly the emotional and motivational aspects of leadership are more fixed – they can be selected for but not developed. Another is that the assessment of competence is far from easy. A third is that there are tensions between using competencies for performance management and using them for development. To put this last one crudely, why would you confess to the need to develop competencies when your pay rise depends on your showing you are already perfect?

- Although many of the skills needed by managers and leaders are common to the whole management population, they need to take different forms for managers at different levels and in different types of organisation. The manner in which the CEO of a major corporation leads change will be different from that of a departmental manager in the same organisation and different yet again for the MD of a small firm. Many competence frameworks used are influenced by American research conducted long ago on small numbers of male senior managers. This is one reason why major companies insist on tailoring their approaches, and often differentiating by level of management.

- Many of the idealised attributes of leaders and managers are not really behaviours rewarded at work. As Keep and Westwood put it there is a 'gulf between what managers do and are required to do by the organisations that employ them, and what theory or even best practice models say they ought to be doing.' This rhetoric-reality gap presents a real problem for the suppliers of management and leadership development. Boyatzis may be witnessing this same tension when his data shows that some managers have the skills to act as leaders but choose not to use them.

Ethnic Minority Groups and Gender Differences

The number of women in senior management roles remains well below that of men (12% of the female population of working age as opposed to 19-20% of the male population of working age). Similarly, there are disparities between the ethnic minorities with some over-represented in management as a percentage of their numbers in the total employed population (particularly Indian ethnic groups) and others (particularly black groups) under-represented. These issues are not easy to address and more legislation is not the answer. The reasons for the differences between ethnic groups in management occupations are little understood. Much more data would be needed to identify key factors. For example, it may be that some groups are over-represented because they tend to start their own businesses and thus become owner managers. The reasons why this might be so in some ethnic minorities but not in others are little understood. There is simply insufficient evidence to say. Similarly, not enough is known about the job choices and career patterns of underrepresented groups. More research is needed if appropriate national strategies are to be introduced.

There are similar problems with gender. Not enough is known about the kinds of jobs held by women. It is possible that they are 'clustered' just below senior management positions and have difficulty 'breaking though' the glass ceiling to rise to the top. On the other hand, it may be that they deliberately choose more 'female friendly' arenas because they seek less competitive and more caring environments than that found in most management occupations. This idea is also reflected in another recent study which explores what it means to be a woman and a manager. The study is based on questionnaires and group discussions with women managers, and finds that women are faced with a contradiction: whether to learn to fit into the dominant paradigm of management, or to play a different game.

Research undertaken among MBA graduates found that there were differences between men and women in the effect on their careers. Other research supports these findings. Nicholson and West found that while men valued external benefits such as salary and status, women placed more importance on working relationships and job satisfaction. Gender differences in the management population arise therefore from a complex set of issues and will not be easily resolved.

MANAGEMENT AND LEADERSHIP DEVELOPMENT

Management development consists of a wide range of activities including the following, Associated with which there are discernable trends:

- Management training given by employers in the form of courses and, more recently, through e-learning. The trend to e-learning as the latest form of distance learning has been a recent one. There has been some pulling back from this after the initial enthusiasm, and the current preferred approach is blended learning – a mix of elearningand face-to-face activity.
- Training provided to employers by private training suppliers. This has been a growing trend and is

linked to the growing business trend to outsourcing, including HRM and other business functions.

- Management education (often associated with Business education) through open programmes delivered in further and higher education and leading to a wide range of qualifications. This has been a growing and expanding activity over the longer term, which has levelled off or even declined in recent years in terms of UK use. For many Business Schools and programmes (for example full time MBA's) the greater use has been international, particularly the economically developing parts of the world that are not yet self sufficient in management education, and from which study abroad is seen as supporting developing business in the global economy. In terms of potential impact on the large UK management and leadership population, programmes from the Further Education sector are of considerable significance.

- Executive education delivered by Business Schools as part of in-company orconsortium activity, which has been an area of recent growth for larger companies.

- Learning in the workplace on-the-job and through career movement, which has always gone on, but is increasingly done deliberately and with facilitation by organisations.

- Management training provided through a wide range of professional bodies as part of accreditation and continuing professional development (CPD). This is an area where there is a significant perceived opportunity, and some initiatives, and one which was identified by CEML as an area of future opportunity.

Some of these forms of management development are easier to quantify than others: We have not included here the literature on organisation development (OD). This has a blurred boundary with management and leadership development. OD interventions may be of considerable significance as leadership becomes more recognised as a collective as well as individual capability in organisational settings.

Brown points to the relative failure of the NVQ structure to impact on management training in the UK. He points to doubts about Standards and the cost/ unreliability of assessment. Thomson, Mabey et al. also point to the 'confused and overlapping qualifications' in management. In spite of the fragmented nature of management and leadership development provision, the CEML advisory group found 'no evidence of a shortage of learning opportunities, though employers often find it difficult to identify provision that meets their needs.'

A parallel CEML advisory group examined the provision of management and leadership development within the HE sector. When it comes to formal training provision by employers, Thompson and Mabey's studies suggest a modest increase in formal management development provision by employers over a ten year period to 1996. They concluded 'the priority given by organisations to management development has increased significantly compared to ten years ago, and is expected to increase further in the foreseeable future.

Of its nature, the volume of work-based management development (i.e. development other than courses) is impossible to estimate. It is important when comparing patterns in different countries to realise that their histories of management education vary very widely. Some of these features are reported by Mabey and Gooderham on the basis of empirical work. The UK spends rather less on management development than the European average in terms of formal training. Some countries, such as Germany, rely on in-company management and leadership development plus career experience to develop their managers. Others, such as Denmark, have strong systems of vocational education alongside academic education, and much management learning occurs in the education system. The UK emerges rather oddly as having vocational qualifications in management, but HRD professionals who ascribe little value to this way of learning management and leadership. The UK also emerges, as so often, as having a shortterm attitude to management and leadership development compared with some European neighbours. It is worth mentioning here that professional bodies in the UK are starting to become more active in the provision of management and leadership development for people who would be classified as 'professionals', more than 'managers'.

- Perren in survey for CEML of 149 professional bodies found that these bodies did see management and leadership as important, but that such skills are not often included in membership entry or CPD. Professional bodies in the fields of policy, administration and business support (e.g. local government, information, personnel, purchasing and supply) placed higher value on management and leadership than bodies representing other fields of work.

- Fox et al. sought the views of a small sample of professionals as well as some professional associations and some development specialists. The terms 'management' and 'leadership' were used interchangeably. The professionals themselves felt that the most important aspects of management/ leadership were interpersonal/ relationship skills and communication skills. The professional bodies and trainers agreed less on what was important. The trainers used mainly conventional learning methods (classroom, courses) but also learning sets or action learning and e-learning. Coaching was also fairly prevalent. Practitioners favoured informal means of development and selected formal learning on an ad hoc basis. Most of the associations had some links with suppliers of management and leadership training. Some accredited university courses in management as part of their CPD offering to members.

As we have seen from the quantitative estimates above, UK investment in management and leadership development does seem to be increasing, albeit from a low base. Although on the whole this is good news, there are still many managers, especially in smaller firms, who have no formal management education or training prior to entering work and little in the workplace. Both shortages of money and of time impede access to management training by some of those who might benefit from it.

There are also changes in the type of management and leadership development activities being undertaken. IES conducted a review of trends in management development, based on literature and seminars held with about 30 major employers. It found that changes in management and leadership activities stemmed from changes in:

- The nature of the challenges organisations perceived for their managers, especially in what might called the 'leadership' aspects of their jobs.
- Changing notions of how people learn, especially higher interest in work-based or action learning, and also types of learning engaging managers at a deeper personal level in their learning.

EVIDENCE ON GENERAL CHANGES

- An IDS review of management development pointed to many of the trends we still see today. There was a strong desire to tailor training and make it useful and this led to arguments for and against on-the-job training as opposed to off-the-job courses. Some companies felt they did best through tailored in-house provision and others joined consortia. MBAs were supported by some companies, with some developing company or consortia MBAs. Secondment was on the agenda in the late 1980s, but mentoring and coaching were not mentioned in this review.

- 360-degree feedback has proved to be a powerful lever for engaging managers with their own need for skill development and at it is most useful when integrated into a development programme.
- Woodhall and Welchman's study on 'work based management development' in 31 organisations concluded there was a gap between all the talk of tailored individual learning in the workplace and its implementation. 'Coaching and, increasingly, special projects are the interventions most likely to be consciously promoted, but explicit guidance on using these learning interventions is rare.'
- A good deal of development activity in the 1990s was directed at the issue of managing or leading change. Doyle found that the impact of formalized management training activity during change was often resisted due to the residual culture and style of the managers. In seeing management development as part of culture change, Holbeche discusses the problem of senior management training as appearing remedial. She argues that feedback can help managers to see the need for change, but their willingness may still be lacking.
- There is considerable interest in the use of e-learning, sometimes presented as programmes or modules within a 'corporate university'. Burgoyne found that companies were seeking to use e-learning alongside face-to-face leadership skill development rather than intending to replace personal contact in management development. Evidence from the CIPD training survey shows that, while e-learning is used by many employers, it tends to be used alongside other

training methods and is more used for IT staff than for managers.

Development for Senior Managers and Business Executives

- Marx and Demby found that that standard development programmes still prevail in most companies, with senior managers rewarded to a certain extent by ttendance at prestigious Business Schools. However, more individually tailored development such as executive coaching is likely to be more effective. They found a growth of consortia programmes designed to broaden the thinking of senior managers by bringing them into contact with people from other organisations.
- Kettley and Strebler echo this in their study of the changing role of senior managers. They note that 'formal business education and training for senior managers is increasingly context specific, delivered in partnership with external experts and focused on new business concepts and strategic learning. Many are experimenting with more individually focused approaches to learning including coaching, counselling and personal feedback.'
- Many companies have defined generic and/or senior management competencies although they vary in the extent to which these really underpin management development. Holbeche identifies many companies using competency approaches, 360 degree feedback, personal development plans and assessment centres to help link their succession planning processes with corporate and management development strategies. Many companies have also determined a set of generic leadership competencies (e.g. BP, Texaco, Smithkline Beecham), but Holbeche warns against 'the limited shelf life of success profiles when business requirements change'.

- Alimo-Metcalf et al. points to some of the same trends in leadership development: emphasis on feedback (including 360 degree feedback), action learning, cross-functional teamwork and the involvement in senior people of delivering development themselves (e.g. as coaches or mentors). Mentoring and coaching have received increased attention in recent years, especially for more senior people at one extreme and new joiners at the other. Ford argues that executive coaching can transform performance by allowing executives to establish their own criteria for improvement.

- Some organisations have used formal mentoring 'schemes' mainly for either graduate entrants or senior managers. Clutterbuck and Megginson identify mentoring as covering a wide range of different support to individuals. Three common roles are defined as executive coach (a short-term help with specific skills), elder statesperson (sounding board and role model), and reflective mentor (increasing self-awareness through constructive challenge).

- Carter in a review of the use of executive coaching, shows that this approach is very popular with large organisations and quite attractive to many managers. However, extending its use to wider populations of managers is limited by its cost and the restricted supply of high quality coaches.

LEADERSHIP DEVELOPMENT AND ENHANCE IN PERFORMANCE

Many would feel that the question 'Does management and leadership capability make a difference to organisational or national performance?' is hardly worth asking. Managers and leaders, it can be argued, are bound to affect performance both in their direct contribution to better business decisions and better-managed people, and indirectly through their impact on wider institutions and policies both at organisational and national level. However, we start examining evidence at this point because the national argument about low productivity and its supposed link with poor quality of management has strongly influenced government interest in issues of management and leadership, as witnessed by the CEML enquiry reporting in 2002.

NATIONAL PRODUCTIVITY

There is persistent concern that levels of productivity are low in the UK. Reports dating back to the 1980s assumed a fairly simple link between national economic performance and a deficit of good managers. Although the evidence of a link between the supply of managers and this economic underperformance is far from clear, the government's interest in this relationship remains unabated.

A recent report from SKOPE also takes a cautions tone. These authors cast doubt upon the efficiency of managerial practices and quote research showing that only a minority of business process re-engineering programmes added to share values. The same was true for mergers and acquisitions. They use these facts to support their argument that management skills are not adequate. Overall, it has to be concluded that there is clearly a great deal that we do not know about how managerial behaviour affects business performance.

DEVELOPMENT CAPABILITY AND ORGANISATIONAL PERFORMANCE

Most of the time we take it as given that the quality of managers and leaders affects organisational performance. However, there is little direct evidence of the extent or nature of this impact. The work of Peters and Waterman was one highly influential example of an attempt to link the nature of management and leadership with organisational culture, as well as with more formal managerial processes and systems. Some of the features of organisations that they saw as causing 'excellence', identified through their case study approach, were motivation, 'bias for action', and productivity through people. By implication they suggest that these in turn are achieved through management and leadership effort. A different and more focused approach to linking the quality of management with business results is shown in the analysis of the employee-customer-profit chain.

The Employee-Customer-Profit Chain

This evidence would tend to reinforce the high interest in managers as motivators of staff who then produce better business results:

- Cockerill tried to link management capability with organisational performance. He sought to validate a framework of seven competencies (information search, conceptual complexity, team facilitation, impact, charisma, proactive orientation, achievement orientation) on 150 managers in 5 organisations. He found that the selected competencies were positively related to measures of organisation performance except one, achievement orientation. Overall, the competence of a manager explained about 15 per cent of unit performance in dynamic environments. In more stable environments, there was little relationship between the high performing management competencies and unit performance. This points to an interesting possibility, that we need managers and leaders more when things are changing. Perhaps the strongest evidence that managers 'make a difference' to organisational performance lies in the research linking HRM with performance. The delivery of people management, as conducted very largely by managers, is now well proven to have a strong association with organisation performance, although proving causality is still difficult.

While much has been written about the broad benefits of investing in management development, what evidence is there concerning the specific impact on organisational performance of training and development of managers? Empirical studies are still small in number.

Training and Organisational Performance

A limited amount of research has been conducted which focuses on the organisational impact of *employee* (rather than management) development or training. Although these studies do not differentiate managers from other employees, they do throw further light on the ways in which development can enhance performance management and leadership development on organisational performance, there is a large and increasingly coherent body of data on the link between HRM practices more widely and organisational performance.

There is a 'double relationship' between management and leadership development and HRM in relation to performance. On the one hand HRM is a major area of the application of management and leadership development – HRM is managed and lead, and the evidence that HRM contributes to performance supports the case that good management and leadership in this area contributes to performance.

On the other side, from a traditional point of view, management and leadership development is one of many HRM practices, and the evidence that it plays a part in HRM effect, alongside other strands of HRM, is also of importance. Finally, the HRM – performance research is amongst the most thorough, extensive, and international, so we can draw important lessons from it methodologically. This field of research is important to the management and leadership development debate in several ways:

- Training is almost always one of the HRM practices associated with superior organisational performance. This makes it very likely that management training, as part of wider training, makes a positive contribution to organisational performance. Indeed, in a synthesis of research in this area, Becker and Huselid identify 'management development and

training activities linked to the needs of the business' as one of four key HRM systems.
- Managers are an input to HRM as well as an output. Nearly all the HRM processes identified as important in this research are ones which managers need to implement through their personal skills *e.g.* high involvement of employees, performance management *etc.*. Managers are also of course important deliverers of training and development to other staff. So these positive HRM practices rely on good quality managers for their delivery. This argument is especially important in some of the most recent research that emphasises the quality of implementation of HRM.
- This field is starting to lay down some clear markers as to conditions under which HRM is most likely to support high performance. These markers mostly concern 'fit' - of HR processes with each other and of HR strategies with business strategies. Again, this work provides stronger support to the hypothesis suggested in the previously that management and leadership development is most likely to need this kind of 'fit' if it is to raise organisational performance.

High Performance HR Practices

The key early studies of HRM and performance were mostly American and looked atwhether certain 'high performance', or 'progressive' work practices were associated with higher organisational performance:
- Huselid examined 13 measures of HR practices for both managerial and nonmanagerial staff in over 900 firms. The practices selected were so-called 'high performance' work practices (quality circles, profit-sharing, appraisal *etc.*). One of these HRM measures was the number of hours training over last 12 months. Measures of HR and financial performance

were reported at company level. Firms employing these practices registered significantly lower staff turnover, higher staff productivity and better financial performance over both the short- and long-term than those firms that did not adopt the 'high performance' practices.

- Another wide ranging study, this time of 590 firms in the U.S. adopting 'progressive' HRM practices, including selectivity in staffing, training and incentive compensation found these practices related positively to perceptual measures of organisational performance.. These effects were similar in profit and not for profit organisations.

- Pfeffer identified five top-performing US firms between 1972-92 based on percentage of stock returns. These companies were characterised by 'high commitment' work practices. Drawing on secondary data from the global automotive industry and other industries, as well as evidence of 'best practice', Pfeffer claimed that people management practices were enduring sources of competitive advantage. One of his seven high performance management practices impacting the bottom line was high expenditure on training. In these HRM-performance studies, training is often measured in very simple ways, most often training spend or proportion of employees receiving training. Sometimes measures are included for both training for new staff and for experienced employees. Although this evidence points to a possible positive link between employee training and organisational performance, training is not often the employment practice *most* strongly associated with performance in these macro studies. Practices around work organisation and performance management usually come out more strongly. These studies also show *association* rather than causal links between HRM and organisational performance.

Contingency Models of HRM

Other researchers have become more interested in the idea that the range of HRM practices which will affect performance depends on the type of business and HR strategies being adopted. They tend to distinguish between 'low road' strategies that rely on cost reduction and 'high road' strategies that focus on quality, variety or service. The empirical evidence here is interesting but less substantial than for the universal 'best practice' approach:

- A longitudinal study of 388 manufacturing organisations in Florida collected data about the age, sales, export performance, life-cycle stage and markets of each organisation, and asked each CEO to judge the degree to which the human resource strategy of his or her company supported international activities. It was found that the most significant predictor of success in exports, as measured 30 months later, was the human resource strategy of the organisations sampled. For instance, if an organisation gave substantial rewards to those who undertook international activities, emphasised this when recruiting and promoting managers, supported training and development in international business and included this as a dimension of any review of performance, then its exports were more likely to be successful.
- Youndt et al. in a study of manufacturing plants, found HR practices aimed at enhancing the employee skill base to have the largest impact on productivity in those plants pursuing a quality rather than cost strategy. Banker et al. found that outcome-based pay schemes were more effective in supporting a customer-focused service strategy where competition

was intense and customers more demanding. They also found that such schemes were more likely to result in performance improvements in firms with lower levels of staff supervision.

- Arthur studied the business performance of Steel U.S. mini-mills. The HR strategies of 30 mills were compared and characterised as 'commitment systems' where attempts were made to shape employee behaviours and attitudes by forging links between organisational and employee goals, or 'control systems' where the goal of HR was to reduce direct labour costs, or improve efficiency by compliance with specified rules and procedures and by basing employee rewards on measurable output criteria. The mills with higher commitment systems (including a higher level of employee involvement in managerial decisions, formal participation programmes, training in group problem-solving etc.) had higher productivity, lower scrap rates and lower employee turnover than those with control systems.

- In a study of 70 automotive assembly plants, representing 24 companies in 17 countries 'lean production systems' were found to be much higher in both productivity and quality than those with 'mass production systems'. Lean production systems aim to create a skilled, motivated and flexible workforce. It was found that the success of these systems depended critically on such high-commitment HR policies such as decentralisation of production responsibilities, multi-skilling practices, profit/gain sharing, a reciprocal psychological contract, employment security and a reduction of the status barrier.

- Delery and Doty found the financial performance of those banks adopting 3 HR practices, namely profit-sharing, results-oriented appraisals and employment security, was 30 per cent better than the average across 219 banks. 'Banks that were able to align their HR practices with strategy are estimated to have nearly 50 per cent higher ROA and ROE than those banks whose HR practices were just one standard deviation out of alignment. Specifically, banks that implemented a prospector strategy involving high innovation, reaped greater returns from more results-oriented appraisals and lower levels of employee participation than did banks that relied on a defender strategy. Banks implementing a defender strategy performed better if they relied less on results-oriented appraisals and gave their loan officers higher levels of participation in decision-making and voice.'.

It is important to note that most of the studies on the link between HRM and organisational performance have concentrated on manufacturing organisations. In manufacturing, the move in developed countries towards high skill strategies and the increased use of technology to reduce employee costs has been prevalent:

- Hoque's study of over 200 hotels shows that the high skill/ high training logic may not always apply in the service sector, where lower skill/ cost reduction strategies can also be common. In this study, hotels pursuing a 'quality-enhancer' strategy, HRM practices are strongly and positively related to HR outcomes. In costreducer strategies, HRM practices do not appear to affect flexibility, quality or absenteeism measures.

The Purcell study also showed that the number and extent of HR practices was less important than the effectiveness of their implementation: 'those organisations with the Big Idea that were value-led and managed were much more likely to sustain their performance over the long-term'. In terms of generating motivation, organisational commitment and job satisfaction, key policy areas were career opportunities, job design, involvement and line manager leadership skills. They conclude that effective firms have a level of sophistication in their approach to people management which helps induce discretionary behaviour (roughly equivalent to 'going the extra mile') and above-average performance.

There appears to be an emerging consensus that there are a number of broad approaches to HRM that can bring performance benefits to most organisations. These include policies designed to build employee commitment to the organisation, and to acquire, build and retain employee knowledge and skills. However, the way in which these broad approaches are most successfully applied is likely to be contingent on the environment, strategic orientation, operational characteristics and history of each organisation. It is the application of HR processes rather than the policy intention which appears the crucial differentiator.

Richardson and Thompson conclude:

- 'It is unlikely that merely adopting a specified set of HR policies is the high road to organisational success'.
- We need more attention to the intervening links between HR policies and organisational performance, and a more specific understanding of the types of policies which are most effective (e.g. what types of training).
- How something is done is often more important than what is done, so we need to look at how clusters of HR strategies are implemented.

Here we turn from an organisational focus to an individual level one. We examine the evidence of a link between management and leadership development, management and leadership capability and individual performance. In doing so we exclude management and leadership development delivered in higher education, partly because the extensive study of the MBA rather eclipses the lack of evidence of the impact of MD more generally. So we are here thinking of management and leadership development delivered by or through the organisation's training function. We are also including management and leadership development which occurs in or very near the job - what we might call 'work-based' learning and development.

Compared with the large literature on how HRM, and to some extent management and leadership development, affect organisational performance, there is astonishingly little evidence on how management and leadership development affects individual capability and performance of managers. Keep and Westwood looking at the same question, find very little evidence that the supply of MLD is addressing the right skills, improving skills, or impacting on performance.

IMPACT OF HRM

Just as there is evidence that HRM relates to organisational performance, so there are some studies showing the link between HRM practices and outcomes at the level of the individual employee. These give us some clues at to the nature of general links which are likely to occur between HRM practices and the performance of individual managers and leaders. A few of these studies have looked at managers, but more have looked at the whole workforce.

It may be that we should not expect to find research that demonstrates a simple link between management and leadership development, capability, individual performance and organisational performance. There are several other factors that are likely to intervene in this relationship.

The HRM literature highlights the likely importance of employee motivation and commitment to the organisation as strong links in the HRM-organisational performance chain:

- Boyatzis used empirical data to show that having leadership competencies does not necessarily mean you will choose to use them. He suggests that the difference between management and leadership is part a matter of attitude, and that more management development needs to be aimed at encouraging people to enact the role of leader, not just giving managers the skills.

INDIVIDUAL AND TEAM CAPABILITY

The link between management and leadership development, individual capability, individual performance and organisational performance tends to ignore the possible importance of how managers work with other people in networks and teams. Organisational culture and its social relationships are likely to influence the extent to which a manager can translate his or her capabilities into performance. Positive cultures, good management processes and networks may make the organisational benefit of capabilities much higher than the 'sum of the parts' of individual managers.

- Day for example imports the concept of 'social capital' into management learning, claiming that management and leadership development is potentially a vehicle for increasing the social capital of the organisation (in the sense of managers having extra collective value through their relationships) as well as its human capital (in the sense of individual capability). So if individuals perform well as a result of development, this may lie in their ability to have improved networks and relationships with others in the organisation (and sometimes outside it too). The organisational benefit may also lie to some extent in this social capital as well as the simple addition of individual capability.

HOLISTIC RATHER THAN MECHANISTIC APPROACHES TO CAPABILITY

Another tension present in seeking to examine the micro links between individual learning and corporate performance concerns assumptions about the nature of individual capability. Some adopt a very analytical approach to individual capability, seeking to find competencies which are linked to particular aspects of individual performance, linked in turn to managerial behaviours of corporate priority. However, there is an equally strong employer interest in much more personal start points for management learning on the grounds that the learning itself will be more relevant and vivid to the individual and therefore has the potential to bring about much greater changes in performance.

Much management and leadership development activity does not attempt precise mappings between individual behaviours and corporate performance, although it may well emphasise a small number of behaviours or attitudes believed to be of increasing importance. We see this more holistic approach in the rapid rise of coaching and mentoring, which inevitably attend to each individual's perceived development needs, even when starting from a competence-based analysis. Some leading employers have invested in programmes which are intensely personal, hoping that they will feed through to corporate performance through their deep emotional impact on the individuals concerned.

The BAe Strategic Leadership Programme, exposing participants to intense experiences of culture in different countries, is an example of such a *'personal journey'*, not designed to have a *'deliverable result in strict business terms.'* The holistic approach does not necessarily mean that it is not helpful to name and assess specific areas of competence and capability, rather it means that we should not see them contributing independently of other competences and capabilities to performance. Any specific competence influences performance through its interaction in a network with other competencies having a joint effect. It may still, none the less, be possible to identify areas of weaknesses in the network of competencies that undermine the effectiveness of the whole.

Here we do not present evidence on the quality and impact of management and leadership development given in further education, mainly because there is very little evidence in this area. A CEML advisory group produced an overview of the very diverse provision of management and leadership development outside HE. Its evidence on the volume of such supply. This working group found it difficult to assess the quality of management education outside HE. It concluded that quality was likely to be very variable. Universities, especially through Business Schools, supply degrees and vocational programmes in Business and Management at several levels. The two prevalent qualifications are first degrees in business and management, and MBAs. Information on the scale of provision in HE, and the various qualifications taken.

EMPLOYMENT AND CAREER IMPACT

There is considerable evidence that qualifications in business and management confer employment benefits on the individual, and that individuals choose such courses largely for vocational reasons:

- Purcell and Pitcher found that 65 per cent of final year undergraduates in Business Studies chose their degree on 'vocational' grounds *i.e.* expecting it to improve their employment and career opportunities. This was second only to engineering and technology. Likewise studies of MBAs in the UK show very clearly that career improvement is a major motivation for such study. There is a reasonable amount of evidence of the positive impact on salary and career progression for graduates of first degrees in Management and Business Studies and MBAs. In comparing Business and Management with other subjects at first degree level in the UK, it is very important to take into account the lower than average entry qualifications of the overall undergraduate intake into Business Schools. Taking this into account, the value of a business degree to the individual seems significant, although it may not outweigh the cost and time of study.

Given the generally positive employment evidence above, especially in relation to first degrees, it is disappointing that employers do not say that they specifically seek graduates with degrees in Business and Management. Rather the general picture is of employers looking for first-degree graduates with good general cognitive and social skills, which they often test for themselves using assessment centres. Employers do not treat business and Management as a 'vocational' degree in the way that, for example, engineering would be *i.e.* placing value on the specific knowledge and skills acquired. Much the same argument seems to apply in the MBA recruitment market, which employers see as another way they can find 'talent', more than specific knowledge or skills. So although Business and Management students seem to fare quite well in the UK labour market, we have no strong evidence that this is because employers value these courses per se or the skills or knowledge gained through them.

Given that, on average, Business and Management Studies undergraduates gain entry with lower than average entry grades, and hence show evidence of added vocational educational value by not being disadvantaged by this later in the labour market, it may also be the case that some employers prefer to recruit people with earlier educational success, who they can train themselves, to those with seemingly more relevant vocational qualification from a weaker previous educational background.

THE IMPACT OF BUSINESS AND MANAGEMENT STUDIES ON PERSONAL CAPABILITY

Some useful studies report on how students of first degrees in business and management and MBAs, perceive their learning, and its impact on their skills and confidence. One key limitation of the research evidence on the impact of Business Schools on individual capability is that it relies so heavily on self-reported assessments of skill. Another is that this research is rarely over significant time periods.

IMPACT ON INDIVIDUAL PERFORMANCE AT WORK

Do those who have undertaken management education actually perform better as managers? This is a central question in the general criticisms of Business Schools in the US. These often revolve around the lack of fit between what is learned on an MBA and what it takes to be an effective leader in practice. There are fewer examples of attempts to link Business School education with individual performance in the workplace. Some examples are given below and show a very mixed set of evidence, far short of a strong case for positive performance impact.

So there appear to be some tensions between the very largely positive feedback from students on their learning at Business Schools and how easily this can be linked to improvements in their performance at work. This is not to say that Business School learning does *not* affect performance, but rather that systematic attempts have not been made to document such a linkage. It may also be that linking learning in higher education back to the workplace is more difficult than we assume.

EFFECT OF LEARNING ENVIRONMENT AND CHALLENGES FACED

There are a number of key factors in the learning environment which will affect how individuals learn. These include personal learning styles, the teaching methodology used and the size of the groups involved. Considerable attention has been given to the notion of learning style mainly originating with the work of Kolb. The main ideas are summarised:

However learning 'styles' are better thought of as learning 'strategies' that individuals can change and develop, and may vary much more with context than the term style, as an individual personality characteristic, implies. In consequence a variety of different teaching methodologies are now being used in management and leadership education and development. Different practitioners favour different options. Methods include simulations, case studies, action learning, and outdoor adventure. Taking the literature as a whole, there is no evidence to show that any one method is the most successful. All indications are that multiple methods will produce the most effective management learning. No one method has the sole answer.

Findings such as these indicate that some teaching tools appear to be more effective than others, at least for some topics and some circumstances. No one strategy will work for all managers and all types of subject area and tailored courses for different contexts and audiences are likely to be the most effective.

FORMAL AND INFORMAL DEVELOPMENT APPROACHES

Mentoring and coaching are referred to throughout this report in the context of other issues. However, it is difficult to find evidence assessing their independent value. They generally form part of a wider portfolio of development opportunities offered by large companies, consultancies and Business Schools. Recent research by the School of Coaching at the Industrial Society indicates that coaching for senior staff has become very common but that the benefits are seldom evaluated.

The very fact of the popularity of mentoring and coaching is evidence of demand and suggests that managers do find them useful. One example of a study of mentoring in Business Schools which undertook research into outcomes did find positive results.

Management Development and Organisational Strategies

Mabey and Thomson in a recent survey found that there had been a shift from informal to formal methods of management development in large organisations over the four years since their previous study in 1996. However, this shift may now have peaked and informal methods such as coaching may be increasing. Evidence for this is so far anecdotal and more ongoing research would be useful in this context. Mabey and Thomson also found that low organisational priority for management development was an important barrier to take-up and identified the importance of both individual and organisational drivers to development.

Mabey and Thomson also found in a subsequent survey that many firms do not have a management development budget. Other studies have also shown that in many companies the link between executive development and business strategy is weak. Looking at kinds of development, Mabey and Thomson also found that most managers preferred a mixture of structured and unstructured development, with some on-thejob elements and some external courses and seminars.

CAPABILITIES NEEDED FOR SPECIFIC ASPECTS

Creativity and the management of change are interconnected issues. The management of change requires innovative (creative) approaches. Similarly, creativity will itself lead to change. Despite a lack of consensus about what creativity is and how it varies between individuals, it is widely believed that creativity can be taught, or at least fostered. Creativity is increasingly becoming part of the curriculum in higher education and there are a number of approaches to how this can be achieved. Some authors are sceptical of these approaches. A recent comment in a report from SKOPE for example comments negatively on management development courses where students play with Lego. On the other hand, other writers such as Chia see innovative methods as necessary for developing the 'entrepreneurial imagination'.

Not only is there debate about how to foster creativity in an educational setting, there is also little known about how to embed creativity within the organisation. This is an area which is little researched. There do, however, seem to be certain factors in an organisation which can promote creativity.

The need to manage change, both that which is internal to the organisation and that which is happening externally in the social, economic and technological environment and which affects the organisational context, will require new management development activities. This is likely to include different kinds of courses, more experiential learning and more focus upon people management skills.

Need for More Than basic Competences

Basic competences are not enough for the changing external environment. A recent review of the literature finds that although Business Schools are able to, and do, teach basic managerial competences, they also need to develop new kinds of products to meet today's needs.

Not everything can be taught, however. Mabey and Thomson found that experience, personality and inherent ability were the most important factors in making an effective manager. Beech's work also provides strong evidence for the importance of innate factors. He found that intelligence is the single most important predictor of management performance. Mabey and Thomson also found that the kinds of skills that will be most needed in this century will be the 'softer' skills - leadership, people management, team working, customer focus. More research is needed into how far these reflect innate factors such as personality and how far they reflect attributes which can be learned.

In addition to having basic management competences, then, managers need 'softer' skills, and also need to be able to innovate and respond to change. The consensus from a number of studies reflects Mabey and Thomson's findings and shows that the key factor for successful organisations in the new millennium will be having leaders who have excellent people management skills and an understanding of behavioural issues. There will also be a need for strategic HR specialists who are able to create an environment of continuous learning and improvement. It is increasingly important that strategic HR factors are input into the formulation of business strategy.

Organisational Context

There is general agreement that learning will be constrained, or enabled, by the nature of the organisation, its structures, size, objectives and people. Argyris draws attention to the informal rules and assumptions which operate in the workplace and the ways in which these affect behaviours. The effectiveness of management development will be facilitated or inhibited according to the context within which it is to be used. The importance of organisational support for development has been indicated by a number of studies. The effectiveness of 360° feedback activities for example has been found to vary with context, and also with individual's beliefs. Similarly, the effectiveness of other programmes was also found to vary with organisational context.

Effects of Transformational Leaders

A recent study by Bono and Judge uses a strong evidence-base to show that transformational leaders do affect the extent to which individuals perceive their activities to be important, feel more job satisfaction, are more willing to help out, and do better at a simple task. Similarly, Shamir et al found that leaders who emphasised collective identity had followers who were more likely to see their work as fulfilling, important and enjoyable. More research is needed into how effective training programmes can be developed to enhance these capacities in leaders. It is also important to involve line managers in development activity if it is to be effective. Management and leadership development affects performance also gives clues as to how the process by which it does so might work. This area of research is revisited here with this 'how?' question in mind, rather than the 'does it?'

HR PRACTICES AND PERFORMANCE

There is a good deal of research indicating that HR practices do impact upon business performance although the methodology is not uncontested. One CIPD overview has found that people management practices do affect performance but that piecemeal change delivers little benefit. HR practices need to be cohesive and aligned with business goals and company strategy, according to the findings of this study. Another key research study, looking at a wide range of companies with over 100 employees from a number of different sectors, similarly found that HR practices are a key determinant of management development processes. It also found that successful firms used a variety of formal, informal and external approaches to development. No one method was seen to work best.

A further study by Winterton and Winterton found a statistically significant relationship between competence-based HRD systems and both individual and business performance. A major benefit of using competence-based systems (job profiles, management development and appraisal systems were all related to competence-based standards in these companies) was that there was a coherent structure, that gaps in competences were more easily spotted, training needs could be specified more precisely, and there were clear criteria for HR planning and career succession. Such systems therefore can have real and measurable benefits. Overall the literature supports the view that business performance is only improved when the right fit between business strategy and HR practices is achieved. There is no one best practice HR strategy that will fit all contexts. Swain takes the view that HR departments need to change their focus from activities to organisational outcomes and instead of asking questions like 'how many were trained?' need to develop measures to find out whether training reflected enhanced performance or had any organisational outcomes. This is an area where more research is needed.

Much of the evidence base for the connection between HR practices and performance is statistical and the *how* and the *why* of what makes for successful outcomes are not well understood. There is a need for further research which will look at the intervening steps and see what mediates between the two variables *strategy* and *performance*. Process-based research of this kind would enable the development of learning tools which would help practitioners to make better decisions about personnel and development investment.

RELATING MANAGEMENT DEVELOPMENT TO PERFORMANCE

Some of the difficulties in establishing a link between management development and organisational performance have already been discussed. It is widely recognised that there has been for some time an overall weakness in the management literature in the area of being able to relate management development to organisation performance. A report from the DfEE in a study of 127 firms looked at the business benefits arising from management development activity. It found an almost universal inability to measure benefits that were directly attributable to management development. A similar lack of evidence of the business benefits arising from Business School activities was found in a report carried out on behalf of the Association of Business Schools. This lack of a clear link may be one of the reasons why some firms are reluctant to invest in management training. This is an area which needs further research. Nevertheless, although there are few well-evidenced studies looking specifically at the link between management development and performance there has been a small amount of research which has succeeded in showing a relationship.

One example is a thorough and strongly evidenced piece of research by Marshall et al 1993 which showed a clear link. The authors found that management training did have an effect on business performance. They concluded that the use of an external consultant in SMEs, who could help them to appraise the business and could also provide management development, was effective in producing business benefits. However, this study was carried out some time ago and more up-to-date research is urgently needed.

There are also other studies looking at the overall link between training (all kinds of training rather than management development) and business performance. Although the link is difficult to demonstrate, there are again a small number of studies which have succeeded in showing the connection. One good example of a well-evidenced study found that training loans did have an effect on business performance. The research looked at SMEs that received government training loans. It found that training loans did have a measurable affect on survival of the business, on growth and on turnover. More research is needed which can look in a similar way at interventions which have concentrated on developing managers rather than the whole workforce in order to provide better evidence that this is also true for management development.

DIFFICULTIES OF ESTABLISHING A CLEAR LINK

It is intrinsically difficult to establish the effects of management development, but some studies are better than others, and we can draw overall conclusions by looking across them. Even when an intervention appears to have been effective, the results may not be reliable. An example of this is another well-evidenced study on developmental feedback systems in an organisation also casts doubt upon the validity of 360° as a development tool. Changes in subjective views (how managers saw their own competence) did not relate to having had the feedback. More longitudinal studies of this nature would help achieve a better understanding of when 360° works and when it does not. At present the research data gives at best mixed results.

While other studies referred to in this report come to more optimistic conclusions about the effectiveness of 360° feedback suggests that this conclusion needs to be taken with some caution. The best overall conclusion is that 360° feedback can have beneficial effects it cannot be assumed that it always does and in all circumstances. Whether it does or not should be taken to depend on features of the situation in which it is used, details of the methodology with which it is applied and the extent of performance gain to be had – with already highly capable managers there will be less scope for improvement. Similarly, a study by Guest et al found that HR professionals and CEOs did not agree either about the effectiveness of HR practices or about how well the organisation was performing financially. These results cast doubt upon studies which rely on asking one or two people in the organisation about the effectiveness of management development or its influence on performance. Research is urgently needed to provide better measures and which can give more reliable results. A recent report from the Kellogg Foundation confirmed this view, indicating that while learning outcomes were often measured, data about impact at behavioural and organisational level were unavailable.

PROXY MEASURES OF CAPABILITY

Although the link between training and development and management capability has proved difficult to establish, there is empirical support for the impact of training and development in general on such things as trust perceptions, job satisfaction, goal and organisational commitment, discretionary behaviour, ability to cope and so on. Factors such as these might be viewed as 'proxy' measures of capability enhancement, and indeed are integral parts of the People and Performance model. This model traces the impact of training (training as a whole, not just management development) upon individuals' skill, motivation and opportunity to participate, which in turn links to commitment, satisfaction and discretionary behaviour to help the firm be successful. Based on a study of 12 UK organisations, the research concludes that sophisticated approaches to people management can help to induce discretionary behaviour in employees and do contribute to above-average performance. Caution must be exercised however in drawing firm conclusions from these results, given that some of the research reported above indicates the possible unreliability of reports about effects.

FACTORS LINKING WITH CAPABILITY AND PERFORMANCE IMPACT

Here we reviews the evidence which demonstrates (or implies) linkages between management and leadership development and enhanced capability at the individual level. Existing literature here indicates a number of features both of the management and leadership development activity, but especially of the organisational context, which make it more likely that management and leadership development will have a positive effect on capability and performance.

Management and leadership development that includes feedback can lead to a number of positive outcomes including improved capability. It might be expected that the use of 360-degree feedback would improve the individual and organisational benefits of management training. This is because such an intervention has the potential for improving capability in at least three ways: increasing the accuracy of training needs diagnosis, deriving a more focused personal development plan and motivating the individual to address their development needs.

Multiple sources of feedback improve accuracy and relevance for the individual, who is then more likely to act upon the data provided by colleagues. In support of this, the improved validity of multi-rater over single-rater assessments has been established and 360 degree feedback has been shown to be predictive of improvement in future performance. 360-degree feedback is primarily a diagnostic tool, and a condition of effectiveness is that relevant training and/or coaching which helps individuals increase their skills and self-efficacy in the development areas highlighted follow it. Alimo-Metcalfe cites a study by Bass *et al* that found an improvement in managers who attended a leadership training programme after receiving 360-degree feedback, but only on those dimensions that the participants had selected to work on.

They conclude that effective learning transfer is highly dependent upon focused effort around personal improvement goals and plans. This finding is supported by a study by Hazucha *et al*. They found that those managers receiving less favourable feedback ratings investing more effort in development activity than those receiving more favourable feedback first time round, and skill increases as a result of 360 degree feedback.

A further condition, leading to improved capability, is the opportunity for participants to discuss their feedback with the individuals who provided it. This enables the manager to uncover reasons behind the ratings given, understand discrepancies between self-ratings and that given by others and to discuss ways of improving certain behaviours in the future.

Siefert et al suggest that repeated feedback is a condition which facilitates individual learning; this is because it keeps the target areas salient, it allows precise tracking of progress on certain behaviours and improves the raters' understanding and appreciation of the skills they are evaluating.

Fletcher and Baldry note that it is possible for greater rater-ratee agreement (congruence) to result from raters' assessments remaining the same on separate occasions while self-ratings move from being more lenient and less congruent towards being less lenient and more congruent as a result of repeated feedback. In other words, a by-product of repeated 360-degree feedback on similar behaviours is to increase individuals' self-awareness, bringing it more into line with the views of their colleagues.

- Managers who have more accurate self-assessments are more likely to be promoted.
- Walker and Smither studied 252 managers who received five annual iterations of an upward feedback programme. Their capability improved more in years when direct reports indicated that the manager held a feedback meeting than in other years. The researchers concluded that meeting with subordinates to discussing their strengths and weaknesses enhances a manager's likelihood of enhancing performance over time.
- In their study of 17 managers in a savings bank, Siefert *et al* investigated the effects of multi-rater feedback and subsequent training on a specific example of managerial behaviour, namely 'influencing tactics'. Eight managers in an experimental group, who had received relevant training following their 360 feedback, were rated as significantly better in the use of these core tactics to

influence subordinates than a control group who had received their 360 feedback, but no subsequent training. This suggests that effective learning transfer for leadership behaviours results when diagnosed by 360 degree feedback
- In Mabey both interview and questionnaire data reveal that, while the content of the 360 degree feedback is unsurprising for the majority of managers, it does have the effect of catalysing more focused self development activities. Many examples were given of managers addressing weaknesses highlighted by the 360-degree questionnaire, making progress in areas of personal development and receiving positive feedback from colleagues as a result. More noteworthy is the finding that participant managers register different aspects of the training and development that they have experienced consistently better than a comparative group of non-participant managers. It can be surmised – though not conclusively – that this more favourable appraisal of development undertaken is due to a more accurate diagnosis and enhanced motivation arising from their 360-degree feedback. Finally and least expected, this positive experience of a management feedback and development intervention leads to significantly more favourable assessments of the organisation as a whole.

THE CONTRIBUTORY ROLE OF ORGANISATIONAL PROCESSES AND CLIMATE

Almost as important as the content of management and leadership development is quality of the management development processes which precede, support and reinforce the development activities. Research suggests that these processes play a big part in capability enhancement.
- Employees produce the most creative work when they work on complex, challenging jobs and are supervised in a supportive, non-controlling way.

- In a UK study, HRD managers were twice as likely to rate management development as having high organisational impact where fast-track development was used. Jones and Whitmore found those engaging in the personal developmental activities recommended by the development centre were more likely to advance in the organisation than a comparator group who were not selected.

- Research on adult learning tells us that development is likely to be more enduring and effective when certain features are in place: these include the timeliness and relevance of the training, opportunities for learning transfer, mechanisms for review and feedback and reward and recognition for any behaviour/attitude modification. When 125 line managers in the Thomson et al study were asked to evaluate their experience of these different aspects of their training and development, just over twothirds were very positive that the development was relevant to the job and that the learning had been transferred from the development to the job. However, generally speaking, they did not believe that developmental progress was reviewed by the organisation, that the reward and recognition policies in the organisation reinforced the training, or that the business impact of the development was assessed.

- A survey of 500 people (managers and non managers) in seven organisations, Tannenbaum revealed that those individuals with a greater awareness of the big picture (clarity about goals and direction; understanding about how their job and unit relates to these goals) reported higher levels of self-competence. High performance expectations, supportive policies and practices and toleration of mistakes during learning were all factors contributing to this big-picture awareness.

- Tafleur and Hyten described the impact of a variety of learning experiences upon job performance, particularly as it related to service quality. Where the learning incorporated task checklists, feedback, goal setting, training, job aids and bonuses for quality, this led to an increase in performance as measured by accuracy, timeliness and overall customer satisfaction.

IN DIFFERING CIRCUMSTANCES

Distinctions are made in the literature, research and amongst practitioners between management, leadership and entrepreneurship, but at the same time it is argued that these are all linked or part of the same thing.

The best conclusion that can be drawn is that there are meaningful differences between the practices carrying these labels, but that they blend together in different proportions in different situations in the work of organising organisations to be effective. On top of this there is considerable semantic overlap. For example the management of innovation has much in common with entrepreneurship, what are often referred to as the soft skills of management (judgement and working through people) have much in common with what is presented as the heart of leadership.

On the other hand when leadership is divided into the transactional and the transformational then the transactional arm of leadership appears to have much in common with what others would label management. On top of this the semantics change over time; for example the discussion in the 1960's and 1970's on management as opposed to administration mirrors the more recent management – leadership debate. In the administration – management debate the former is the maintenance of useful routines, the latter to do with messier processes of change and dealing with people.

In the management – leadership debate management is cast in the administrative maintenance role, and leadership takes on the role previously attributed to management. In addition to this there are cultural variations in the acceptability of terms in different economic and work sectors. For example, outside the world of private sector business: the public sector including health and education and the professions (which can be extended to include knowledge worker based organisations) the term leadership tends to be more acceptable than the term management which has had a very mixed reception in these domains.

To add to the complexity a more international perspective, which may be necessary in the context of globalisation even if the prime concern is with the organisational performance in the UK economy and society, shows that that terms like management and leadership do not necessarily have direct equivalents in, for example French, German and Japanese languages, and the work labels given to those involved in organising organisations in these nation states and cultures are different.

Finally, there are other work terms, like Director, Chief Executive, Chief Executive Officer used differently within Anglo-American culture to refer to people and roles that we would associate with leading and managing. For the purpose of this analysis, we suggest that the CEML position that it is unhelpful to split management and leadership (and by extension entrepreneurship) is the most useful one to take, but within this broad family of activities concerning the organisation of organisation there are some differentiated activities, which ultimately integrate, which are work considering separately but with this in mind.

ENTREPRENEURIAL SKILL

The question of entrepreneurial skill and how it can best be developed is a key issue in the current policy and economic environment. While the development of skill is part of the overall learning situation and can be taught in a variety of ways, skill development is also dependent both upon the context in which it is taught and the context in which it is used. Little is known about the nature of entrepreneurial skill and whether it can be taught or is innate. If entrepreneurial ability is not innate, then it can be developed. One report has studied entrepreneurs and found that rather than being highly risk-taking individuals as has previously been thought, in fact they have different cognitive perceptions of business situations to those of others.

They perceive opportunities where others see risks, rather than actively seeking the risk and being natural 'risk takers'. This finding has implications for management development. Whereas personal propensities such as a tendency to risk-taking are believed to be innate and largely impervious to change psychology suggests that cognitive processes *can* be developed in learning situations.

If successful entrepreneurs are operating by different cognitive processes and these processes can be identified and taught, then their successfulness is likely to increase. As Palich and Bagby say "It stands to reason that those who seek opportunity are likely to find it."

LEADERSHIP SKILL

A great deal has been written about the nature of leadership and the skills and behaviours leaders need to have. Horne and Jones in a strongly evidenced study found eight key characteristics of leadership of which inspiration was seen as both the most important and the most lacking. A considerable range of methods was considered effective for leadership development.

Leadership lies not only in the quality of the individual but also in the situation. There may be many effective styles of leadership. It follows therefore that in some cases rather than seeking to develop different leadership behaviours in people, a leader can instead be appointed to a position which suits their leadership style. Organisational culture also matters. Leaders must be able to adapt to change and will be more effective in an organisation where the organisational culture responds positively to change than in an organisation where change is resisted. Leadership can also be *transactional* or *transformational*. In transactional leadership leaders use power to achieve task completion by followers. In transformational leadership, the leader motivates followers and engages them in the processes of the work to be completed. There is however no single consistent definition of a successful leader arising from the literature.

There are no clear answers. There is widespread belief that interventions (training and development activities) will help to develop and improve leadership within organisations. On the other hand, trait theories show that there are significant correlations between personality traits and successful leadership. As personality traits are stable over long periods of time, this suggests that innate personality traits are an important part of leadership capability.

Other recent theories suggest that leadership is no longer a process in which leaders are individuals who have followers, in a situation in which dominance and/or influence are the primary vehicles of leadership. Instead, leadership is seen as a social process where leadership involves coordinating efforts and moving together as a group. Whereas in the past, leaders used to direct and command, it is suggested that now they need to influence and support.

WHAT MANAGERS NEED TO LEARN?

A considerable body of theory exists about what managers need to learn and the competences they need to acquire. For example, Senge in his seminal work found that managers need four kinds of learning: to attain personal mastery; to surface mental models and challenge them; to build shared visions; to facilitate team learning. As has already been discussed above, Business Schools are able to, and do, successfully teach basic management competences. However, as has also been discussed above, managers need a wider range of skills than those that can be taught through formal courses. Argyris and Schön made a classic distinction between *espoused theories* and *theories in use*. They found that managers need development which will help them become aware and responsive to feedback through what they call *double-loop learning*. Managers often only look for, and are only able to accept, feedback that fits in with their pre-conceived notions. Management developers need to help managers to step outside their taken-forgranted world and seek genuine feedback about the outcomes of their actions.

CHANGING MANAGEMENT SKILLS

A report for the Skills Task Force found that the managers of the future will need to be able to respond to continuously changing environments. They will need both formal and informal learning processes, and will need both know-how (skill, competence, tacit knowledge) and know-that (propositional, cognitive knowledge). There has been a shift away from manufacturing and primary industries and this is expected to continue as is the shift away from manual and low skilled occupations and towards professional and managerial occupations. These authors quote data to show that employers systematically under-estimate the difficulty they will have in recruiting to managerial positions. They also show that there have been increasing difficulties for employers in recruiting to managerial occupations.

They suggest that these data indicate that there is a shortage of managers. In addition, qualifications among managers have traditionally been low in the UK although it is not clear whether this reflects a lack of skill or simply a different pattern of qualificatory behaviour. However the proportion of qualified managers is rising. Johnson & Winterton also conclude that different skills are needed by managers in SMEs to those needed in larger organisations. They point to the high failure rates of SME start-up as evidence of the management skills gap in SMEs. On the other hand, Storey and Westhead find that there is no clear empirical evidence to support the view that increased management training in SMEs will result in improved business performance. This must be seen therefore as an area of conflicting views in which firm conclusions are difficult to draw.

MANAGEMENT AND LEADERSHIP IN THE PUBLIC SECTOR

It is widely believed that public service management is not as good as it could be. A recent research study undertaken by the PIU concluded that the public services do not attract or keep the best leaders. It also reported that there is little data in the public sector about the career progression, turnover or wastage of public sector leaders. Partly in response to such concerns, there are many new leadership colleges being set up for the public sector. There is however no evidence at present as to how effective they are. The report recommends a number of strategies for the public sector including more active recruitment of leaders, better selection processes, better rewards (not only financial but in terms of recognition and other benefits), a secondment scheme, and new strategies to develop leaders so as to widen the pool available. It has also been suggested that generic competences are not applicable across different sectors.

Much more research is needed about what is effective in terms of development for leaders in the public sector. Research undertaken by the Association of MBAs (AMBA) has suggested that public sector managers tend to leave the sector when they gain an MBA. It is not clear why this is so but it seems likely that they choose to take the MBA with a view to moving into the private sector. If so, this has worrying implications for management capacity in the public sector. It is also the case that the public services have seen many reforms in recent years. These reforms are based on principles of accountability, the development of a framework of standards, more devolution to local levels, building local capacity and offering more choice for customers. To respond to these changes and pressures, managers in the public sector need different skills from managers in the private sector. This is particularly so in the areas of partnership working and dealing with the political dimension.

A wide range of performance indicators has been put in place in the public sector, but there appears to be little or no research relating these to management or leadership development. This is an area in which further research is needed. Charlesworth's report indicates that leadership in the public sector is seen as poor, that leadership development in the public sector tends to be old-fashioned and out of date, and that leadership development is given a low priority in the public sector. Leaders in the public sector need to learn how to work in partnership with other organisations, to work with the political dimension, and to develop frameworks that put users and citizens as the heart of their change agendas.

Outcomes in the voluntary sector are even more difficult to assess than in other sectors. This is a specialised area and one where additional research is needed. The Kellogg report found in the USA that community leadership outcomes are the most difficult to evaluate. Community programmes usually have little prior assessment of capacity and find it difficult therefore to determine whether there has been any impact. Similarly, in the UK, more work is needed to identify the development needs of voluntary organisations and to look at how their effectiveness could be assessed.

SIZE OF ORGANISATION

A significant body of literature indicates that the management development needs of small firms are different to those of large firms. Details of some of the literature on this topic are given in Perren. The literature he review suggests that SMEs find management development too 'supply led', that informal approaches to management development are highly valued, that 'learning through doing' may often be the most appropriate for SMEs, and that there are unique features of business support required by small firms. This evidence is largely based on the views and perceptions of small business people themselves. Whether they would benefit from more formal development if they were willing and able to use it is an open question but the reality is that they do not use them very much, and this is not for the lack of them being on offer.

The practicalities of being away from work for significant periods, and costs in many cases, are barriers, and it certainly appears that small business people tend to have developed the learning strategy and style of learning by doing and seeking informal support and advice from those that they know and trust in their personal social and business networks. In addition for many (but not all) small business people the attractions of gaining qualifications in management and leadership are less than for managers in larger organisations where formal qualifications may be more important for getting selected for jobs and career progression within organisations. The CEML conclusion was to offer more support for approaches that 'go with the flow' of informal support for learning and learning by doing. Following up the initiatives that are known to have followed from this would be a useful future evaluation research activity.

Overall, the literature suggests that the best approaches to management development for small firms will lie in the short course or individual business coaching models. It has been known for some time that it is difficult to get SMEs to engage in management development. Henderson et al in a small descriptive study found that time rather than cost was the limiting factor for SMEs in undertaking management development. Other writers have suggested that SMEs would undertake management development if they saw the value of it and if it served their interests. An interesting case study of an initiative involving business coaching found that this was an effective way of gaining the interest of SMEs. These findings showed that the key factor was trust and that where a relationship of trust was built up between the company and the coach, effective change and learning did take place.

It has also been found that managers of SMEs have different needs to those of other firms. Gibb showed that owner/managers have very different attitudes to development from those of managers in larger firms. The owner/manager is unlikely to view development as a personal gain, or as career development. He or she is not looking for the same kinds of rewards or returns from development as a manager in a larger firm. Rather, development is seen in terms of gains to the business and only development that is seen as directly related to this will be valued. Similarly, managers in micro-enterprises have their own particular needs. Little work has been done on micro-enterprises, but one interesting study in Ireland (where 90% of firms are micro) of firms with ten or fewer employees found some interesting results.

DOMINANT ORGANISATIONAL CULTURE

A large literature exists on the 'learning organisation' and the nature of organisational culture is widely understood as being crucial to management effectiveness. Kilmann offers the following definition of a learning organisation: A learning organisation describes, controls and improves the processes by which knowledge is created, acquired, distributed, interpreted, stored, retrieved and used, for the purpose of achieving long-term organisational success. He draws both on TQM (total quality management) and BPR (business process re-engineering) in his discussion of the factors which are relevant.

Bramley found a number of factors in the organisational context which are more important than managerial skill in determining how the work will be done. These factors included the structure of the organisation (who reports to whom), the organisational climate (how people relate to each other, whether individuality is valued, what support and encouragement is given), the design of the work (whether it is stress-inducing, what aspects are seen as key results areas), and whether good performance is actually rewarded (both in terms of recognition and praise as well as promotion and pay).

These things will affect how managers behave far more than the knowledge and skills they may acquire through development. What is needed therefore in his view is development related closely to the workplace, focusing on giving feedback on performance and working towards individual development plans. Another study, this time a case study of training in a large organisation, found that contextual factors were highly significant in terms of learning. Although this study was not a study of managers but of training for all employees, it is included here as illustrative of the kinds of contextual factor which may be important. It is not known if these factors also apply to managers but if they do, there are clearly important implications for training and development. This study found that informal and tacit learning was more important than formal, 'embrained knowledge' as a source of innovation. Much learning at work was found to be informal and socially produced, or else socially constrained. Greater weight therefore needs to be given, conclude these authors, to how group and organisational variables influence learning when designing learning interventions. These findings corroborate the views of situated learning theory and the analysis by Blackler of different kinds of knowledge.

Blackler distinguishes between embrained (cognitive) knowledge and the embedded knowledge of communities of practice which is both informal and tacit. Senge has argued that knowledge creation occurs in working teams and that individual learning is frequently a by-product of what goes on in really innovative teams. Senge points out that individual self-development and learning is not the ultimate goal, and that if it becomes so, the organisation is vulnerable to having that knowledge leave with the individual.

4

The Purposes and Nature of the Appraisal

Any strategy for any organisation has to build from what that organisation is, which means that the first task is to understand the present strengths, weaknesses, capabilities, resources and vulnerabilities, in relation to the external environment in which it operates. Neglect of this basic step can result in strategies which appear well founded in relation to the market and the assessments of the future environment, but which cannot be implemented because of ill-founded implicit assumptions about the organisation itself.

The early books on strategy stressed the importance of what, depending on the whims of the author, was called the corporate appraisal, the position audit, the situation audit, or the assessment of strengths and weaknesses, opportunities and threats. All divided the task into two: the internal appraisal and the external appraisal. However, although there are different elements to be addressed, these two sub-tasks are not totally independent of each other.

The internal aspects have to be interpreted with one eye on what is going on outside, and the external have to be related to what is happening inside. Some authorities tried to put their own stamp on the concept of strengths, weaknesses, opportunities and threats, developing mnemonics around various combinations of the initials, or some-times around the initials of synonyms. Thus we had SOFT (strength, opportunity, fault, threat), TOWS, WOTS UP (weakness, opportunity, threat, strength, underlying planning) and SWOT. The only combination we did not seem to be offered was TWOS! For some reason SWOT has been the winner and is the term in most common use today. There can be few managers who have never been involved in a SWOT analysis. However, there has also been a change in what is meant by SWOT.

The analytical foundation that was the intention of the early writing has disappeared in many modern books, and, more importantly, from what managers actually do in many organisations. SWOT has become a process of asking managers what they believe are the strengths, weaknesses, opportunities and threats for their part of the organisation, either as individuals or in discussion groups, when strategies are under consideration. Managers do have insights that can be important, but they do not always have accurate factual knowledge, so if they are unaware of the importance of various matters, or of what is actually going on in the organisation, they will ignore these things. So the results of the common approach to SWOT may contain nuggets of gold, but are often so mixed up with iron pyrites, fool's gold, that they can be misleading and unhelpful. This is not an inevitable outcome, but is one which is highly likely.

We have seen many SWOT analyses developed in this way, and have seen numerous occasions when they have missed the critical issues, or totally misinterpreted the strategic situation. Frequently, managers find it hard to identify true strengths, and we have seen statements that show only two: one praises the skills of the chief executive, and the other refers to the competence and dedication of the management team. Weaknesses listed often encompass minor operating issues, rather than the main strategic matters, and result in numerous action plans, few of which are relevant to the long-term strategy of the firm, and most of which are never implemented. We have also observed the opposite, when an organisation has undertaken a comprehensive appraisal, and as a result has completely changed its strategy.

Sometimes this has been a result of a management consulting assignment, but it also happens when managers themselves are given the opportunity to make a full assessment. The executive MBA programme of Copenhagen Business School has as its main final assignment the completion of a full strategic appraisal of the students' own organisations, incorporating various analytical approaches which will be discussed later in this book. As the students are usually senior managers, they are in a position to use the results of their work, and there have been many situations where this exercise has caused a total rethink of the strategy. Despite good management information systems, and a deep knowledge of their business and its markets, many have found critical information from approaching the task in a thorough and holistic way.

There may be several reasons why the corporate appraisal has become corrupted to an "ask the managers" approach. They include:

- *Lack of Guidance on how to do it:* Despite the emphasis on the appraisal in the earlier literature, there are very few books which attempt to explain how to undertake an appraisal. It is also true to say that many MBA programmes spend very little time on this. Being told that something is important, but not the detail of how to do it, certainly makes it harder to do the job well.

- *Better Management Information Systems:* Managers today have access to better, more comprehensive and more up-todate management information systems than was the case in the past. This can greatly facilitate the corporate appraisal, provided the right information has been collected in the first place, which does not always happen. Regular access to information can mean that managers really are informed about every important aspect of their business, and therefore do not need special exercises: it can also lead to complacency and a situation where critical factors are not related to each other, or thoroughly understood.

- *Pressure on Managers.* The pressure on managers for immediate results has always been high, but is now greater than ever. It is certainly much quicker to ask managers to define the corporate strengths and weaknesses than to spend precious time on special analyses. Therefore, managers have to be convinced that the extra time is justified. The pressure for a quick fix means that managers will often be tempted to reach for a technique, instead of going back to basic principles, although this is rarely the most effective way to deal with a strategic problem.
- *The Complexity of Many Companies:* Many companies are very large and complex, which can make the task of carrying out a comprehensive appraisal seem rather daunting, and, with the decline of large strategic staff departments, the task of organising such a study is devolved to busy line managers. We hope that this book will show that it is a task which lies within the competence of most managers, and that if approached in a sensible way it need not be overwhelming.

NEEDS OF AN APPRAISAL

This is a question which has a number of answers, because an appraisal may be needed in several different situations. They are discussed here in order of probable frequency of occurrence. The importance of various aspects of the appraisal may vary with the purpose, but the overall concepts are applicable to all.

Preparation of a Strategic Plan

We do not assume that all organisations will want to produce a written plan, either as a one-off event or as part of a formal procedure within the overall group. However, we *know* that all organisations have to think about strategy, and that effective strategy is unlikely if divorced from the realities of the present situation. We can draw a parallel with a personal decision. Let us assume that you want to take an energetic holiday with a group of very fit people exploring remote high mountain country in South America. You may not have taken very much exercise in the last ten years, and may never have walked in mountains before. The penalty of being considerably weaker than the group would vary from embarrassment at causing delays to others if you could not walk as fast as they could, to putting other people in danger if you collapsed or caused such delays that you and others had to walk in rugged country after nightfall.

Faced with that sort of holiday, and knowing what you know about your state of health, you would review your fitness. If you were pretty healthy generally, you might decide to do some training before leaving, to get fit enough for the trip, and indeed you might leave the decision on whether to join the party until you had seen how well you could cope walking long distances on day trips to smaller mountains which are closer to you. You might also want to have a medical examination, to confirm that you had no underlying problems which you did not know about, and which might be exacerbated by strenuous activity and altitude.

If you were irresponsible, you could just sign up and go, without doing any appraisal or taking any remedial action. But to do so would increase the risks of failure, and could even become a disaster. The sensible person would do a self-appraisal, add expert opinion where needed, and take remedial action as necessary. The risks of failure would be much reduced. In one sense the corporate appraisal has a similar purpose to this personal appraisal. It checks out the organisation's fitness for specific strategies, by testing the things you think you know already, and by taking steps to uncover things which could be critical, but which are currently hidden from you. But the corporate appraisal does more than this, in that it may help the identification of opportunities.

We are not arguing that the corporate appraisal will deliver a total strategy to you. We are emphatic that it is an essential first step to such a strategy. analysis (and the corporate appraisal is but one of many essential analytical tasks) is only one of five critical factors that are essential in attaining an effective strategy.

It is not a sequential model, in that it does not argue for any particular order for these factors, nor that one has to be completed before another can begin. But strategic success depends on all of them. At the heart of the diagram is the calibre of senior managers, for weak management can defeat the best strategy, and may prevent you even finding a good strategy. Around the outside of the model are analysis, creative strategic thinking, the way strategic decisions are taken, and implementation. The model implies that a failure to undertake the corporate appraisal could have an adverse impact on the strategic decisions that are ultimately taken. In addition, it could affect the ability of the organisation to implement those decisions: if - for example - assumptions were made about corporate competencies which were erroneous.

Review of a Strategic Situation

A similar situation arises when a manager takes over a new responsibility. We use a new chief executive as an example, but the same sort of situation can apply with managers at lower levels than this. One of the first tasks of a new CEO is to review the strategies of the organisation, and this includes a need for a detailed corporate appraisal. Sometimes consultants are used for this task, which may be to preserve objectivity, or because of a shortage of resources which makes it sensible to use outsiders. Speed is often very important, particularly if the company is failing. Although any newly appointed CEO, particularly if brought in from outside, would be well advised to undertake such a strategic review, the task becomes unavoidable in the failing or underperforming company. The order in which the elements of the appraisal are tackled may not be the same as the order in this book, since attention should be focused on the obvious problem areas first, but the approaches discussed are all relevant. The main difference lies in the speed with which decisions have to be made, partly because of external pressures, and partly because a company that is losing cash has an immediate need to do something about it. Not surprisingly, in such situations, the now traditional SWOT approach by asking the managers is unlikely to achieve the results: if they knew where the problem was, they would presumably have done something about it before.

Acquisition or Merger

There have been numerous surveys, stretching back to the early 1970s, which show that there is a high failure rate for acquisitions and mergers. Until recently, if anyone had asked us the chances of success, we should have said it is the same as if you toss a coin. In most surveys success was judged in one of two ways: the organisations' own assessments against the original objectives, or whether the acquisition was subsequently closed or sold off when this was not the original intention. The reason we have not referenced these surveys is because of a more recent study which measured shareholder value. On this criterion only 17 per cent of acquisitions could be called a success, in that they increased value, 30 per cent left the value unchanged, and the rest reduced value. This is a far higher failure rate than had been indicated by the previous less-objective criteria, and comes dangerously near calling tails when the other person is using a double-headed coin. Interestingly, 82 per cent of the companies in the sample believed that the acquisition had been a success, which was almost a mirror image of the true position. This research identified a number of keys to success, only two of which are of concern here: detailed synergy evaluation and due diligence. Synergy evaluation requires a detailed knowledge of your own operations as well as those of the potential acquisition, and the KPMG report argues that the evaluation should be undertaken before the deal is struck. The emphasis should be on what can be delivered, not what is theoretically possible. The detailed knowl edge that comes from a corporate appraisal is essential for synergy evaluation. Due diligence, as KPMG found, is widely undertaken, but is not always comprehensive. For example, 54 per cent of cases did not cover management culture, 35 per cent excluded HRM, and slightly under half included IT (these were aspects specifically covered in the survey questions, and the results do not mean that all other areas were comprehensively included). KPMG states:

> Sophisticated and forward looking recipients use a "springboard" approach to due diligence which often encompasses a range of investigative tools designed to systematically assess all the facts impacting on value. This can include market reviews, risk assessments, and the assessment of management competencies, as well as areas to concentrate on for synergies or operational impact.

Ideally, similar information should be obtained to that described in this book. When the due diligence is undertaken from outside the target company, as in a hostile bid situation, it is unlikely that such comprehensive information can be obtained, and standards have to be lowered. However, in a friendly acquisition the situation may be different and there may be access, possibly via a consultant, to internal data.

Divestment

Although we do not wish to labour the point, sometimes a corporate appraisal is very helpful in getting a good price for an activity which is to be divested. One company we are aware of undertook a synergy evaluation in reverse to determine which potential buyer could gain the most value from buying the subsidiary it wished to sell. This could not have been done without a detailed knowledge of their own organisation and those of competitors.

WAYS OF LOOKING AT AN ORGANISATION

There are many different ways of looking at an organisation, each of which can yield different insights. The triangle looks at total performance of the organisation under study, which could be an overall group, a strategic business unit (SBU) within the group, or any self-contained business within the SBU. So in this study we would include items like the overall profitability, shareholder value measures and growth.

Using one or more of these integrative concepts does not invalidate the functional view, but may add additional strategic insights which might otherwise be lost in the gaps between the functional chimneys. The diagram shows an integrated organisation, but we could have positioned a number of SBUs side by side, with the bars overlapping all or several of these. Technologies, for example, may stretch across several SBUs within the organisation, and this may be part of its strength.

- *Competencies:* Are shown by the first bar. Hamel and Prahalad stress their belief that top managers should view the organisation as a portfolio of competencies. They see a competence as a "bundle of skills and technologies", and add the phrase "that enables a company to provide a particular benefit to customers" when describing a core competence. Every year since 1993 management consultants Bain & Co. have undertaken an international survey into the use of tools and techniques in companies. The survey covers the top 25 topical tools and techniques which are of value to top management. Core competencies were used by 63 per cent of companies which took part in the 1998 survey, and were ninth in order of popularity. However, no one should view the core competence approach as a stand-alone technique which is not part of a wider corporate appraisal. The development of new core competencies is s strategic activity that should follow a careful appraisal of the current competencies, whether core or non-core. And the appraisal of the competencies requires a careful study to decompose the firm's "economic engine".

- *Capabilities:* Represented by the second bar, are a concept which appears to have been derived from the core competencies method. Stalk, Evans and Shulman argued that the really important thing was not competencies, but capabilities, defined as "a set of business processes strategically understood". The authors use many of the examples given by Hamel and Prahalad in their works, arguing that it is capabilities rather than competencies that has led to their success. The main thrust of the argument is that it is not just the individual processes but how they are bundled that really matters.

- *Processes:* Have long been seen as offering a different way of looking at an organisation, and approaches like total quality management (TQM) and business process reengineering (BPR) in their different ways are dependent on identifying and understanding the current processes. We have included the value chain approach under the process heading, although it is different from merely identifying what the processes are, and its focus is on what delivers value to customers.

- *Technologies:* Are a part of the core competence approach, but also need to be looked at in their own right. It is easy to see how a critical aspect of the technologies owned by an organisation could be overlooked unless an organisation-wide examination were made.

Although this may be less likely in a small organisation, it would be a real danger in a large multinational operating with several SBUs.

SOME FOUNDATION QUESTIONS

Although each element of the appraisal has to be looked at individually, and in relation to the purpose of the appraisal, there are some basic questions to be answered which, with common-sense variations, can be applied to every element of the appraisal process. They provide a mindset which is helpful, whether we are looking at overall performance, undertaking a functional analysis, or taking one of the other ways of looking at the organisation which were discussed above.

The following list is quoted from Hussey:

1. What are we doing now?
2. What are we achieving by doing this?
3. Why are we doing this?
4. Does what we do fit the customers' requirements?
5. How do we know this?
6. How does what we do compare with competitors, in so far as we are able to deduce this?
7. Are there other ways in which we could achieve the same benefit?
8. Should we be doing these instead?
9. How does this contribute to our corporate success?
10. How does it help the corporate vision?

THE "INSIGHT" APPROACHES

Earlier we pointed to the deficiencies of approaches which relied on management insight and opinion, but nevertheless said that there could be some value in the "ask the managers" approach. Although the focus of the book is on analytical methods, we are ending with some ideas on how to get more out of approaches that tap into what the managers know or believe are the strengths and weaknesses. Results are likely to be more useful if attention is focused on a specific issue or problem, rather than asking managers to identify all the strengths and weaknesses of the firm, which often leads to superficial answers.

For example, if a probable strategy of the firm is to expand the geographical operations of the organisation, managers might be asked to define those things about the company which could be used as building blocks for this strategy, the things that act as constraints that would have to be dealt with, and the new skills and competencies which would be needed.

Another approach might be to take the two or three major competitors and ask in which areas they are better than us, where they are thought to be worse, and where we are all about the same. The problems and issues chosen must be believed to be relevant to the managers involved, if they are to put their minds to the task. Another tip is to do some work first, so that key findings from the management information system are provided as part of the process of discussing strengths and weaknesses. There is a very simple, but useful, tool called the equilibrium approach, which is based on force field analysis, and is intended to aid discussion with groups of managers. The following extract is taken from Hussey.

The objectives of equilibrium analysis are:

- To achieve a common understanding of strengths and weaknesses.
- To identify strengths as well as weaknesses.
- To decide priorities for corrective action.
- To identify corrective action.

It is a very simple concept which can be taught to any group in a matter of minutes. The horizontal line represents the present state of anything that is to be studied: labour turnover rates, market position, cost structures, profitability, etc. Focus should be given by posing a question such as: "Why is our market share 15 per cent?" The base line then represents the current state – a market share of 15 per cent. It is as high as 15 per cent because certain positive features support it. It is as low as 15 per cent because certain negative features hold it down. The trick is to get the meeting to identify these two groups of factors, writing them in heading form at the top and bottom of the diagram, across the page.

If too many weaknesses are identified attention can be changed to strengths with a remark such as "Now I can't understand why you have any market share at all." If too many strengths come up one can ask why market share has not risen to 50 per cent.

Criteria for successful use of the approach include a group of people who know the situation, and preparation for the meeting by an analyst who has looked at the factual base available. The analyst should be prepared to challenge (e.g. if the group insists that a plus factor is the firm's reputation, whereas market research shows that it is almost unknown, the factual position should over-ride the impression).

The next step in the use of the technique is to rate the relative significance of the various factors identified. This is the reason for the scaling on the vertical line.

Once the information is displayed it is possible to use it:

- Would the position best be improved by strengthening a positive factor or removing a negative one?
- Are there any factors which cannot be altered by the firm, and which should not receive more attention?
- What can be done about the really important factors?

The equilibrium approach could be used again if it was decided to tackle the high sales force turnover, and used to try to identify the factors which attract sales people to the firm, and those that cause them to leave. If the assessments move from the known base of fact, it may be useful to accept them for the time being, but to check them out after the meeting.

REFLECTION

Certainly a well-run modern organisation will be able to obtain much of the required information from the management information system, but our experience is that there are always critical aspects, in even the best run organisations, which are not covered in the optimum way for a strategic appraisal, and there are always critical areas which are overlooked. Because organisations are changing fast, their capabilities, resources, strengths and weaknesses also change rapidly, and even well-informed managers can base strategies on out-ofdate understanding: a problem which we hope will be avoided by those who follow the advice of this book.

ASSESSING FINANCIAL PERFORMANCE

Any appraisal of a business should start with the overall financial performance. Whether the organisation is large or small, financial performance gives an indication of overall success or failure. How success is judged will vary between different types of organisation. The public quoted company may see its market value as the most important dynamic; the small business may interpret success as the provision of acceptable salaries to its owner-managers; the not-for-profit organisation may be more concerned to ensure that it is able to continue to meet the needs for which it was established.

There are various standard ways of doing this. Many readers will be familiar with the common methods and ratios, and because most organisations will regularly use at least some of them. This makes it easier for those who do not wish to read the definitions to skip them. The value of any ratio is much reduced unless it can be compared to something. The comparator may be internal (e.g. performance for prior periods, or performance of the various units of the group, or the target), but we would argue that more often it should be external (e.g. competitors or companies which the stock market sees as similar). Without the comparison any ratio loses much of its power, as it is harder to judge whether it is good or bad.

However, there is a note of caution, in that there are organisational differences in acceptable accounting treatment within any one particular country, and variations in generally accepted accounting practice between countries. So if comparing a return on investment ratio, for example, with that of a competitor, it is prudent to read the notes to the annual report, and to try to identify as many of the differences as possible.

APPROACH OF THE ORGANISATION

Earlier we mentioned that we expected that most organisations would, as a matter of routine, keep tabs on the overall measures of financial performance. Behind this truism lies the fact that not all organisations will do this in the same way. For example, a company that has growth in earnings per share as its driving force is likely to take different actions, and to judge its own performance differently, than if it were using one of the value-based methods.

In the first case there would be emphasis on growth in earnings, with a tendency to choose debt rather than raising funds by an issue of new shares. In the latter, the emphasis would be on cash flow, the market value of the company, and the rate of return earned compared with the overall cost of capital. Both these methods will have different implications on how business units within the group are managed and their performances judged.

It follows that one early question to determine is which of the methods the organisation uses as its main driver. Logically, the next step is to assess the advantages and disadvantages of the chosen method, and to consider the implications of a change in thinking. So there is value in assessing overall financial performance by several different methods, to see what additional insight can be gained. In addition to gaining a picture of the overall performance, the overall financial appraisal can provide a first idea of where the profit is coming from. Initially this will be at the level of SBUs or operating companies; later we will suggest how the analysis should be taken to a lower level of resolution. Again, we recommend that a number of measures be used, and the figures displayed for each. As a minimum we recommend growth in revenue and profits.

Return on assets, and a measure of cash flow. In this case too, ratios make more sense when compared with various comparators, one of which should be the weighted cost of capital.

Market Valuation

The organisation's performance in the stock market should be tracked, and the variations in market value calculated. It is easy to argue that, as so much of what affects the share price is outside the control of the organisation, managers should have little concern with it. True, the stock market does sometimes appear to be irrational, but we have to remember that it is driven not just by past performance but by expectations of the future. In all companies, management is to a large degree shaping those expectations, and in companies that follow a value-based approach the choice of strategies is made in a deliberate way with shareholder value as the main determinant.

When the British supermarket chain Somerfield acquired a rival firm Kwik-Save in 1998, the market capitalisation was reported as £1.26 billion. It had soared to £2.2 billion by the end of that year. In November 1999 it had dropped to £409 million, and at this point Somerfield hoped to raise some £400 million by selling some of the stores in the group. By March 2000, when it was announced that the chief executive was leaving the company, the market value had fallen to £283 million. It looks as if this acquisition was one of the more than 50 per cent which destroy shareholder value. Undoubtedly there were performance problems, which meant that the deal did not deliver its promises, and performance problems frequently lead to cash flow difficulties. Unexpectedly high levels of debt always mean that there are additional costs before any earnings are available as dividends. Share prices, which rose dramatically on expectations of high profits from the merger, fell equally dramatically as the actual results of the merger became clear, putting more pressure by shareholders on the management. What might come from an examination of market value in the financial appraisal is an appreciation of whether the shares are over- or under-valued, and the vulnerability of the organisation to a hostile takeover bid. In a multi-business organisation, it is also worth trying to establish whether the whole is worth less than the sum of its parts, which could lead to actions such as divesting or floating off certain activities.

FINANCIAL RESOURCES

The appraisal is not just about performance and expectations, but should also establish the financial resources the organisation can muster. As a first step the conventional gearing and liquidity ratios should be calculated, to give an indication of the flexibility the organisation has to raise further debt financing if required. When looking at these ratios, it is sensible to look at seasonal patterns, as what is an adequate level of finance for most of the year may be inadequate for the peak periods.

A higher level of liquid capital than is needed for operations may be a strength, in that it gives strategic flexibility, but it can also be a serious weakness, making the organisation a target for corporate raiders and depressing the overall rate of profitability of the whole organisation. The next task is to assess the flexibility the organisation has to raise additional equity There may be several strategies available. At this stage the aim is not to make choices, but to understand the limitations of the organisation, in relation to the likely capital requirements of the near future.

Clearly an organisation's ability to grow is affected by its capacity to finance its strategies. In the appraisal the aim is to understand the degree to which the organisation's financial strength (or lack of it) is a help or a hindrance. This understanding is even more useful if it is placed in the context of the organisation's current pattern of needs. One useful method is portfolio analysis. This of course is not just a financial tool, and can be one of the bases of a corporate strategy. In the financial context here, it is a way of looking at all the units of an organisation in relation to each other to see which are expected to consume cash and which to generate it.

Although we do not believe that portfolio analysis should be used in quite the way suggested by its early exponents as the main determinant of strategy, it is extremely useful as a way of getting an overview of a complex multi-business organisation. We have used black circles for businesses losing cash in the last financial year and open circles for those gaining it. The figure for cash gain or loss is written against the symbol: the second figure shown is the average for the last three years. Any information about known commitments for the future which will alter the pattern could also be signalled on the chart. An example might be a contract agreed for the building of a new factory in the following year, the capital costs of which have not yet hit the books.

Of course, it would be possible to do a simple listing of businesses detailing this information. The value of a portfolio chart is that it gives some indication of the quality dimension of each business, and although unspecific about future capital needs, it does distinguish those businesses likely to be heavy cash consumers from those that are not. The key point is that profits and cash generation are not always synchronised: a very profitable business in a high-growth situation may be going through a period where the annual cash used, for assets and working capital, may be greater than the cash generated.

USING ROI CHART

A useful method for showing the economic structure of a business is the ROI chart, sometimes called a Du Pont chart after its leading initiator. The ROI chart combines the income statement and balance sheet, and gives a broad indication of the sources of profits and, ideally, the utilisation of financial resources.

Contribution to Profits and Central Overheads: Be used instead of profit, as in many organisations head office costs are allocated and apportioned to businesses on a somewhat arbitrary basis. This can make a business appear less profitable than is the actual case, but - worse than this - can make it appear that closure of the business is a sensible strategy: this is only true if the head office overheads also disappear. Frequently this does not happen, as they are not true direct costs, and this means that the same costs are now allocated or apportioned over a smaller base of businesses, which makes these businesses look less profitable. Using contribution instead of profit can therefore give a truer economic perception of the value of each business. The ROI chart is an ideal tool for an organisation with five or six SBUs, or for an SBU with a similar number of sub-units. It becomes cumbersome with large, complex organisations, and may become difficult to read, although it may still be valuable at SBU level. Similarly, in small, single-business companies it may add nothing to what can be read off the final accounts. As with all ways of displaying information, the decision to use it should be based on the situation of the organisation.

THE SOURCES OF PROFITS

At this stage of the appraisal we should have documented the overall position of the organisation, and know the cash generating or cash consuming propensity of each of the SBUs. We would also have first impressions of the level of profits, profitability and contribution of each SBU. Performance ratios will have been looked at against various internal and external comparators, so that we have an understanding of whether they are good or bad. We would also know our overall financial strength or weakness. The next stage is to gain a deeper understanding of where the profits come from. This means getting to the level of products (or activities in the case of service businesses) and customers. And the first thing to do is to check out the way the organisation calculates the costs of products.

To managers used to taking the cost accountants' figures as accurate, this may seem like heresy. In reality it is not the accuracy of the calculations that should be questioned, but the validity of the assumptions that lie behind them. The following extract from Hussey explains the issue.

In many cases the apportionment of costs between products is on some form of allocation basis. It is worthwhile studying the basis of apportionment and allocation since although suitable for many purposes it may be inadequate for this study. Many allocations assume that costs fall in a normal distribution; for example, that invoicing costs are a fixed percentage for all products. Inventories may be treated on the same basis. If costs are reallocated on the basis of actual transactions two things may become apparent:

- A skewed distribution between products.
- A skewed distribution between different customers.

An example may make this clearer. A firm offering a lorry sales service is likely to express its sales/delivery costs as a percentage of the sales value, say 5 per cent. The assumption is made that every £1 of sales bears the same percentage of cost: in other words that a normal distribution applies. In fact, everybody really knows that it costs less per unit to sell one customer 100 units than to sell 100 customers one unit each. In addition everybody knows that it takes more time and effort to reach a customer 10 miles away than one who is only one mile away. In other words costs do not fall in a normal distribution. Yet not all organisations arrange their cost data so that they can make any decisions on this basis.

One of the first people to argue for a different basis for costing was Drucker who suggested the transaction basis for cost allocation mentioned earlier. An example of this would be to allocate invoicing costs on the basis of the number of lines on the invoices when looking at products, and the number of invoices when assessing the costs of customers. This gives a much closer interpretation of the true costs than apportioning by value.

The transaction idea has been given a modern interpretation in the concept of activity-based costing (ABC). This tackles the indirect costs, by seeking to understand how they are generated (which enables them to be better controlled) and relating them to specific processes, activities or products. ABC assigns costs to products and/or customers upon the basis of the resources that they actually consume.

Thus an ABC system identifies costs such as machine set-up, job scheduling, and materials handling. These costs are allocated according to the actual level of activities. All overhead costs are thus traced to individual products and/or customers, as the cost to serve all customers is far from equal. As a result, ABC forms an integral component in the strategic planning process and unlike conventional accountancy, provides a vehicle for assuming future costs rather than purely measuring past history.... . ABC permits managers to identify actual cost drivers and address these, and so reduce fixed costs.

Any remaining overheads which cannot be allocated on ABC principles should not be apportioned. Contribution to these overheads and profits, rather than an arbitrary profit figure, should be used instead. The nonsense that can result from apportionments is illustrated by an experience David Hussey had while undertaking a corporate appraisal with the UK company that made Ovaltine, among other things. On the UK market at that time there were two types of labelling, the large volume being in the label for the normal retail trade.

The other, which was low volume, was for supply to hospitals. The only difference in the product was the colour of the label. Hospital Ovaltine was sold at a much lower price, and the only reason for the different pack was to prevent hospitals selling the product on to the retail trade, although why anyone should have thought that this would happen is a mystery. However, the accountants were well pleased with the hospital product, because the cost schedules showed that the factory cost was so much less than that of the retail variety, so despite the lower selling price, the gross margin was higher. All anyone had to do to know that this was rubbish was to watch the product being made. As the only possible difference in costs was the paper label, the figures had to be wrong. But they were checked twice by the accountants, who confirmed their findings. Closer examination found that indirect factory costs had been allocated to all products on the basis of realisation, so the cheaper the price, the less it appeared to cost. What happened as a result of this was that the special label was dropped. As there were several pack sizes this also reduced the inventory of finished stock. This was some time ago. Do any companies make similar errors today? Unfortunately, the answer is yes.

Another extract from Hussey shows one of the disturbing things found when he undertook an appraisal of a management consultancy on his appointment as its managing director.

The example comes from a management consulting firm: the figures are made up for the example but the method of calculation is real, as are the two overhead burden rates. This firm used an absorption costing system, where all overheads are charged to "products", in this case consulting assignments. The example is of the choice facing a project director who has gained an assignment to start immediately, but has the choice of two ways of staffing it. One uses the project director and another employee: the other uses an equally competent external part timer, who is only paid for work performed. The accountant's schedule shows that more profit is earned if the outsider is used. The main reason why it works out this way is that the 115 per cent overhead is not added to the outsider. There is logic in this, as this burden is partly the cost of the consultants' downtime, and partly a share of space and secretarial costs: the outsider is only paid when employed by a client so no downtime is incurred, and works only on the assignment so uses (in theory) none of the space and support costs. So the accounting conventions tell you to use the staffing of case 2, to make more profit. But a moment's thought tells you that you earn less in this way than in option 1, because you have £4,000 additional expense going out of the business.

You still have to pay the in house consultant who would not be used in example 2. So in the circumstances I have described it would be a silly choice.

This example shows the danger of using figures without thought. If the firm had conducted an analysis of its customers calculating the sales to and profit earned from each, and used these conventions, it might also mislead itself. For various reasons the client providing the highest accounting profit, might not be the most valuable client to the firm. Clients giving a lower profit might provide a greater contribution.

Although option 2 would not be in the economic interests of the firm, it is worth mentioning here - although HR issues are the subject of a later - that the reward system drove project directors to make this choice. Total profit earned in the year on projects managed, as defined by the accountants, was one of the criteria by which performance was judged. If an organisation already has an ABC system, this stage of the appraisal will be much easier to conduct.

In the many which do not have such a system there will be much more work, which can bring a very different perception of the value to the business of products and individual customers, and may even change the perception of the profitability of the SBUs. In addition to the new strategic insight, which often challenges the existing perceptions held by managers, our experience has been that many immediate actions to improve results are identified and implemented.

We are not suggesting that all organisations have only seven products, nor do we imply that every minor product should be examined with the same intensity. The analysis cannot be completed entirely from looking at the accounting information. In fact, only the columns looking at sales, profit contribution and financial assets could be filled in from what has been discussed so far. The point of the form is that it draws together a wide spectrum of information so that it can be looked at simultaneously. The first two columns of each line are identical, and the repetition is to make it easier to read the form, as the width, which is restricted by the size of the book, and the need to avoid confusing readers with the abbreviations that would be used in practice mean that the rows have to be divided.

SPECIFIC AREAS OF RISK

The financial appraisal should also cover areas of real or potential risk. This is where certain events and trends in the external environment meet the internal elements of the organisation. The type of issue we have in mind here is the depth of exposure to exchange- rate fluctuations, or the assets and profits at risk through investments, major contracts or major customers in politically or economically unstable countries. The aim here is to identify the big risks, and quantify them as far as is possible. It hardly needs saying that an organisation with half of its assets and earning power in a combination of Russia, Serbia, Indonesia, Sierra Leone and Zimbabwe would be facing more risk than a similar sized organisation whose efforts were concentrated on the EU, the USA and Japan.

THE FINANCE AND ACCOUNTING PROCESSES

So far we have looked mainly at the position of the organisation through its financial figures. However, in doing this we have also touched on matters which stand behind the figures, and which cause the organisation to interpret its results differently, or to behave in a particular way.

Examples are the particular way in which the organisation judges itself (e.g. earnings per share, valuebased strategy or some other approach), and its concept of cost accounting (e.g. absorption costing, ABC). Competitive advantage can be gained or lost through the choices the organisation makes, so an important part of the financial appraisal is to identify these policies, concepts and conventions.

It should not be assumed that the organisation's current choices are the best, and although all have advantages and disadvantages, in every unique situation some are better than others. The evaluation of whether what is done is the best choice has to take the context of the organisation into account. One illustration of how the accounting system can become a weakness is indicated by research by Kaplan. He found that many organisations have a "fundamental disconnect between the development and formulation of their strategy and the implementation of that strategy into useful action". Four major barriers to effective implementation were identified:

- Vision that could not be actioned, because it was not translated into operational terms.
- Strategy that is not linked to departmental and individual goals (incentives are tied to annual financial performance instead of to long-range strategy: only 21 per cent of executive management and 6 per cent of middle management have objectives that are tied to the strategy).
- Resource allocation is based on short-term budgets and not the strategy (only just over a third of organisations have a direct link between the strategy and the budgeting process).
- Control is directed at short-term performance and rarely evaluates progress on long-term objectives.

METHODS FOR MEASURING FINANCIAL PERFORMANCE

Earnings per share (EPS) This is calculated by dividing the after-tax profits attributable to ordinary shareholders by the number of ordinary shares. The difference between the EPS at the start and end of a period shows the growth or decline. This method provides a measure of the value provided to shareholders, expressed in an easily understandable way that can be compared with other companies. However, EPS is based on accounting conventions, which can vary between organisations, and does not take account of the market value of shares.

Margin on Sales Net Profit Divided by Sales, Expressed as a Percentage: Market value (of a quoted company) The generally accepted definition is the current stock market price per share times the number of issued ordinary shares. Price/earnings (P/E) ratio Market price per ordinary share is divided by the earnings per share, to give a ratio which takes account of share prices. However, it has the deficiencies of the EPS method, plus the fact that the method of calculation in the financial press uses the last reported EPS, and it is making a big assumption that this figure is a constant until the next company report.

Return on investment (ROI) There are several different ROI methods, but they are all based on calculating profit as a percentage of capital. It is the definitions of these which vary with the purpose. The ROI can be calculated both pre- and post-tax: traditionally British companies have preferred the former, and US companies take the latter as the norm. Two of the most used ROI measures are given here, but there are others.

Return on assets (ROA) Net profit as a percentage of total assets. It measures the profitability in relation to the assets, without being concerned with how those assets are financed. For this reason it is useful for comparing the performance of units within the organisation, when these units have no responsibility for how the finances are organised. Return on owners' equity (ROE) Measures the return gained on the shareholders' equity in the firm. It is a performance measure which is of interest to senior management and shareholders, although it does not measure the full extent of shareholder value.

SHAREHOLDER VALUE METHODS

There are a number of methods which examine strategies for their value to shareholders. They all start from the economic premise that cash flow is what is important, at the level of the whole organisation and of each of its business units, thus avoiding many of the traps. They use discounted cash flow (dcf) methods to evaluate the future cash flows of the strategic options, which is similar to how dcf has been used, for around

40 years, for the assessment of capital investment projects. This approach therefore takes account of the time value of money, and also insists that all strategies are designed to earn more than the organisation's cost of capital.

Cost of capital The weighted average cost of capital is the most commonly used method. This takes the cost of debt, preference shares and equity, weighted by the proportions in which they occur in the capital structure of the organisation. Debt and preference shares can be costed relatively easily. Equity is somewhat harder, as it represents the opportunity cost to shareholders, or what could be gained by investing in other organisations with similar risks. It can be argued that for equity there are three components to consider: the interest rate that could be gained from a risk-free investment, compensation for the expected rate of inflation, and a risk premium which is related to the additional risks of this investment.

Valuation Methods

Equity-spread Approach: The equity-spread approach to valuation focuses on the difference between the return on shareholders' equity (the change in share price, plus dividends, divided by the initial share price) and the cost of equity (the shareholders' expectation for return, based on the element of risk). If the equity spread is positive, then shareholder value has been created; if negative, then it has been destroyed. Share price theory assumes that the share price is influenced by a company's expected equity spread as well as its growth prospects. Managers will do best, then, to focus investment for growth in positive equity spread businesses. The technique's value is limited because it is based on accounting value, with likely distortions. It also ignores some very important sources of value, such as deferred taxes and terminal value at the end of the planning period, and is also very sensitive to financial leverage.

Market value Multiples: This approach seeks to find a business unit equivalent of the market/book multiple. This approach lends itself to simulating both the beginning and ending market values of a business unit on the basis of the book value of its assets. To establish the multiple it is necessary to determine what are the measurable indicators or drivers of the market value. These variables (combinations of returns, growth, R&D expenditure, etc.) are given weighted values, with the help of specially developed models and databases to help predict share price based on book value.

The key advantage of this approach is that its accuracy can easily be tested with historical data. A test of a sample of 600 US firms found that value-creation estimates based on multiples of either assets or sales corresponded more closely to actual shareholder value creation than the accounting measures of ROI and EPS. One of the disadvantages of the method is that book values (the base to which the multiple is applied to predict the "value") can be affected by many accounting factors which could distort the picture, so it does not necessarily prove a reliable base.

Economic Value Added Approach: The economic value added approach is the product of the equity spread (the difference between return on equity and the cost of capital) and the total capital employed in the business. The objective is to increase the economic earnings derived from the existing or projected capital bases. (Unfortunately, if the equity spread is negative, then the approach is "economic value lost'). This approach is frequently used at the portfolio planning stage; and some companies only use it for making strategic decisions at the group level.

POSITIVE-VALUE AND NEGATIVE-VALUE BUSINESS UNIT APPROACHES

These approaches are simply the opposite sides of the same coin. Like the economic value added approach, they are used to make portfolio decisions about business units, and in making acquisition and divestment decisions - adding to or growing those businesses for which economic returns exceed the cost of capital (positive net present values). Businesses with negative economic values will be restructured or eliminated, with capital diverted to positive-value business units, The Q-ratio approach The Q-ratio approach also focuses on economic value. Developed in the 1960s by James Tobin, the Nobel Prize winning economist, the approach calculates the relationship of the market value of a company's assets to the cost of replacing those assets in current money. This Q-ratio is, thus, an M/B multiple with the book value of assets in the denominator adjusted for the effects of inflation. The rationale is that investors adjust their expected returns for anticipated inflation when analysing alternative investments. Therefore, the true or "real" value of a business should also reflect this inflation factor.

SOME LIQUIDITY RATIOS

- Current ratio (expressed as a ratio) Current assets divided by current liabilities.
- Debt/equity ratio (expressed as a percentage) Total liabilities divided by shareholders' equity.
- Debts/capitalisation (expressed as a percentage) Non-current liabilities divided by (non-current liabilities plus shareholders' equity).

THE MARKETING AUDIT

Managers may have a number of reasons for undertaking a marketing audit. Among them might be:

1. The introduction of a new product.
2. As part of a profit enhancement exercise.
3. Assessing whether the firm has:
    - the right pricing policy,
    - the bundle of goods and services appropriate for the market,
    - an appropriate channel strategy.
4. As part of a regularly scheduled marketing planning process.

The marketing audit is a comprehensive and structured examination of the firm's market and the forces impacting the market, the firm's activities and performance, as well as the processes by which marketing decisions are being made. The outcome of a marketing audit should highlight the opportunities and challenges for the firm's marketing and suggest recommendations for improvement, and a plan for achieving superior performance. It is necessary to follow a structured approach when assessing the company's market performance. This helps the marketing audit team work through a comprehensive and systematic diagnosis.

The audit will generally start with a meeting of the marketing audit team and key officers of the firm, in order to establish the initial reason the for audit and the objectives to be answered by the marketing audit. Limitations in terms of depth, coverage, reporting format (written reports consume many resources; effective presentations few) and time period to be covered should also be agreed up-front. Such a meeting should be followed by a detailed plan, under considerations of timeliness and costs.

THE MARKETING AUDIT PROCESS MODEL

We believe the marketing audit process should follow a five-stage process. Each phase consists of a number of elements that must be investigated in detail. The first step, the marketing audit, can generally be divided into two parts: external and internal analysis. These two parts cover six key areas of analysis:

1. *Customers:* This part of the investigation must cover an analysis of the current, past and future customers, their needs and preferences, segment differences, demands of different segments, buying patterns, development in application of core and augmented products, and similar issues.

2. *Competitors:* Who are the major competitors, current and future? What are their strategies and objectives, competencies and capabilities, market share, profitability, and technology base?

3. *Channels:* How are products and services brought to market? What are the channels? What is their share, concentration, ownership, profitability, efficiency, ability to satisfy current and future customer needs, trade practices, and similar issues?

4. *Context:* This element covers the macro-economic, demographic, political, ecological, public and regulatory conditions under which the market is operating. For firms operating internationally, this element must be reviewed with care, as it can be particularly tricky for the marketing activities of the firm.

5. *Company's Competencies:* The firm's own strengths and weaknesses must also be considered as part of the marketing audit. Not only must the competencies be evaluated, but also their relevance in terms of generating competitive advantage. The firm's organisation, structure, marketing information, reporting, planning and control systems are also important.

6. *Costs and Profitability:* What are the profitabilities of the firm's different market segments, products, territories and channels? What is the cost structure and how does it compare to competitors?

The first four elements are part of the external analysis and the last two part of the internal analysis. Conveniently, all six elements start with the letter "C", and marketers often refer to the list as "the 6 Cs of marketing". The marketing audit results provide the input for assessing the potential and sustainability.

ASSESSING THE POTENTIAL AND USTAINABILITY

Based on the 6 Cs analysis of the marketing audit, the task is now to establish the basis for future demand and competition. The key questions to answer from the previous analysis are:

1. What will be the forecast for our products and services if we continue to conduct business as usual?
2. What happens to the future demand if we improve what we are currently doing?
3. What would happen if we started to do business in a very different way?

As part of this analysis, we must also examine the sustainability of performance. To what extent is the current level of performance dependent on unique technology, cost structure, trade relationships, or customer "lock-in"? The fundamental issue to be addressed is the *attractiveness* of the market and the segments being served. By attractiveness, we are considering the fundamental growth and profitability. If the answer is positive, the following question is, of course, what forces might threaten the attractiveness. If a negative response is concluded from the analysis, we must ask what can be done to make the market attractive.

BUSINESS DEFINITION, GOALS AND RESOURCES

The previous analysis provides the basis for examining the fundamental business definition and the stated goals, and assessing the resources made available. Here a number of questions may challenge the current definition of the customers, the market coverage, the technology base, the aspiration level and the means to reaching the goals. Typically, the auditing team will ask questions, such as, "How do we define our business?", "What do we want to make our business?", "How do we want to conduct our business?" etc. This discussion will naturally be linked to a fundamental discussion on the objectives which the key decision makers believe will be necessary to achieve at the behest of the company's shareholders. However, the discussion must also include other important constituents, such as employees, customers, partners in the distribution channel, local, national and international governments, suppliers and other "stakeholders'.

The establishment of specific goals will naturally flow from an examination of the relevant sets of objectives. The goals can be quantitative as well as qualitative. In recent years, more firms are starting to consider a broader set of financial as well as nonfinancial measures. Even with the financial goal set, we are starting to see firms use a more sophisticated set of measures, which are then linked to the remuneration packages of management. For the marketing management team, this means that merely achieving sales targets will likely be inadequate. Achievements of market share, channel penetration, shelf position, brand recognition, customer loyalty indices, sales force effectiveness, advertising effectiveness, repeat purchase benchmarks and similar factors may also be part of the goal set. The evaluation of the firm's goal set, and particularly of their prospects for achievement and their future relevance, will necessitate a discussion of the current resource allocation, as well as the likely resource availability. This will, in turn, create a new discussion on the future goals to be achieved.

ASSESSING THE MARKETING PLAN AND KEY MARKETING DECISIONS

The discussion of goals and resource utilisation is essentially a prelude to an assessment of the current marketing plan's effectiveness and efficiency. This phase will also include an examination of the firm's segmentation approach and the choice of the target customers. The marketing audit provides an overview of customer developments, but an analysis of the chosen segment and developments for this group of customers will also be necessary, for several reasons:

1. The firm's marketing activity may have altered customer expectations, and new initiatives will now be appropriate.
2. Competitors' actions may have changed the dynamics within and between segments.
3. Customer preferences may have developed due to outside trends.

New technological and channel developments may also be part of the forces that have challenged the assumptions that were the basis for the firm's current marketing plan. In light of the market developments of the preceding period and the prospects for the future assessed in the marketing audit, it behoves the audit team to analyse the specific aspects of the company's "marketing mix". The marketing mix is a term used by marketing professionals to describe the critical marketing decisions which in concert are the manifestation of the firm's marketing strategy. The marketing mix is generally thought to consist of five critical decisions, all of which flow from the marketing audit:

1. *Positioning Decision:* This decision relates to the distinctive perception desired of the firm's bundle of goods and services, in the minds of customers in the chosen market segment. For example, Volvo's positioning, in the minds of its chosen customer group, is that of a safe family vehicle.

2. *Product/service Decision set:* The decision concerns the bundle of product features and augmented service offerings that the firm has chosen to be part of its commercial endeavour. The decision include both the depth and range of the product/service portfolio and must include not only an evaluation of volume, profitability and development, but also an assessment of the fits with customer needs and expectations for the chosen segment.

3. *Pricing Decision Set:* This decision set focuses on the firm's pricing strategy, but must also include assessment of volume discounts, year-end bonuses, trade support, non-financial incentives, return policy, financing offerings, back-purchase etc., which may all influence the customers' cost experience.

4. *Promotion Decision Set:* This decision deeply concerns the firm's efforts to communicate its value proposition to its targeted customer group, including

public relations efforts, general awareness creating activities (such as television promotions and print media activities) and interest enhancement efforts (such as trade shows, dispensing of sales force campaigns and in-store campaigns).

5. *Place/distribution Decision set:* The decisions concerning the management of the firm's channel strategy must also be examined. The impact of the Internet has made these decisions more difficult today, and in previous years. Rooted in the customers preferences of where and how they choose to buy the firm's offering, the channel strategy must manage the potential conflicts among the various avenues to the end customer. These five critical sets of marketing decisions, often referred to as the 5 Ps of marketing, must be viewed in totality, and thus examined for their internal consistency. The segment choice and the totality of marketing decisions in unison form the marketing strategy of the firm. The marketing audit team must also consider the robustness of the current plan, its internal consistency, and its analytical and creative composition. The group may examine whether alternative strategies are available to the organisation, and the reasons for selecting one as opposed to others. Contingency plans are an inherent part of the general plan, and should also be evaluated.

EVALUATION OF EXECUTION

The final phase of the marketing audit process is the examination of the firm's execution of the marketing plan. The basis for this phase rests in the key marketing decisions that are the core of the marketing plan. The execution is grounded in the specific programmes and projects of the critical marketing decision frame. The auditing team must consider the consistency and relevance of the programmes and projects, and how each initiative links the decisions to the goal achievement. The associated budgets for each programme and project should also be evaluated against the actual resources expended, and the goal achievements associated with each programme or budget. Finally, the delegation of responsibility for each programme or project, the timeliness, and the desired impact will also be part of the marketing auditing team's scrutiny.

THE MARKETING MANAGEMENT PROCESS

The marketing audit is not merely intended to examine the achievement of current marketing results and suggest changes in the decisions which may have led to the marketing results. The marketing auditing process should also lead to an evaluation of the firm's marketing management, the processes used to generate market intelligence, and the processes for analysing and disseminating the results to the relevant decision makers within and outside of the marketing function. Recent research suggests that these processes are vital to spur market orientations in firms, resulting in higher business performance, greater customer satisfaction and more satisfied employees, but also examine the degree to which the market intelligence and analyses are used in responsive decision making.

As suggested this research suggests that three key drivers are vital to achieve market orientation. The first driver is a set of senior management factors. These factors are mainly about the senior executives' concern and involvement in ensuring that market intelligence is undertaken in a timely fashion, that the analytical work has a sufficient level of rigour, and that key decisions are being supported by facts and analyses and not merely anecdotal evidence. In the words of one executive, "If the top doesn't ask the question, nobody will provide the answer". The auditing team must address the issue of senior executives' drive for market orientation, and suggest any desired corrective action. The second critical set of factors relates to the inter-functional dynamics of the firm. To what extent do serious functional barriers prevent information from flowing between departments? Do different professional groups have the social and linguistic ability to cross functional demarcation lines?

The third driver of market orientation consists of various organisational and systems factors which may impact the market orientation. The firm's organisational structure, the budgeting and planning process, the reward and remuneration systems, and the IT system may all impact the degree of market orientation of the firm. The marketing audit should also address these fundamental drivers of market orientation as part of the review process.

This has covered the marketing audit process, and has discussed the critical areas of analysis to be performed during the various phases of the process. The extensiveness of the marketing audit is a function of the specific needs of the firm and the purpose decided on prior to the start of the process. The process can be performed by an internal team. However, following good auditing practices developed in accounting, it is very useful for one or more outsiders to participate or to monitor the efforts.

APPRAISING PRODUCTION

Production, as used here, is the process of making the product or service. For some organisations it may mean manufacturing, which is perhaps the first image that conies to mind when we read the word. For a supermarket it is the retail outlets and the warehouses that support them. In a management consultancy, it is the service that is actually provided for the customer. In civil engineering contracting it is the building of roads, bridges and other structures. So whether the organisation makes products or provides services, there is a process of production, which requires analysis during the corporate appraisal. Not all organisations may think of their activities in quite this way, as the critical factors vary immensely between different types of industry, and different sizes of organisation within each industry. Success for a hairdresser depends more on the skills of the person providing the service than on the limited equipment used in the process.

This makes a dramatic contrast to a Ford or a Nissan, which takes a global view of its production, with factories in various locations, all coordinated as part of a global sourcing programme. The enormous variety of companies and industries makes it difficult to give guidance that can be applied universally. The approach taken here is to make manufacturing the prime example, but then show some of the variations that would be applicable to different types of service business. From this we hope that the reader will be able to derive a satisfactory investigation of his or her own business.

CRITICAL FACTORS IN PRODUCTION

A recommended first step is to define the critical factors, which are derived from the critical success factors for the business as a whole. These are the things which production has to get right, if the organisation is to satisfy its customers, develop its competitive position and achieve its overall goals. The critical factors provide one standard against which actual performance can be compared, and are a useful starting point. Although there may be some factors that are common to many businesses, there will be others that are more specific to the particular business. For example:

- *A Manufacturer of Lifts:* Two critical factors are on-time delivery and quality performance. The factory has to be in a position to ship all the required sub-units of a contract to the field installation unit at the date specified in the contract. The sub-units might include several lift cars, doors, architraves, controllers and motors. If the factory is late in delivering even one sub-unit, it may delay the completion of the whole building. The same effect can be caused if one of the sub-units does not meet the quality standards and has to be replaced. Besides losing the goodwill of the contractor, architect and building owner, delay means additional costs in the field, and exposure to penalties.

- *A Contract Packer of own-label Detergents:* Own-label manufacturers provide a substitute for branded products. Their customers include the major supermarket chains, whose brands appear on the products. Critical factors for this business include flexible production, so that requirements for new products can be met speedily, manufacture to a tight production cost and the ability to meet the volume requirements of customers.

- *A Management Training Organisation:* Two critical factors for an organisation providing in-company training courses, in addition to the expected capabilities in training skills and subject knowledge, are about keeping customers. A feature of this type of consultancy is a relationship with the client, which can last for many years. So the first production criterion is to be able to meet each client's needs for the number of times a course is to be run, and the time and place where it is to be run. This does not mean that there will be no flexibility at all over dates.

But if the client's needs cannot be met there is a high chance that another consultancy will be brought in instead. It is better to decide not to bid to a new client than to decline to teach some of the programmes an existing client requires. A second criterion is continuity of professional staff. This does not mean that no changes can be made over time, but changes that are over-frequent, or the withdrawal of the professionals who have built the relationship, can cause dissatisfaction. In a well-run organisation many critical factors will have been included in the formation of the management information system. However, they may not all be easily capable of conversion into routine summary information. For example, the contract packer needs a careful approach to continuous production planning to ensure that customer volume needs can be met, and bare performance statistics will not replace this.

When the appraisal is part of a due diligence study, the buyer has to be careful not to fall into the trap of assuming that what is critical in his or her business is all that matters for success with the acquisition. This can be a particular danger when the business being acquired has similarities with, but is not the same as, the business of the buyer.

It is not just that the wrong criteria can be used for assessing production performance, but any wrong assumption may lead to poor post-merger integration actions, and ultimately disappointment with the acquisition. If there is any doubt about the critical production factors, you may gain inspiration. This shows what Johansson et al call the new metrics for establishing customer value. If you know which of these are critical for your organisation's strategy, you should be well on the road to determining what the critical requirements from production really are.

GETTING THE FACTS

There are two different areas to audit: the basic facts, which include the operating results, and the production strategy. Although logically the facts are the outcome of the strategy, they also indicate its effectiveness, so looking at these first makes the task of appraising the strategy somewhat easier.

CAPACITY OF THE PRESENT PRODUCTION UNIT(S)

This is a relevant question for both service and manufacturing units. It is not always an easy question to answer, particularly in a manufacturing plant where the same machinery can produce different products, some of which may take longer than others. There are often trade-offs; for example, the plant can produce either 100 units of product A or 200 units of product B. There are other qualifying statements to be made, such as the number of shifts worked, or maximum production with and without overtime working. In a manufacturing environment, there is a finite capacity, even if it is difficult to quantify.

In service operations capacity is also fixed at any one time. An airline has a finite number of seats available on each flight. This can be reconfigured, within limits, to allow for more or less space per passenger according to class of travel, but - like manufacturing - at any one time there is a finite capacity. The same sort of situation applies whether the organisation is a retailer, a professional undertaking such as a firm of solicitors or general practitioners, a hotel, or a central heating service engineer. However, there may be a difference between theoretical capacity, and practical capacity.

For example, the theoretical capacity of a consulting firm might be taken as the number of working days in a year, multiplied by the number of consultants in the firm. However, in practical terms it is not possible for every consultant to work on client assignments for 100 per cent of the working days in any lengthy period. To do so assumes that no person has any gaps between assignments and that no clients ever change dates of appointments, and it allows no time for gaining new work, administrative tasks or personal development.

So the practical capacity is somewhat lower than the theoretical. Capacity can be expressed in physical terms, in money (e.g. factory cost, revenue earned or gross margin). And, of course, any organisation may have more than one unit of production making more than one product or service. Only in the simplest of organisations would we want to look only at a total figure, something which becomes even more important when we seek answers to the next question.

What Was the Capacity Utilisation?

Capacity utilisation is obviously important, and, like capacity, there may be several ways of looking at it. For example, an organisation with several plants making the same product may have had a reasonable average capacity utilisation, but there may be a different interpretation if the analysis shows that for individual plants utilisation varies between 20 per cent and 100 per cent. And the interpretation could be different if the market is expanding than if it is contracting.

Then there is seasonal variation in utilisation in some industries, and it is possible for production to run below capacity for half the year, yet not be able to meet demand in the other half: a typical problem in, for example, the holiday hotel industry. And just to complicate things further there may also be a seasonal variation in capacity, because of the impact of holidays.

Implications for Increasing or Reducing Capacity

The capacity utilisation figures should be supported by an understanding of what is required to increase capacity (or reduce it, if this is more relevant to the situation). The relevant issues to consider are the minimum size of increments in capacity, costs (capital and revenue) and the time needed to bring more capacity on stream. To these we should add opportunities for outsourcing, and actions such as extra shifts. There is a vast difference in time, costs and minimum increment from, for example, extending capacity in an oil refinery, compared to a professional services firm. An airline may be able to charter extra planes quickly, depending on the state of the charter market and its landing rights, but a comparable option may not be available to a hotel whose attraction is its building and location.

Productivity

Everyone would agree that the recent trends in productivity, and the indications for the future are important. What is more difficult is how to measure it. If asked, most of us would probably say that it is our output in relation to the inputs we have to provide to attain it. A survey gave examples of some of the measurements found in practice:

- Output value/labour cost
- Output volume/material cost

- Plant availability
- Total cost/unit of output

Total factor productivity (TFP) was suggested by Hayes, Wheelwright and Clark as a means of measuring the overall performance of a factory, department or other productive unit. Although they were writing about manufacturing, the method can be used in service businesses. The final analysis is expressed in terms of money, at the values of the base period taken for the study, in an attempt to remove inflation. The formula is expressed by Hayes, Wheelwright and Clark as:

They suggest that output be the number of units valued in real terms at either manufacturing cost or sales price. The four inputs are materials, energy, labour and capital. The first three are first expressed in physical units, and valued (with adjustment for inflation. Capital, under their definition, is net book value of machinery (their preference, although gross book value could be used).

It is valued by first adjusting the value for inflation, and then calculating the annual cost of this capital by multiplying the capital value by the firm's cost of capital (inflation adjusted). The reason for this is that it approximates the period costs of the machinery. Ratios of output/input can be calculated for each of the four factors, and for the total, and the base period can be compared with subsequent periods, and the improvement or deterioration expressed in percentage terms.

Although productivity calculations are at their most complex in a manufacturing organisation, or in a service industry with an industrial type of environment, they are equally important for most other service businesses. However, more imagination may be needed to determine ratios that make sense in situations where output cannot be converted to money. For example, we would not argue that a teacher is now three times more productive because someone has increased class sizes from 25 to 75 pupils: it ignores the results which cannot be measured in money, and are related to personal development of the pupils within the limits of their individual capabilities and potential.

DELIVERY PERFORMANCE

This was mentioned earlier and may not be critical for every business. Where it is important, performance data should be included in the appraisal THE PRODUCTION STRATEGY There are numerous options within a production strategy, whether for a manufacturing or a service organisation. Understanding the path that is being followed, and considering whether it is the most appropriate way of doing things, is a valuable part of any appraisal. There may be strengths in the way things are done, but there may also be weaknesses. There has been a tendency in Western business to assume that "either manufacturing was totally compliant to the requirements of marketing or finance, or that its contribution to new thinking would be relatively limited". Although Pendlebury's comments refer particularly to manufacturing, they are relevant to many service businesses as well. Our approach is to discuss a few concepts which seem to us to be particularly important, and to follow this with a broader checklist which suggests rating what is done using a scale of the competitive advantage gained.

World Class Production

World class performance should not be restricted to production. Knowing whether you are world class or not is just a comparison, but a decision to become world class is strategic. Knowing where you are requires comparisons, not necessarily against competitors, as other organisations with similar processes may be more effective in those processes than competitors. Moving on from merely comparing ratios to attempting to understand how the results are achieved, and bringing the lessons back to the organisation, is called benchmarking. Benchmarking is not necessarily a signal that the organisation is striving to become world class, as it can be used to seek improvement without any long-term aim. A determination to be world class implies a longer term strategic commitment.

Hayes, Wheelwright and Clark define world class manufacture as "Basically this means being better than almost every company in your industry in at least one important aspect of manufacture.". This definition need not be restricted to manufacture.

A four-stage journey to being world class was postulated by Hayes, Wheelwright and Clark:

- *Stage 1:* They term "internally neutral". The task is seen as just to "make the stuff", or provide the service without surprises. The organisation at this stage is likely to set its standards on the basis on its own past performance. It may be seeking to improve its performance, but without reference to anything outside the organisation's own interpretation of what should be achieved.
- *Stage 2:* is "externally neutral". The reference is taken with regard to competitors and the industry, and the task is seen as to meet the standards of main competitors, following industry practice, and using the same materials and suppliers of plant as the industry. Many organisations at stage 2 restrict their comparisons with competitors to those manufacturing within the country.
- *Stage 3:* Is "internally supportive". It is no longer seen as appropriate just to copy competitors, and the organisation moves beyond this, with its actions being related to the specific strategies of the whole organisation.
- *Stage 4:* "externally supportive", is when the whole organisation seeks not merely to be better than competitors, but to be the best in the world in every important thing that it does. The comparison is no longer just with the industry, but with any

organisation from any industry that is best at any of the relevant processes. However, being the best means much more than copying. It requires continuous, creative attention to every aspect of the organisation.

Global or Local Production

Global thinking is well established in many organisations, but this does not always mean that production has kept up with the changing requirements. We can imagine a continuum which has purely local operations at one end and full global integration at the other. Two points could be marked on this continuum: the most appropriate position for the organisation, and where it actually is. Ideally, the two points would be identical, but in practice this is not always so.

The factors which lead to the appropriate position on the continuum begin with the requirements of customers, and are followed by the nature of the technology. Production has to meet the needs of the customers, yet itself is subject to a number of factors which affect its optimum organisation.

Factors which are purely related to production include:

- *Scale Efficiencies:* High efficiencies of scale bring an economic incentive for a few large centres of production. Very low efficiencies of scale remove this incentive.

- *Procurement Economies of Scale:* Where these are low, the incentive for concentration is low. The converse applies when they are high.

- *Experience Curve:* The experience curve means that production costs in a plant fall as cumulative production volume rises. Where the curve is steep, such as in the manufacture of many electronic products, there is another incentive to concentrate in a few factories.

- *Nature of raw Materials:* Where the raw materials are perishable, as in the quick freezing of vegetables or the production of wine, the economic incentive is likely to be the sources of raw materials, rather than seeking the benefits of global production.

- *Transport Costs:* High transport costs in relation to the value of the product are likely to pull the decision towards local plants. Where costs are low, there is less disincentive for fewer plants operating on a global basis.

The factors listed above are more likely to be relevant for manufacturing, where industry after industry has moved further towards the global end of the continuum (for example, motor cars and consumer electronics). This is because customer requirements can be met from this type of industry regardless of the location of production.

Globalisation takes a different form with many service organisations, where production itself has to be local because of customer needs. What often happens here is that although the service has to be provided locally, the customer organisation may be global and requires the same service across the world in all its locations.

This brings a need for coordination of multi-local operations, with common standards of service, and the ability to meet the client's global needs. Many firms in many industries increasingly operate in this way: examples can be found among accountants, advertising agencies, hotels, car hire and business travel agents, as well as numerous other industries. In manufacturing, the incentive to move towards the global end of the continuum is driven by customer requirements, technology and manufacturing advantages. In service industries the driver comes mainly from the customer or, less frequently, the technology (for example telecommunications).

The Focused Factory

The idea of focus in manufacturing is not new, and the quotation used here comes from Skinner from concepts developed as long ago as the 1960s. Our reason for including the concept, is that it is still being "discovered" by various organisations. Skinner argued:

A factory that focuses on a narrow product area for a particular market will outperform the conventional plant, which attempts a broader mission. Because the equipment, supporting systems, and procedures can concentrate on a limited task for one set of customers, its costs and especially its overheads are likely to be lower than those of the conventional plant. But more important, such a plant can become a competitive weapon because the entire operation is focused to accomplish the particular manufacturing task demanded by the company's overall strategy and marketing objective.

Focus avoids at least three manufacturing problems:

1. Equipment is obtained which is optimally suited to what it has to produce. Where there is no focus, equipment bought for a different manufacturing task may be used, and although the product can be made on it, it is not necessarily the most effective method of production.

2. People who are trained to be excellent at a particular thing may be expected to change their standards when making the next product. Defence and aeronautical parts may have to be made to extremely high tolerances and with zero defects. The machinery may well be capable of making products which require less stringent standards. To produce them to the higher standard means that the cost of production is higher than it need be, but to keep telling the workforce to change the standards they apply depending on the type of contract causes confusion and leads to failures in both product areas.

3. The main line of importance may have to be interrupted because of a need to make other

products. This causes more downtime and set-up costs, as well as disruption. A common example is the production of spares on the main line used to produce the original equipment, particularly as the spares may be for products that are no longer made. A result is failure to meet the manufacturing objectives of either, and there is often a conflict over which to produce. The issue is not what can be produced on any given line, but what should be produced. Skinner recognised that it was not always possible on volume grounds to have completely separate plants for every different product line, and suggested that when this was the situation the concept should be extended to establishing "plants within the plant". In other words, parts of the factory would be dedicated to specific products, and operated as if they were completely separate plants. The "plant within a plant" concept may make sense for smaller organisations, but the expansion of global operations means that more organisations have the volumes needed to set up focused plants. An example is Ford, which is transferring car assembly from a factory in the UK to Cologne in Germany, but is making the UK plant a centre of world excellence for the production of engines. The concept of focus is not restricted to manufacturing. It may also be appropriate for industrial-type service businesses, and for other service activities like transport and warehousing. There may be marketing reasons why other types of service business focus production. But the concept has its widest application in manufacturing, and if your organisation takes pride in the fact that it can meet any challenge in any of its plants, this is probably a weakness and not a strength.

Outsourcing

Organisations have always bought in some products and services which they could have made themselves, usually because it is cheaper to do this, or it avoids a capital investment. Additional reasons for outsourcing have developed over the past 10 to 20 years, related to the total quality management (TQM) concept of cooperative relationships with suppliers, which treats suppliers as if they were more strategic partners than adversaries. Although it is convenient to consider outsourcing, on the appraisal of production, it is a corporate-wide concept which is by no means restricted to production. Services that have been outsourced in many organisations have included internal audit, security and the routine parts of information technology, as well as many aspects of production. The main reasons for considering outsourcing, and why the current situation should be assessed as part of the appraisal, are:

- *Flexibility.* The problem of managing peaks and troughs is reduced as far as the organisation is concerned, because its own employees are fewer in number. The problem of managing the fluctuations is shifted to a specialist supplier.

- *Reduction of Risk:* This may be related to flexibility, but may also be a reduction in exposure. A highly integrated operation means that a number of corporate eggs are in one basket. If some of these can be removed, and the risks passed to someone else, the organisation may be in a healthier position.

- *Cost:* An external organisation which is focused on a particular product or service can often deliver cost reductions because of the economies of scale it can achieve.

- *Inventory Reduction:* In some situations outsourcing can lead to a reduction in the inventory of raw materials and work in process, particularly if just-in-time methods are used.

- *Focus:* The removal of important, but peripheral, areas of activity means that the organisation can focus on the things that are important, and which it can really do well.
- *Quality:* Specialised suppliers should be able to provide products and services to a high quality standard.

There are pitfalls to avoid. Things which are core to the organisation's future success should be protected, and should not be outsourced. This includes core knowledge. The last thing that is wanted is to set up a new competitor. The appraisal of outsourcing should look at the current state of affairs, the opportunities for further outsourcing, and areas currently outsourced which are core and which should be brought back into the organisation.

AUDITING TECHNOLOGY AND INNOVATION

We have included technology and innovation because they are often, but not always, related. However, we should make it clear that this does not cover information systems/technology, which, because it is a requirement of almost every organisation. Not all industries will have technology high on the priority list, and certainly not all will be innovators in the development or application of technology. But when technology is important, it can be a critical factor. Those organisations in high-tech industries depend for their survival on the application of complex technologies. But they are not the only industries where technology is important, as products with lower levels of technology may use up-to-the-minute technologies in the production processes. For all these industries, future success may depend on the strategies developed for technology, and the way technology is integrated into the total corporate strategy.

Of course, an organisation can employ a mix of technologies, and still not be particularly innovative, just as it is possible for innovation to occur in organisations or functions which have little connection with a particular technology. All organisations should be concerned about innovation: many should be concerned about technology. Despite their many differences, it is easy to see that corporate success will be affected by the choices organisations make about the technologies that lie behind their products and processes, and their capability to innovate. Both are important, and both are often neglected areas of the corporate appraisal. From first-hand experience in both areas, we believe that the technology aspect is neglected in many organisations which should give it more attention because it is difficult and moves into realms of uncertainty. Innovation is often excluded because of a common misconception that it is the same as creativity. Creativity is a key component in an organisation's capability to innovate, but it is by no means the whole story.

TECHNOLOGIES

Let us begin with a dictionary definition: Technology: "the practice of any or all of the applied sciences that have practical value and/or industrial use: technical methods in a particular field of industry or art." (Chambers Twentieth Century Dictionary) Although our focus is on the internal aspects of the appraisal, technology - like marketing - is a topic where we have also to look outside the organisation in order to be able to interpret what we have found. An example of this comes from our collective experience, a consulting assignment at corporate level with a merchant banking organisation which had a number of subsidiaries in various industries.

One of these subsidiaries was a photographic processor, which at that time provided central processing services to many of the high-street shops. This subsidiary was seen as very effective in its technology, and indeed it had to be in order to keep its contracts with the big high-street names. At that time there was a commercial vulnerability, in that there was a high dependence on a few key customers, who had the resources to set up their own central processing laboratories. There was also a concern over the potential impact of the emerging digital technologies (at that time it was video). All this was enough for the decisions that were made at the centre about whether it was time to sell what was currently a profitable business.

However, there was another threat which emerged later: the change in processing technology which has enabled fast in-store development of films and the production of photographs. We do not know whether the management of what had been the subsidiary saw this change in good time, but it is easy to imagine the uselessness of assessing the current technological competencies as strengths without taking into consideration the impact of the emerging changes in technology. In broad terms, what is needed is a way of auditing the technology situation and then identifying the strategic implications of what has been uncovered. The principle is similar to the approaches taken in various other facets of the corporate appraisal. The difference lies in the peculiar complexities of defining technologies in useful ways, in classifying them and in constructing useful quantitative information which is not always readily accessible.

TECHNOLOGY AUDIT

A number of authors have written about the technology audit. We have found the books and articles mentioned here of particular value. Because the approaches are all somewhat different, there is something of value that can be found in all of them. Henry suggested a four-step approach to looking at technology:

1. Technology audit
2. Strategic implications of the technology portfolio
3. Technology implementation plan
4. Technology monitoring programme.

Our concentration is on the first two steps, although we find it easier to think about them together. However, for those who have a need to make the technology audit a continuous part of the management process, the rest of his framework is of interest. Henry argues that technology is a value-adding activity: an asset which enables organisations to leverage resources to meet the needs of the market. He looks at the chain which stretches from the factors of production (labour, materials/natural resources, and capital) to the final consumer. The steps in this chain move from material acquisition through all the activities of productions, distribution and marketing.

At various points there are nodes, where technology is used to connect various business links to improve efficiency or give a particular advantage. A technology-asset audit focuses on determining the real or perceived value that any technology node, or its individual technology links, has in the business benefit-cost chain - from raw material acquisition, to the supply of the produce or service, to the customer. Henry suggests that comparisons should be made against the competitors, and offers a checklist of questions that should be considered:

- What are the basic technology assumptions in the company's current business strategy?
- What are the basic technology assumptions in competitors' strategies?
- Is the customer's perception of the technological qualities of the company's products important?
- What value, if any, do the customers place on the technological qualities of the competitors' products?
- Is corporate R&D contributing to improvements in the company's current technology position, or are improvements starting to take longer and cost more?
- Are competing technologies becoming costs-effective?
- Are competitors making gains ahead of the company?
- How does the company manage information related to these questions?

Lindsay provides a statement of the objectives of a technological audit which is helpful here:

- To identify and evaluate the organisation's technological resources and capabilities.

- To assess and evaluate the market significance or potential of the organisation's strategies.
- To assess the organisation's competitive position in its technologies.
- To understand and identify how the organisation can develop and exploit its technologies in order to build and maintain sustainable competitive advantage.

Ford offers a framework and a number of questions which need answering. We have followed some of his thinking in our own advice on the technology audit. He too makes the point that the audit should become a continuous management process.

CONTENT OF THE AUDIT

Product or Production?

The key technologies may be used in the production methods the organisation uses, or they may be the products it offers, or a mix of both. A critical success factor may therefore be the way technology is applied to make the product to higher quality standards and at lower costs.

An example is the modern steelworks, where complex technology is used to produce what is a lower technology product. In another organisation the basis of success may lie in the ability to offer something unique in the product itself. An organisation concerned with the application of engineering principles to new applications, up to and including the installation of the proven prototype, may produce a new application of technologies, such as a new method of tethering North Sea oil platforms. It is the application of the product, rather than the production processes by which the prototype is made, which gives the strategic advantage. The processor used in PCs offers an important technology to those who buy it, and at the same time can only be made using key technologies. In such organisations, the strategic advantage may be gained through both the production and the product, and the organisation may have patents for both. When we begin to audit the technologies in an organisation, a first step is to separate our findings under these two headings.

Further Classification

Ford suggests looking at technology under three headings: the technologies which are *distinctive* to the organisation, those which are *basic* (without these the organisation could not enter its markets), and those which are *external* to the organisation. The distinctive technologies are the ones which are the foundation of the organisation's success and which give it distinct competitor advantage. Basic technologies are important, but the organisation is a user rather than a developer. External technologies are bought in, for example as sub-components, and are not the area where the organisation gains distinctive advantage.

Personal computers offer an example. It is possible to find small organisations which will assemble a computer for you. Every component is external bought-in technology. The main basic technology is the ability to mix and match the various components and assemble a finished product which matches the customer's requirements, and works. There is no distinctive technology in either the production or the product itself. At the other extreme there are the large organisations like Compaq, IBM, Dell and Gateway. These, too, rely on many external sources of technology. In addition they have certain distinctive technologies which are important to their success. These may lie in the area of production, design or in some of the elements that make up their computers. Although they all have access to the same component suppliers, and the same basic technologies, the distinctive technologies are among the tangible factors which enable them to differentiate their products.

If these three headings were applied to the two main groupings of production and product, the result would be a strategic understanding of what each technology means to the organisation. But this begs another question. How do we identify technologies?

Identifying the Key Technologies

One of the practical problems is to desegregate generalized descriptions of technologies into more precise elements which have meaning in the organisation. This can be very difficult for a non-technical person even to attempt, so one of the first requirements is that the team undertaking the audit should include members who have knowledge of the technologies. Nakamura illustrated one approach, using similar but slightly different groupings to those suggested previously. It takes the form of the technology tree. The roots are the basic technologies which provide the firm with a foundation for technological development. The trunk represents the core technologies which are growing out of these roots. The branches are the derivative technologies growing from the core. Leaves and fruits are the products which have sprung from each derivative technology. His description envisages the fusion of branches, to develop more applications.

The figure comes from Nakamura's consulting assignment with a particular Japanese company, and the published version does not give away critical confidential information. Some organisations have several technology trees, from different strategic business units (SBUs), and one role of the audit should examine the degree to which the trees themselves intertwine. Our experience is that it can be very difficult to obtain synergy in technologies between different SBUs, even when there are certain similarities in the technologies applied.

Although the numbers on Nakamura's tree are somewhat sketchy, it is possible to see how the concept could provide a technology analysis of products, which would enable quantitative information to be derived showing the significance of the various technologies through their impact on sales and contribution.

Hussey describes another approach: Illustrates a way of trying to define and examine technologies across an organisation. This particular example is derived from an assignment of mine in an unusual organisation which was a cross between consulting engineering and process engineering, although neither term is an accurate description of the activity. In essence the business was concerned with the application of engineering principles to new applications, up to and including the installation of the proven prototype. The technical strands of a business such as this are of great importance in defining future strategy. To preserve confidentiality I have extended it to a completely different industry. The figure relates the technologies to the products and their different markets, and it is possible to calculate the significance of the technologies by inserting the numbers for sales and contribution. Not too much should be made of the specifics of the illustration, as it is only to show the principle.

The Costs and Benefits of the Key Technologies

This point deals with innovation. Failure in capitalising one's own technologies can be because innovations are killed by the internal inertia, and the good ideas never reach fruition. On the other hand, success may occur because there is something about the way the organisation is run that enables sound ideas to be properly tested and evaluated, and ensures that the winners are backed. 3M is the world's prime example of an organisation that is able to benefit from its distinctive technologies, and develop new areas of distinction. However, failure may also occur because of problems with R&D. If new products or processes with commercial value are not developed in good time, or are not effective when put into use, the problem may lie with the objectives given to R&D, the resources allocated to it, the calibre of the researchers or the way the function is managed. In the audit we need to try to look at past patterns of costs and benefits, to collect quantitative data to support the analysis. For example:

- Number of patents registered (but remember that patents are a means, not an end in themselves).
- Annual contribution from new products.
- Annual contribution from process improvements.
- Annual income from licence agreements granted.
- Annual costs.

Past and current performance is helpful in highlighting strategic issues, but should be expanded by notes which relate the results to the current strategy that is being followed.

Does the company fully exploit its technologies? This question may be more important for a multi-SBU organisation, where there is potential synergy to be obtained between the technologies of various business units, but somehow this is not obtained. Sometimes the reason for this lies in the difficulty of defining technologies in precise enough terms, so that the possible areas of congruence are not perceived. Sometimes the problem is organisational, in that no one has time to coordinate technology with other businesses, and there is no one with overall responsibility for doing this. There may be "not invented here" attitudes, or a belief that "this SBU spent the resources to develop its present position, so why should it hand the results to someone else?". The audit should first establish whether there are unexploited opportunities, and then explore why they are not exploited.

There is a related issue. Can we release value on some of the patents and know-how which we possess? This may be through sale or licence, or it could be through joint ventures with other organisations, or setting up a business to use some of the technology. Examples of the latter are the Danish brewery which has a subsidiary offering an independent consultancy service to the industry, and the airport operator which acts as a consultant in airport design and operation.

The Life Cycle Position of the Key Technologies

This is a requirement which is rarely capable of a precise answer, but it is still an important issue to consider. The approach suggested would give a view of the current importance of each technology to the organisation, although it needs to be qualified by information about any changes that are expected in the near future. For those technologies which are seen as key, it should be possible to assess where the technology life cycle is, if only on one of four points: emerging, growing, maturing or declining.

The results of this assessment feed back into the assessment of the organisation's R&D activity, discussed under heading 4, above. Although precision in this analysis is difficult to attain, it is not hard to see how the audit might bring to top management attention various situations which should be dealt with. Between us, we can think of a number of examples from client organisations where there was an apparent lack of awareness that a shift in technology was taking place. For instance:

- A company that made bottle washing equipment, and had failed to consider that the growth of the non-returnable plastic bottle would change their market for their product. In fact it was worse than this because the son of a director had been foisted on them. Management resented and disliked him, and so chose to disregard a study that he had made of the likely effect of the then new bottle.
- The manager of a manufacturer of machines for printing tin plate for cans made on a three-stage process, who was in denial that the then recently introduced two-stage aluminium can, which printed the can as it was drawn, would have any impact on his market.

Emergent Technologies

It is self-evident that this is an important question for many businesses, but it is not always one that can be answered easily. There is a relationship with the previous point, in that one reason for a change in the life cycle position of a technology could be because of new technologies. Indeed, both the examples were of organisations that had either not seen, or would not see, how a new technology was affecting the life cycle of their product. The aim is to see the situation before it becomes critical. However, the ability of an organisation to do this depends on information, so the audit should consider the management process. How do we keep informed about emerging technologies, changes in current technology, likely developments for the future, and the position on the technology life cycle? Relying on people to dredge up an assessment for the annual planning cycle is a recipe for missing much of what matters. So the intelligence needs to monitor patents, other competitor activity, changing customer needs and new research trends. This requires technically qualified people, leavened by others with knowledge of markets and products. The questions that need answering are what sources of information are used, how regularly the intelligence is reviewed, who does it, and what happens to the results.

Phases of a Development Project

This point was inspired by Gluck and Foster. It requires looking at the phases of development (study, design, development, production, marketing and post-marketing). Top management can exercise most influence on the final outcome if it is involved most heavily in the first two phases and the early stages of the third.

In many companies this is the opposite of what happens and most top management effort is put into the final three phases. However, by this time, the major technological strategic decisions have been taken, usually by someone quite low in the organisation. It reminds us a little of a presentation once given by a mid-level person from a city's town planning department. He declared that he alone determined the whole town planning strategy. Yes, there were elected councillors, he had several managers above him, and they thought they were making the decisions. But he set all the assumptions on which the strategy was based, and no one had ever questioned them. These assumptions determined the strategies that could be followed, and eliminated many others. In technology it cannot make sense for the paths that the company will follow to be determined by people who have no responsibility for the overall vision and strategies of the firm.

Ford argues that initially a firm which develops a new technology will posses a much greater level of knowledge about that technology than the customer, and because of this may be able to charge a premium price because it sets the standards. As customers gain in experience, and begin to add developments of their own, the gap narrows and the customer begins to find other sources.

The margin therefore tends to drop. Following this argument, it is useful to obtain a view of where the organisation is in relation to its customers. However, there is a counter consideration, which is that if the gap is too wide, customers may be reluctant to buy the product, because of uncertainty over the benefits of the technology. It is difficult to see how this information can be more than an estimate of the gap, and the trend it is following, so it has the dangers inherent in all such assessments, that wishful thinking can affect the result.

The dangers of thinking of the world as you would like it to be, rather than as it is, are illustrated by this example from the chemical process contracting industry. The particular organisation had high standing in the industry, and following a change of policy by one of its important customers was bidding to be the preferred supplier in its particular field. It had worked with the customer as a leading supplier for many years, and there had been some cross-licensing of technologies. They were convinced they would win. You can imagine the blow when they lost out to another supplier. The reason for their failure was nothing to do with their performance. It was simply that the customer did not want a closer relationship with an organisation that believed that in all areas it had greater technical knowledge that its client. Possibly in these particular areas it had once been ahead of the client, but those days had passed, although the organisation had not noticed.

EFFECTS OF CHANGES IN TECHNOLOGY

It may be tempting to think that an audit of technology is only a matter for the high-technology companies, and can be ignored by all others. This is true only for as long as the technology stays static. A few examples worth mentioning of where new technologies have taken over a market, and frequently led to the collapse of some or all of the traditional players, are typewriters, which have been to a great degree replaced by computers, electromechanical telephone exchanges, which are now an obsolete technology, and home cine cameras and projectors, which have almost completely given way to video. At the low-technology end, plastic windows frames and doors have replaced wood to a large extent, and with plastic cladding on exposed wood on buildings have reduced the volume of business available for professional house decorators.

The task of painting the outside of a house may not on the surface appear to be affected by leaps of technology, but the available market has certainly changed. One purpose of the technology appraisal is to help the organisation "leverage the company's technology assets to meet tomorrow's business objectives as defined by the current strategic plan".

However, we believe that the need is more complex than this, in that the results of the audit should be used to help identify where new strategic decisions need to be taken. Current strategy may be a useful basis of comparison, but the analysis should also highlight areas where current strategy may appear to be inappropriate. The purpose of the appraisal is to assist in the development of sound strategic decisions. At one level this means the strategic decisions appertaining to technology, in order to make a success of the corporate strategy - a reactive role. At another, it is the way technology will influence the overall corporate strategies – an active role. While the purpose of the appraisal is not to make strategic decisions, it will have little value if it does not give a clear indication of where there are issues that should be considered.

Matrix Techniques

Various matrix techniques have been proposed to enable organisations to look at the technology implications of the portfolio in ways that gives different perspectives to the types of analysis we have looked at so far. Neubauer suggests a technology grid. This has *technology position* on one axis, moving from weak to strong. The other axis shows *technology relevance* ranging from low for old technologies of little value to high for new technologies where many applications are possible. The factors suggested for each axis are:

- Technology position
- Patents
- Licences
- Development lead times
- Personnel
- R&D budgets
- Relevance
- Breadth of application
- Speed of acceptance
- Developmental potential
- Application in other industries
- Environmental acceptability

Each SBU is plotted on this matrix. In our opinion, although the SBU may be appropriate in some situations, there are others when positioning in this way is to combine chalk and cheese. In these cases it may be desirable first to plot the main product groupings of the SBU, and then to combine these into larger "bundles" which share common characteristics. Otis Elevators could be seen as an SBU of its parent United Technologies, in that all of its products have a strong potential relationship with each other. It is possible for a large building contract to require lifts, escalators and moving walkways (think of an airport). However, the technologies of electric lifts, hydraulic lifts, escalators and moving walkways are not the same, and combining them on the Neubauer matrix could conceal valuable information.

The suggestion is that the final matrix would be used to check that current investment in technology matches the need, and that priorities are shifted; for example, to reduce investment in lowrelevance technologies, and increase it in businesses where the company needs to catch up or maintain leadership. Rowe, Mason and Dickel suggest a slightly different matrix. This positions the portfolio according to technical position and technology importance. It may be that for one axis both authorities have the same thing in mind, and that we should not read too much into the different meanings of relevance and importance. There are differences in the position index, where Rowe, Mason and Dickel use a concept of high = leader and low = follower. They offer a different perception in the labels attached to each of the four boxes:

- High importance/high position: a *technological leadership* position, which has to be pursued aggressively if it is to be maintained.
- Low importance/high position is labelled *over-engineering*. Businesses in this category may well be spending more than is appropriate, and should consider reducing the level of technological commitment.
- High importance/low position: *catch up or get out*. The argument is that this is not sustainable in the long term, and that either resources have to be committed to moving technology into the high position box, or the activity should cease.
- Low importance/low position: *technology adopter*. Businesses in this box beg questions about how the technology should be supported. The initial implication is that it should be acquired from external sources, and that major internal resources should not be spent on this area.

The questions raised from these and similar matrix analyses are indicative. The purpose of the corporate appraisal is to provide one of the foundations for strategic thinking. Although we are not treading much farther along the path of actually forming technology strategy, we will conclude with a few more ideas.

Ford suggests three different types of technology strategy. First there is a technology acquisition strategy. He adds the caution that there is a need to examine the position on the life cycle of the technologies or sub-technologies acquired. There also needs to be a strategy for exploiting technology. This goes deeper than the issue of the strategic business portfolio, and includes an aggressive approach to finding other ways of gaining benefit, such as licensing others to use the technology. Finally Ford suggests that there is a need for a strategy to manage technology, which implies making decisions on all the issues identified in the audit process.

INNOVATION

Innovation may well have been covered in part by any organisation that has appraised its technology, but even in these organisations there may be innovations that are not related to technology, which may require objective scrutiny. All organisations rely on innovation to a greater or lesser extent to ensure that they renew themselves. The two aspects to audit are whether the organisation is innovating as successfully as it should, and, if the answer to this is negative, whether the management processes in the organisation are appropriate for the task.

CREATIVITY

It is reasonable to suggest that creativity is a prerequisite for innovation, but it is not reasonable to assume that all an organisation needs to do to improve the quality and quantity of innovations is to harness creativity. Somehow the two are often confused. This is a point which we will come back to, as it lies at the heart of any attempt to audit an organisation's ability to innovate. In normal usage, there are many meanings to the word creativity, and it is easy to slip into the trap of thinking only of the creative genius of a Leonardo da Vinci, or an Einstein, forgetting that quality of imaginative thought which is possessed to a greater or lesser extent by all human beings. Jones suggests: "Creativity is a combination of flexibility, originality and sensitivity to ideas which enable the thinker to break away from the usual sequence of thought into different and productive sequences, the result of which gives satisfaction to himself and possibly to others".

Creativity needs to be taken in context. Almost all of us have a creative spark within us, but the context in which this bursts into flame is not always that of the organisation. The cleaner may appear to be a stolid, plodding, work-horse in the office, but at home may produce delicate embroidery or tend a beautiful garden. What is happening is a harnessing of creative ability to a degree of technical mastery.

These manifestations of creativity may have no value in the organisational context, but in any case would be unlikely to flower in a situation where work is routine and without stimulation, there are few problems to overcome, and expectations of the contribution of the worker are very low: which is precisely how we perceive and manage many office cleaners. Of course the degree of creative ability varies from person to person, and the highly creative individual may be in the minority. Although those endowed with a high level of creativity may produce more and better ideas and concepts, it is also possible to harness the latent creativity of the less well endowed. This is one of the benefits that may spring from a well-run total quality management (TQM) concept. Although few of the many innovations that may result are likely to be of major strategic value, the cumulative impact of many small innovations can be significant.

Maslow argues that the fullest (and healthiest) contribution to creativeness may be expected from people who have reached the self-actualisation stage: that is, their physiological, safety, love and esteem needs are already met. Perhaps we might simplify this by arguing that empowered people who operate in an organisational climate which encourages creativity are most likely to be able to produce creative solutions for the benefit of the organisation.

The need for an organisational climate which fosters creativity is important, and there are differences between the creative organisation and others which are more stolid in their acceptance and application of the new. One of the reasons behind the need for a sympathetic climate is that the creative process is not completely logical. Although parts of the process can be directed so that the mind is focused on a specific problem area, the solution cannot be guaranteed. Indeed, it is uncertain whether an idea of any value will emerge at all. Motivation and the encouragement of creativity are important elements in the process, and will not occur in a hostile environmental climate. An innovation might be described as a creative idea that has been made to work. Webster says:

Simply put, innovation is a better thing to do, or a better way to do it, that increases an organisation's ability to achieve its goals. This does not mean change for change's sake. To qualify as an innovation, a change must be visible to others and must offer a lasting impact. Innovation can occur, and should be encouraged, at all levels within a company, from top level executives to lower level managers and individual contributors. An innovation can be as basic as a procedural change in a distribution system or as complex as entry into a whole new market.

So an innovation may be a product, a process, a method or a system, but is more than an idea. It has to be converted from the idea to action. Some years ago Drucker commented on the fact that creativity was not the bottleneck: "There are more ideas in any organisation, including business, than can possibly be put to use. What is lacking as a rule is the willingness to look beyond products to ideas. Products and processes are only the vehicle through which an idea becomes effective". Although this management classic might be considered old in terms of the speed at which management thinking has developed, his statement is remarkably similar to the conclusions from her research which led Webster to her definition. It was not lack of ideas that was the problem, but the ability to convert them into innovations.

The entrepreneurial process means that an idea has to pass rigorous tests. Drucker emphasised that it has to have operational and economic validity, and must meet a further test of personal commitment:

- The idea itself might aim at social reform, but unless a business can be built on it, it is not a valid entrepreneurial idea. The test of the idea is not the votes it gets or the acclaim of the philosophers. It is economic performance and economic results. Even if the rationale of the business is social reform rather than business success, the touchstone must be ability to perform and survive as a business.
- The strategic importance of innovation is emphasised by Drucker, who sees ideas as part of the process of making the future: "tomorrow always arrives", and those companies which fail to innovate will suddenly find that they have lost their way. This is a rephrasing of the words of the sixteenth-century philosopher Sir Francis
- Bacon: "He that will not apply new remedies must expect new evils: for time is the greatest innovator".

ORGANISATION AT INNOVATION

This is the first question that the appraisal should attempt to answer. It is not always easy to quantify the answer. Although it may be relatively simple to look at the number of new products launched in a period, and the sales and contribution gained from each, this begs the question of whether they were copycat products or something which had genuine originality. This means that each new product should be looked at objectively, to see whether it counts as an innovation.

But as we saw from the Webster definition, innovations can also take place in systems, processes and the machinery used to make products, and not all will be as visible in the accounts as a new product. To help us interpret information on successful innovation, we also need to know about the attempted innovations that fell by the wayside. And to have real meaning we should look at the phase where they fell, and also look at the patterns of success or failure of the new products. The phases of an innovation might be considered under the headings of:

- inspiration (having the idea),
- initiation (getting the idea accepted),
- implementation (putting the idea into practice),
- inspection (checking that it has produced the expected results).

Since, in most organisations, the available information will not give insight into every phase, the only solution might be some sort of survey, either through getting selected managers to complete a formal questionnaire, or by arranging meetings with groups of managers and other key people to complete the analysis as they see it.

Pinpoint precision is not needed. In the end we need to have a view of whether the organisation is innovative enough for the conditions in which it operates, and the success rate of new innovations.

In order to be able to examine the processes of innovation in an organisation, we have to think about what the processes are. The outline here is based on research undertaken and concepts developed by management consultants Harbridge House, modified by our own experience. There are three elements to consider.

The Individual, Alone or in Small Groups

This is where the inspiration starts, and the main requirements are creativity, any appropriate technical competencies and various individual characteristics (such as a willingness to challenge the status quo).The components of this activity cover the initiation, implementation and inspection phases. The activity here is a form of change leadership, complicated by the fact that few of the people who have to go along with the change report to the initiator, and many may be senior to him or her. The initial letters of the words chosen to describe the steps in the change leadership process spell EASIER.

- *Envisioning:* This is the process of developing a coherent view of the nature and importance of the innovation. The vision may cover such things as size, what the innovation will do for the organisation, its future scope, and how it fits the overall corporate vision. It is the person who is responsible for moving the idea to an innovation who should define this vision, and the greater the potential opposition to the idea within the organisation, the greater is the need to give attention to this part of the process. The leader who cannot articulate the vision in a way that has meaning to others will find it harder to ensure that everyone pulls in the same direction. It is particularly important when the driver of the innovation is not at the top levels of the organisation, because it will be necessary to carry more senior managers along. 3M, which has an enviable reputation for innovation, is reported to have a system in which the originator of every potential major innovation has to have a Boardlevel sponsor. Getting over even this first hurdle is difficult unless there is clarity of vision.

- *Activating:* Envisioning is a difficult process, because the border line between empty platitudes and meaningful descriptions is very narrow. Activating is even harder. It is the task of ensuring that others in the organisation understand, support and eventually share the vision. The vision cannot be understood unless it is communicated, and it cannot be communicated unless it is defined in a coherent way. Initially the task is to develop a shared vision among the key players in the task of implementation, but in many organisations there are benefits in reaching deep into the organisation. A widespread commitment to the vision makes it easier to see the relevance of the innovation, and underlines the importance of coordinated efforts. The well-known story of Post-it Notes at 3M shows that the approach to getting commitment to the vision of the prospects for the product can itself be creative. The glue on these pieces of paper, which many of us now find indispensable, was reputed to be a failed research product, but someone saw the potential for a permanent, but removable, marker for documents. The recognition of the possibility is accredited to an employee who wanted something to mark the places in his hymn book when he sang in the church choir, and from that those involved formed a vision of a wider potential. To gain commitment to the product against initial opposition, they made up a stock of the little pads, and issued them to various managers in the company. Once everyone was hooked, they discontinued this special supply, and said that the product would not be available unless it was launched. By this time everyone in the company was convinced that the product was essential, and would succeed.

- *Supporting:* Good leadership is not just about giving orders and instructions. It is much more about inspiring people to achieve more than they otherwise might have believed possible, and providing the necessary moral and practical support to enable this to happen. The envisioning and activating steps in implementation are about sharing and sustaining inspiration. The supporting step is about helping others to play a key part in the implementation process. To achieve this the leader has to have a strong empathy with the people he or she is trying to inspire, and the imagination to see things from their point of view. There needs to be an understanding of both their present capabilities and their potential. While giving support to help a subordinate reach a tough new goal, the leader has to be able to recognise the problems the person faces, without ever implying that there is the slightest doubt that the person will succeed. Supporting needs a base of respect, trust and integrity, and fails when these essentials are lacking.

- *Installing:* This is the process of developing detailed plans to enable the innovation to be implemented and controlled. The nature and shape of those plans will vary with the complexity of the innovations, and their nature. In only rare circumstances will it be a task that should be totally undertaken by the leader of the innovation project, and in most cases the process would benefit from the involvement of the key people who are expected to carry out the actions that will implement the innovation. The instruments that may be used will also vary, depending not only on the complexity of the strategies, but also on the time scale for implementation, but the basic reasons are constant. They are to:
  — ensure that all the consequences of implementing the innovation are understood, in so far as they can be foreseen.
  — This includes the impact on the organisational variables discussed earlier.
  — identify all the actions that have to be taken to bring about the change. This usually requires much more attention to detail than would be appropriate for any formal strategic plan or boardroom presentation.
  — allocate responsibility for the various actions that have to be taken.

- establish the priorities of the various actions, in particular those that will hold up the whole process if not done to time.
- provide the budgets needed to ensure implementation of the plans.
- set up the teams and structures needed to implement.
- allocate the right human resources to the tasks (if necessary recruiting additional people or using consultants).
- determine any policies that are needed to make the implementation process work.

There is nothing unique or special about any of these individual requirements, nor the instruments such as plans, budgets, critical path analysis, Gantt charts and other tools which have to be developed to ensure that nothing is overlooked, and that everything is coordinated. These are all the regular instruments of management. In most organisations this stage will require a hard-nosed view of the economic prospects for the innovation. 3M, which does more than most companies to stimulate the creative process, even to the extent of expecting that everyone will "bootleg" a significant amount of time to the development of new ideas, has the final check where the Board considers the business plan for all significant new activities, and nothing sloppy is likely to pass this scrutiny

- *Ensuring:* Plans, structures for implementation and policies may be formulated, and on paper the organisation may have covered everything. But this is not enough, and consideration must be given to the monitoring and controlling processes that will ensure that:
    - all actions are taken on time, unless there is a conscious, justifiable decision to change the actions.
    - where actions are changed, there is both good reason for the change, and re-planning for the new circumstances.

- the results of actions are as expected, and if not corrective action is taken.
- plans are still appropriate if the situation has changed.

All organisations have monitoring and controlling processes, but those that currently exist may be inadequate to monitor the new strategies. One of the actions in the implementing phase might therefore have been to establish supplementary controls so that timely information is made available on a regular basis.

Monitoring and control processes also provide a reason for the various players in the implementation game to meet, thus providing another way of reinforcing the commitment to the vision.

- *Recognising:* This means giving recognition to those involved in the process. Recognition may be positive or negative, and should be used to reinforce the change, and to ensure that obstacles to progress are removed. Although recognition may include financial reward, this may be the smallest part of what is needed. Public recognition (among peers and senior managers) of the part played by a particular manager may show that what has been done is appreciated. That small word "thanks" may have great motivational value when expressed sincerely by a leader who is respected by the person.

The Organisational Context

Every organisation establishes a context within which everything has to work. This context may encourage innovation, be neutral or actively prevent it. The three elements to consider are the organisational culture, the structure, and the strategic direction. The best way to appraise the innovation process and the organisational context is to track through how a few recent innovations, or attempted innovations, have been managed. What you find can then be compared with the approach recommended here, and any significant areas of concern noted.

5

HRM, Management Effectiveness, Culture and Structure

Although the four areas are by no means the same thing, they are related, and human resource management (HRM) appears first because, to a degree, it touches on all of them. In all four areas there is a case for comparing some of the performance measures against external criteria, but it is even more important to evaluate the policies and actions against the vision, values and strategies that the organisation is pursuing. It is this strategic comparison which is often overlooked.

Models like this have been around for some time, the most famous being the McKinsey 7S model, but we believe the originator of this type of thinking was Leavitt. He argued that structure, task, people and technology were closely related, and that actions taken on one of these had an impact on the others. The main difference in our model is that *technology* has been subsumed into the broader term *strategy*, and *culture* and a number of different aspects of *systems* have been added.

The argument summarised through this figure is that the intended strategy should drive the other organisational variables. If there is a mismatch, the other variables may instead supplant the strategy. In other words, what happens will not be what was intended to happen. Obviously there are degrees to which a mismatch can be tolerated, but everything that works against the strategy makes implementation more difficult, and increases the possibility of a total failure of the strategy. If the corporate appraisal is made before a new strategy has been decided, the comparison can only be made against the current strategy, and it would be desirable to re-examine the conclusions in the light of any major changes that might afterwards be decided. However, much of the work will have been done, and it should be possible to make the reassessment with a minimum of delay. The methods described here should bring strengths and weaknesses to the surface. In many organisations the problems lie concealed in the background where they cannot be recognised and solved. It is easy to see how the combination of the information coming from accounts and the reward system was driving behaviour in the opposite direction to the strategy. The research in Kaplan demonstrates that a mismatch of processes and the strategy is by no means an isolated event. It happens in well-run organisations.

HUMAN RESOURCE MANAGEMENT

We begin, as we did with finance, by establishing the factual base. Although not all HR strengths and weaknesses can be read from looking at figures, many can. For example, recruitment and labour turnover figures can reveal whether the organisation has difficulty attracting and retaining particular types of employee, and high absenteeism figures may point to various other problems. The following description of the minimum information that should be collected is adapted from Hussey. Most organisations know how many people they employ, but even that is sometimes an easier question to ask than to answer, because of definition problems and timing issues. But there are legal requirements which demand that these figures are available for at least some points in the year. For a detailed understanding of the organisation we need to have much more statistical data than just total numbers. In fact the use of totals without an underlying depth of knowledge can mislead. A simple example is that a bald employment total gives us no idea of how many people we might expect to have to recruit next year, just to maintain the same size. And the real-life situation is much more complex than this. In all cases the statistics are more helpful if they are in a time series, so that a run of several years can be compared and, where there are seasonal factors, relevant lesser periods, such as by month or by quarter, can also be examined.

Analysis of Actual Employment Numbers

Employment numbers should be broken down by business area, country, location within the country and department. The reason for this group of headings is obvious. If you do not know how the employees are dispersed by location and organisational unit, it is not possible to assess the impact of some of the changes in activity which are intended to take place. Similarly, the fact that there is a full complement of highly skilled people in the US operation does not solve a shortage in a third-world country. There are other headings that should be investigated to give more insight into what the numbers really mean. For example, it is important to get an understanding of certain types of employee in the overall totals. Traditionally many organisations have kept statistics on the basis of direct and indirect employees, hourly paid and salaried, productive and non-productive. In the USA there is also normally a breakdown of exempt and non-exempt, which is a legal requirement related to terms and conditions of service. These breakdowns take us a little further forward, although most emerged more from an accounting need for cost information, than for HR actions. The separation of *direct* from *indirect* workers is less meaningful than perhaps it once was, because of the replacement of numbers of direct production employees by automation, which requires the support of more indirect experts. The next level of resolution is concerned with seniority and skills. The first point can be more easily covered if the organisation has a grading system, because there is at least some chance that every employee has been put into a grade. This gives us some good information to build on. However, information on level in the organisation does not tell us what people do, and it is not really meaningful to combine sales managers, when sales managers are easy to recruit or promote from within, with scientists on the same grade, when there are few others in the organisation with the same disciplines and there is a world shortage. In this situation, we could double the number of sales managers without a problem, but this may not be true of the scientists. So we need to have access to some statistics which describe jobs in a broad but meaningful way that is suitable for aggregation.

It is possible to go further, to try to break down employees by skills and competencies. Such databases can be very useful but are also extremely difficult to establish and keep up to date, and unless there is such a database already it may be impracticable for a larger organisation to make this analysis. It is also harder to keep the information in the same way as the other statistics, as each employee may fall under several headings in the analysis. A simple example is that when I used to analyse the saleable skills of employees of a consultancy which I managed, I always had more skills than people. When we added language fluency the list extended again. This was a useful and simple exercise in a consultancy employing 20 full-time staff and about 10 part-time associates, where all the people knew each other, but would be very complex and more difficult to apply to a very large business.

The final levels of resolution are gender and ethnic minorities. The main purpose is to ensure that the organisation's antidiscrimination policies are operating in a satisfactory way, although the statistics are not the whole answer to this question. However, they will give a preliminary indication of whether the organisation operates a "glass ceiling" with few women or people from ethnic groups able to move beyond a certain level. Such statistics have to be read with care, as the fact that a plant in Bradford has more employees from minority ethnic groups than another in

Horsham, West Sussex, may be more to do with the make-up of the population in the area than any policies applied by the organisation.

Age and Length of Service

Other statistics are needed to give more insight into potential human resource issues and problems. A starting point is an analysis of age of employees by grade and by length of service. It is deliberately kept simple, and assumes that the organisation has three grades of manager plus a managing director. Grade 3 is the most senior grade, and these are the executive directors. If we relied only on the bottom line of totals by grade, we would see that there is an issue, in that the proportion of women moves from just over a third in the lowest grade to nil in the highest, but it would not give any insight into where to look next, nor would it have given any indication of the other problems that can be seen from the age analysis. What the detail shows is that the organisation seems to have done something about achieving a measure of parity in the entry-level grades, but there it ends. It also suggests that unless particular attention is given to this issue, it will be many years before there is a more appropriate proportion in the next grades. A companion lengthof- service analysis would bring more insight. If, for example, it showed that in grade 1 75 per cent of the 36-40-year-old males had at least ten years' experience, but that 50 per cent of women had less than five years, it would indicate that either the organisation has greater difficulty in retaining women, or that when vacancies have arisen it has taken deliberate efforts to have a fairer recruitment or promotion policy. In grade 2, we would make different deductions if the length-of-service analysis showed that most of these managers had spent their whole careers with the organisation, than if there were a healthy mix of service periods, which showed that not all promotion was from within. The main strategic problems revealed are around management succession, impending changes at the top, and the potential career management issues for those in grades 1 and 2. Lengthof-service statistics would give further understanding. Apart from the insight such analyses give to the organisation, they provide a basis for calculating retirements, and may indicate weaknesses in succession planning.

Labour Turnover Analysis

There are two elements to labour turnover statistics: how many people leave and why they leave. Statistics should be capable of being presented under all of the headings discussed so far, so that it is possible to compare areas of the organisation, grades and age/length of service. For forecasting and for policy purposes it is important to know the broad reason for leaving, such as death, retirement, health, redundancy, other organisational initiative and resignation. Although not representing termination from the organisation, it is useful to be able to add those who have left a grade or area on promotion (or for other reason) elsewhere in the organisation, an analysis which might have more complexity in a multinational that moved people into different businesses and countries. The cause of the turnover is very important. Projecting historical ratios of all turnover is not safe when there is an abnormality in the situation. The retirement pattern of the past few years may not continue, for example, because the organisation has had a policy of early retirement and there are now few people left who are over 50 years of age: there may have been major redundancies in each of the past three years, but the organisation is now slimmed down, and these abnormal events are not expected to recur.

What is revealed about resignations at different levels or areas of the organisation can be important for the understanding of the situation. It may also indicate a need for further investigation, such as surveys to find out why people resigned. Turnover by grade and age can be particularly revealing, in that an apparently healthy rate for the whole can conceal major problems in certain areas. An overall rate of 10 per cent might hide the fact that in some areas it exceeded 100 per cent. While turnover rates should be expected to vary across the organisation there are limits to what should be seen as healthy.

Overtime

This has been a long-standing way of giving some flexibility of resources to the organisation, and boosting the income of employees. Typically, figures will only be available for overtime for which the organisation pays and therefore excludes most management and much clerical and secretarial time. Extra time, willingly given, to deal with a particular problem or project may be a sign of a motivated organisation. A situation where people stay at their desks, regardless of whether there is work to do, so that they are seen to be there long after closing time, is a sign of low morale and an unhappy, distrustful atmosphere.

Lost Time Analysis

Time may be lost for unavoidable reasons. However, sometimes it can be as a result of either low morale, or the working situation itself. It is important to know the patterns of time lost in different areas of the organisation, and whether these can be changed. Because there may be large differences by location, grade and type of job, it is not appropriate to assume that overall ratios can be applied universally. Categories under which information might be analysed include days lost because of:

- Industrial disputes
- Accidents.
- Occupational illness.
- Other illness.
- Time off in lieu of overtime (where the organisation has such a policy).
- Other approved reasons (e.g. unpaid leave, education).
- Absenteeism.

Holidays have not been included in this list because they are an entitlement.

Non-employees

Most organisations have people working on site who are not employees, but for whom some services have to be provided. They may be temporary staff, who are the employees of an agency, contract staff, some of whom may be self employed, but where the organisation has responsibilities to collect tax and national insurance, and contracted-out services, such as security, internal auditing and IT operations. It would be wrong to ignore these categories of people, and I would suggest that the minimum information needed is the total hours they provide, and the maximum and minimum numbers of people each month.

Remuneration Levels

What is needed here is not great schedules or what the organisation pays its employees in cash and benefits, but a summary analysis which explores the variation between practice in the organisation and the industry. For certain level of people, such as senior managers, and skills which span many industries, a broader basis of comparison may be needed. The figures cannot be interpreted in isolation from the profit situation. For example, an organisation which pays the highest rate in the industry for its factory workers and has the lowest profitability of the industry may have a serious weakness: however, if its profitability were to be higher than any other firm in the industry a high wage policy might be a strength.

THE EXTERNAL ENVIRONMENT AS IT AFFECTS HRM

Although generally in this book we have not tried to cover the appraisal of the external environment in all its aspects, in the HR area it is not always possible to interpret the internal statistics without some consideration of what is happening externally. For example, an inability to recruit sufficient numbers of people with certain specific skills could be because:

- the organisation offers remuneration packages which are below the average; or
- the organisation has a poor reputation as an employer; or
- there is a national shortage of people coming out of the universities with the appropriate qualifications.

One of these causes is totally internal, another may be a mix of internal and external factors, and the third is related to wider environmental issues. Of course it should be amended to fit the particular situation, and you will need more space than we have provided to record the answers.

HRM, VISION AND STRATEGY

Earlier we stressed the need to compare current HR policies and practices with the requirements of the vision of the organisation and the strategies it was following. Here we suggest a number of tools which will assist this process, and later we will suggest the steps needed to look in depth at one area of HRM, management training. With modifications, this way of thinking can be extended to other HRM activities, and we believe that the detail we provide on management training will point the way.

A Diagnostic Questionnaire

The first tool is a diagnostic questionnaire which can be used at corporate or business unit level. It examines the overall philosophy of HRM in the organisation, and can give a good indication of the degree to which HRM is a good strategic partner to the other management functions. Although this could be completed by one person, more might be gained by having several managers in the organisation fill it in from their own perspectives. Some thought should be given to each of the questions: if no one in the organisation can see their relevance, you can assume that HRM does not act strategically, and is not allowed to do so anyway. More can be gained from the questionnaire than the crude scores suggest. It is separated from the questionnaire to ensure that it does not influence initial thinking about the questions themselves.

Contribution of HRM to the Business Needs

It offers one way of beginning to get into the detail, and if required can be used in a working session with managers to crystallize their perceptions. The headings to the rows can be adapted to include other areas of HRM activity. The space under each row heading is intended for the specific detail of what is being considered, as the headings are too broad to be useful. For example, the reward system might be considered under headings like top management, first-line managers, sales and shop floor.

Management training might also be considered by level. What is actually listed should be related to the needs of the organisation, and it is unlikely to be the same for every organisation. Once the areas to be explored have been identified, the next question to ask is whether what is being done helps or hinders the organisation's strategy. A rating scale is suggested. Identifying an issue in general terms is not always helpful, so the next question invites specific attention to what could be improved. The final column identifies obstacles. For example, it might be that a new agreement would have to be negotiated with a trade union, or solving a problem faced in department A would cause a problem for department B.

The summary represents, should not lead anyone into the trap of a simplistic form-filling approach. Those using this tool must have knowledge of the HR activity being considered and of the strategy it is being examined against. Clearly if there is no knowledge of either, this particular approach will not be useful.

Using the Integrated Organisational Model

The model presented is more than a concept, and can be actively used in a detailed analysis of the components of HRM. This model to explore what new needs are called for as a result of a new strategic initiative. With adaptation it could be used to review an existing strategy. It is not just the strategies that might change, so the recommendation is that the analysis covers vision, values and objectives as well. We define these as follows:

- Vision is top management's expression of what the organisation is striving to become, and incorporates what in earlier literature used to be called mission statements. A vision is semi-permanent. It is likely to outlast any strategic plan that may be prepared, but will not last forever.
- Values are the moral and ethical principles which guide the organisation in its decisions and actions.
- Objectives relate specifically to the key targets for each of the next few years, set in the context of the vision, and which are markers that help indicate progress towards the vision.
- Strategies are the means by which an organisation moves to attain its long-term aims.

Relating HRM to the Business

It illustrates another approach, which will be discussed further in the detailed examination of management training which follows. It requires that the organisation has some clarity in its strategic thinking: if no one can define the elements of the strategy, it will not be possible to look at how it might impact each of the areas of HRM. The intention of the approach is that the key elements of the strategies, values, visions and objectives would be written out in the left-hand column. Strategies appear first, not because of the logic of how they were formulated, but because they should be more concrete than values in HR terms, and values in turn are likely to be more concrete than vision. There may indeed be little to write at all under objectives, since all the actions may already have been identified at an earlier stage. The HR area headings are indicative, and should be changed and expanded to fit the particular business. The figure does not attempt to list them all. The space under these headings is intended for the specific issues to be recorded. We would not attempt the impossible, to literally write in every detail in a minute space, and instead would prepare a separate schedule of each of the HR activity areas. The summary chart would use symbols to show the state of the issues found in the supporting analysis: none, minor or serious.

In broad terms we know that every one of the activity areas is likely to be relevant to every strategy, but what we are looking for is three specific things:

- A mismatch of the current HR policy with a particular strategy etc., on the lines of the integrated organisation discussion given earlier.
- An aspect of a current strategy etc. which should lead to specific HRM actions, but has not done so.
- The implications of new strategies, and the impact these might have on the existing situation.

AUDIT OF MANAGEMENT DEVELOPMENT

A really serious appraisal should go somewhat deeper into each HRM activity area. The sort of analysis described above should provide considerable insight, but there will also be many activities within HRM which should be probed in depth. The ideal would be to undertake a complete audit of each activity area, but if this is not practicable we recommend a selective audit of those areas which are like icebergs, and have much more of the detail hidden than is visible. And like icebergs they have the power to do damage to an organisation. Management development is only one of many activity areas which could have been chosen to illustrate a detailed methodology for an audit. We selected it because it is an area which could contribute more to strategic success than is the practice in many organisations. It is also an area where organisations spend considerable sums of money without knowing whether they are receiving any benefit. Because there may be thousands of different initiatives ongoing, many of which may have become institutionalized over the years, it is usually an area which will repay study.

The framework and questionnaires used here can be modified easily to fit other activity areas and indeed may need to be modified for any particular organisation. The bias here is towards management training.

AN OVERALL FRAMEWORK

It provides an overall framework which describes the logic of the steps outlined here. Although only the top four elements of the model are about the audit itself, in the interest of completeness we touch briefly on the remaining parts of the model. Our bias is to drive the audit by the needs of the organisation. This does not mean that we will ignore the needs of individuals, but we will look at them in a particular perspective.

Step 1: What the Organisation Needs?

The questionnaires discussed earlier are appropriate here, and should have yielded information which is directly relevant to this HR activity area. When considering the needs of the organisation which may be met through management development, it is worth remembering that management training, for example, can be used to help people understand and become committed to a significant change, as well as providing skills and competencies that are important if people are to be able to play a full part in making the change a success. Matrix approaches can be helpful in analysing the implications for management development of particular aspects of vision, values and strategy. An example of one matrix (in simplified form) is given for illustration and this is followed by a blank form for completion. The example assumes that the organisation has three new strategic actions: a major expansion into Europe, delayering the organisation and the building of strategic alliances. Real-life situations are more complex and subtle than this, and more than one matrix may have to be developed. The principle remains valid. Be ready to develop a more detailed analysis showing the number of people who require the skills listed. Also consider whether a management training or other development initiative might deliver added value to the organisation as a tool to help implement the strategies. For example, if new strategic alliances are forged, would a joint workshop of managers from both parties help both sides to understand cultural differences, and as important, to begin to develop a working relationship? In a real situation we should expand the analysis to include vision, values, strategies and objectives. This is what and its supporting questions attempt to cover.

1. Use the concepts of the blank to begin your analysis.
2. What are the implications of your findings?
3. For each of the organisational needs identified, list the skills and knowledge that are required at each level of management using the form below. Use the following letters to indicate whether these are new to the organisation (N), already existing but in need of enhancement (E), or already existing but needing to be maintained (M). Modify and extend the form for your own situation and the levels of management in your organisation. You may need to break skills etc. into competencies.

Step 2: What the Organisation Already has?

In this context we mean the skills, knowledge and competencies that are already possessed. It is possible, for example, that all the requirements identified are already possessed, in which case the organisational need is to maintain those skills, and equip people for promotion. For corporate appraisal purposes it would be a great strength, albeit a somewhat unlikely one, if all the requirements were in place. There could also be a major weakness revealed if the organisation were setting off on complex strategic paths without having people with the right skills in the right numbers. During this step we have to uncover what skills exist, and what training needs have been identified. Initially this means reviewing the sources of information available inside the organisation, although it may indicate a need to undertake special studies, and to change the regular methods the organisation uses.

Task 1: Determine which of the following methods your organisation uses:
- Annual appraisal of subordinate by his or her boss.
- Special training needs assessment surveys.
- Assessment centres.
- 360° annual appraisal systems.
- 360° feedback systems for collecting training needs information.
- Other (specify).

These sources will indicate identified training needs which may or may not match with the strategic requirements identified. They will also identify a number of requirements for the future development of people, and what we might term "maintenance requirements", needs which may not appear to be strategic, but which are important to enable the organisation to continue to operate effectively.

Task 2: list the training needs identified, by level of management. Classify these into those which:
- meet the identified organisational needs (S).
- meet longer term needs such as developing people for promotion (L).
- meet the personal objectives of managers, but are peripheral for the organisation (P).
- have no obvious value (O).

Task 3: assess the implications of the analysis so far.

Task 4: what can be concluded about any organisational needs which have not been identified in the assessment? Is this because they were not considered in the evaluations, or is the organisation already proficient in all these areas.? Or do we not know? We need to reach a decision. It may be necessary to undertake an additional survey to establish the facts.

Task 5: Assess the implications from the analysis of what the organisation has, and identify actions that should be considered.

Step 3: What Are we Currently Doing to Close the Gap?

Actions already being undertaken may include training and development programmes, coaching and the recruitment of people with additional skills. Before we can begin to assess the gap between what we have and what we need, we need to audit the actions already under way. The concentration in this checklist is on training and education, but in real situations the other initiatives should also be considered. Typically, an organisation has many programmes and initiatives in place, aimed at various levels of management. The questions below concentrate on the training and education aspects of development, but the concept should be extended to other management development actions.

Task 1: analyse the present, past and planned future annual expenditure on management training and education. The following format provides a guide. In theory this should be an easy analysis to make. However, we know from our own experience, and from various published surveys, that not all organisations could easily turn up these figures from the management accounts, and if your organisation is one of these you will have identified a serious weakness. Part of the reason why some organisations do not appear to have a full understanding of their total expenditure on management training is the multiplicity of ways in which costs are incurred for each initiative. Some costs are incurred by head office, and may or may not be charged out to profit and cost centres in various ways. Others are incurred directly by the cost and profit centres. Some are mixed: for example, the costs of the programme itself may be funded centrally, but the travel and accommodation costs may be paid by the participants and repaid by the unit where they work on an expense claim. Ignorance of the full picture often means that poor economic decisions are made. Very few organisations outside the civil service and professional services firms like management consultants have any idea of the cost of those who attend programmes, and even fewer attempt to consider the opportunity cost.

Task 2: audit the overall training programme. An examination of the total spend should yield useful information, but there is much more that we need to know. Expenditure and effectiveness are very different things, and what we have to begin to establish is:

- What did we get for our money?
- Did the aims of the initiatives match the strategic needs of the organisation? (Did we spend money on the right things?)
- Did the right target population attend the programmes?
- What were the real benefits achieved from each initiative?
- (Were the benefits what we expected?)

To answer these questions requires a detailed operational analysis, as well as an examination of information from the management accounts. A number of organisations would have difficulty answering these questions without a number of special exercises, which is surprising considering that large organisations may spend many millions of euros on management training and development. Typical findings in practice are that with some work the costs of the various initiatives can be calculated. However, although the aims of some programmes match the corporate need, many do not. Often the programme is set up in relation to the needs of specific people, but it is others who attend the programmes, so the real need is not met. And in most organisations the only assessment made is the completion of happy sheets, at the end of each programme, which measure neither learning nor changes in behaviour The analysis suggested overleaf is not meant to imply that all organisations run only two programmes, and in real situations the number of columns should be extended and additional pages should be used. Some of the questions posed in the example are to establish the basic facts: others are detailed probes into every aspect of the programmes the organisation is running. It would be appropriate to include initiatives planned but not yet run, although in these cases some of the questions would remain unanswered.

Not every point that needs investigation is included in the above example, and there are a few more that require attention.

- In support of the analysis so far we need to establish the topics in each initiative and the time given to each. This is because otherwise we may not be able to match programmes to the strategic needs which we have identified. It is also possible for a topic to be covered, but not with the depth that is really required.
- What are the present policies for training? This question should be divided into general policy, provision of training and assessment of benefits.
- Who decides what new training initiatives are needed? It may be that the decisions are being taken at the wrong levels, and that because of this training is not reaching its target population.
- How does the organisation ensure that the right people receive training? It may be that a measure of compulsion is needed.
- What is the policy for who pays for training (corporate, divisional, business unit, individual etc.).
- How is performance of the training unit measured? (If the only measure is the average number of training days per person provided you will know you have another weakness).
- How are the benefits of initiatives determined?
- What is the policy on personal development (e.g. professional examinations, sponsored degree courses etc.)?

Step 4: /Assess the Management Training Gap

It is now time to interpret the gap from the analysis undertaken so far:

1. What organisational needs are not being met?
   — Needs What should be done?

2. Which needs are only being partially met?
   - Needs What should be done?
3. Which initiatives fully meet organisational needs?
   - Initiatives What should be done?
4. Which initiatives partly meet organisational needs?
   - Initiatives What should be done?
5. Which initiatives do not appear to meet any needs?
   - Initiatives What should be done?
6. Which policy areas require review?
7. What solutions other than training may be used to fill the gap?

The Remaining Steps

It includes three further steps which might loosely be called implementation. They cover the actions which are likely to result from the appraisal. The first of these steps is called revised management development policies. The appraisal could, of course, demonstrate that all the current policies are appropriate, but frequently changes will be indicated. For example, there might be a need for a different policy towards development which can be directly related to corporate needs, than towards development which meets only the personal aspirations of employees. Such policy changes might cover the nature of the development which will be offered, the proportion of the budget which will be spent on each, and changes in how people are selected to receive the development. After the policy changes, the next logical move would be the detailed actions to support the policies. In the training example we have been using, this might mean dropping some of the training programmes offered, changing the content of others, adding new programmes, altering the target participation and changing the frequency of events. It might involve replacing some training events with a different method of management development. The final stage of the model is to implement these plans, and to monitor the results.

CONCLUSIONS TO THE HRM APPRAISAL

We hope that the brief coverage of the HRM appraisal has shown that not only is there a lot to do, but that the conclusions reached can have a far-reaching impact on the future of the organisation. This is particularly so if the organisation has not previously taken a strategic approach to HRM. It is not just strengths and weaknesses which will be revealed, but areas where costs can be saved, money spent more effectively, and more accountability placed on HRM.

Our remarks should not be read as applying just to the HR department. In many organisations some HRM activity is delegated to operating management and to line managers. The principles described here are relevant, no matter where in the organisation HR is managed, or how that responsibility is divided.

MANAGEMENT EFFECTIVENESS

The effectiveness (or lack of it) of the management resource is one of the most important strengths or weaknesses of any organisation, but is probably one of the most difficult things to assess. Most modern companies have performance management systems, which will provide very useful data, but not always what is required. One reason for this is that performance is generally assessed in relation to the current job, whereas the corporate appraisal should be looking forward in the light of the new challenges the organisation may be expected to face. A second reason is that, generally, one could expect that problems of effectiveness identified by line managers will have mostly been dealt with in the normal course of events. Following the logic of this, some might argue that there is nothing to appraise, because the performance management system will have ensured that all problems are solved. So by definition, no organisations have weaknesses in management, only strengths! And if you believe that, you will believe anything. We have covered part of the problem through some of the suggestions made for auditing HR against the vision and strategies of the organisation, but here our emphasis was on the skills, knowledge and competencies needed. The underlying attitude was that anything missing could be solved by recruitment, development or outsourcing. We were not particularly discussing how effective the key managers were, only whether they had the capabilities needed. Effectiveness is about how those capabilities are applied. The driving force of any organisation is provided by the top management teams at the centre, and in each of the major business areas, and it is these people whose effectiveness to take the organisation forward is our main concentration. This is what makes it difficult, as these are the same people who might already have decided that the major corporate strengths are the competence of the chief executive and the top team.

One method that might be used might be for the chief executive to look at every member of this top team, against the needs of the organisation as he or she expects them to emerge, and from this assessment we might come to a fair understanding of the strengths and weaknesses of this team. However, the validity of this exercise would depend on the competence and objectivity of the chief executive. If he or she is not up to the mark, we are unlikely to find out much by this method.

A variation on this approach might be for the appraisal to be undertaken by a task force of non-executive directors. Provided they really understand the business and the directions it is moving in, this could be the best approach to use. Certainly it is practical, and can be done quickly. A more accurate method might be to run assessment centres for all the top team. The disadvantages are that this would be costly and time consuming in any organisation of size.

CULTURE

Culture is intangible. We know it is there, and we know that it affects how a company performs. We know that cultural differences between two companies which come together in a merger or strategic alliance can be a cause of failure. In a way, it is a little like temperature: we can tell whether it is hot or cold, but can only find a precise way of defining these terms when we have an instrument that will measure temperature with some precision. Until we have this, how we judge the temperature is affected by personal differences in whether we feel hot or cold, whether we are mobile or static, and our state of health. In addition, there is no precision in our feelings about what the temperature really is. It is possible to make a judgement about culture, to know that the way people behave as a general rule in the organisation is helpful or a hindrance to the strategies the organisation is trying to follow. Observation will tell us in broad terms whether the culture is bureaucratic or entrepreneurial, or if people normally take decisions or avoid accepting responsibility. However, it is usually difficult to determine what needs to be done as a result of such judgements, they may not reveal important differences between the various business units and departments within the organisa tion, and it may be ifficult to gain a shared understanding of what the culture is, because of differences in how various key managers perceive it.

Any serious appraisal of culture has to find the equivalent of a thermometer so that measurements can be taken. There is no one standard measuring instrument for culture, and generally the methods advocated are proprietary, although the principles behind many of them are more widely available. It is possible to take measurements of attitudes (in which case it is necessary to decide which attitudes would give a valid interpretation of culture) or of behaviour (but which behaviours are important?). The method used here for illustration is by no means the only one available, and was used for many years by management consultants Harbridge House Inc. What was measured was climate, effectively a dimension of culture, which describes the way it feels to work inside the organisation. Climate was found to be largely caused by the management practices of the leaders (at various levels) within the organisation. The extensive research behind this concept found six aspects which were significant components of climate:

- *Structure:* Clarity of roles and responsibilities.
- *Standards*: Pressure to improve performance coupled with pride in doing a good job.

- *Responsibility:* the feeling of being in charge of one's own job.
- *Recognition:* The feeling of being rewarded for a job well done.
- *Support:* The feeling of trust and mutual support.
- *Commitment:* A sense of pride in belonging to the organisation.

Under each of these headings key management practices were defined. Measurements are taken using feedback instruments. At a minimum these are completed by the subordinates of each manager in the survey, and often in addition by peers, the manager of each manager, and possibly by customers and suppliers. All questionnaires are handled in confidence, with each manager receiving an aggregate report of his or her practices, without knowing what any one person has reported. These aggregate reports are confidential to the individual, and what the company receives is an overall report, which could be developed for each relevant organisational unit.

The advantages of this method are that differences in various areas of the organisation can be studied, a comparison can be made with what is a desirable profile for the climate, and because the assessment is based on how managers manage it becomes easier to develop strategies to change management behaviour. Change management behaviour in the critical areas, and you change the climate. Bedingham describes another approach, the Organisation Culture Inventory (OCI). This uses 12 styles of behaviour as the basis for defining culture. He explains that the instrument can be used to identify a target culture, as well as to measure the curent culture. He states:

Creating the target culture comes from an examination, by the senior management team, of the organisation's strategy, mission and values. They are then able to describe how things need to be done in the organisation in order to achieve the strategy with the highest level of effectiveness and efficiency and with the minimum amount of pain.

These are converted into a profile, based on the standardized items within the OCI instrument. These same items are used to survey the organisation to measure the current culture. The result is an ability to compare the culture of the organisation as a whole and by relevant sub-groups, with the target culture. If there is someone in the organisation who is competent to assess culture, and has access to an appropriate instrument, there is no reason why this cannot be undertaken in-house. However, it is an area where lack of skill or knowledge may be dangerous, and it is one of the few areas discussed in this book where we should advise that serious consideration is given to using an external consultant.

STRUCTURE

The structure of an organisation can facilitate or restrict the development and execution of effective strategies: frequently there is a trade-off, in that the structure is beneficial in some aspects and harmful in others. An example is the structuring of the organisation into SBUs. This can facilitate the exploitation of market opportunities, but may make it harder for the maximum synergy to be gained from the development of technologies which are relevant to more than one SBU.

The first task is to collect information on how the organisation is structured. In most organisations this will already be defined, both in policy terms and in organisation charts. We say most organisations, because our experience includes quite large organisations that do not have this information readily available, although of course a de facto structure does exist.

Structure defines:

- The way the organisation positions itself towards its markets.
- How it coordinates its activities.
- Where decisions are made.
- Responsibilities.
- Reporting lines.

Once the current structure has been established the appraisal should assess its appropriateness in the light of the organisation's vision, values and strategies. The following suggestions are made:

- Adapt it to help determine which elements of the structure help, hinder or are neutral to the business needs.
- It may be useful to relate this exercise to specific elements of the vision etc., in line with the examples given earlier for a strategic approach to HRM. This may be particularly necessary if significant changes in strategic emphasis have been taking place, such as a global expansion.
- Assess the role of the various elements of the head office organisation. How are these elements contributing to shareholder value? Do they duplicate what is going on elsewhere in the organisation?
- Determine how the structure aids or hinders the development of synergy between the various components of the organisation.
- What problems have been encountered in practice, which are caused by the structure?
- Are there too many layers of management in the structure?
- Is the structure compatible with the culture that the organisation requires?

6

Information Systems for Capability Management

Any company analysis must include an investigation of the firm's internal and external information generating capabilities, analytical procedures for converting data into useful information, ways of disseminating this information to relevant departments, and the firm's practices for using information in decision making. Any firm will as a minimum have an accounting system at the very core of the management information system (MIS). Needed for legal reasons in even the smallest of firms, this system should have evolved into something more comprehensive to provide management information, about, among other things, costs related to relevant activities and information that can be used in the subsequent adjustment of resource allocation. Even in small firms it is observed that the accounting system created at the very outset of the firm's existence often does not evolve with the firm as it grows.

This principle problem is similar to that of much larger enterprises, where the management information systems of yesteryear are ill equipped for the decision making of today and tomorrow. It is therefore necessary for an evaluation of the firm's information system to consider not only the existing context, but also the evolving needs of the enterprise -

something of a challenge with today's evolving computing and communication technology. How to transition the gap between the company's current information systems and new generations becomes a challenge of monumental proportions for executives (just ask any executive how recently they have attempted to install an enterprise resource planning system, such as SAP).

IT SYSTEMS IN MERGER AND ACQUISITION

A report quotes Thomson Financial Securities Data which gives the value of annual global acquisitions as more than $2.2 trillion. The record of corporate success in M & A is not good. The same report by KPMG measured the impact on shareholder value of M & A initiatives across a sample of companies in Europe. The bad news was that, measured objectively in this way, only 17 per cent of deals increased shareholder value, 30 per cent left it unchanged, and 53 per cent decreased it. Failure to consider IS/IT at an early stage is often a contributor to loss of value (there are other causes as well, of course). A previous survey found that the IT systems of both organisations had been integrated by 37 per cent, the acquired company's systems were discarded by 25 per cent, and a completely new system for both companies was developed by 15 per cent. Despite this, only 7 per cent of organisations had allowed for a budget for restructuring IT. A small proportion of respondents (12%) identified the IT strategy at the outset, but it was left principally to the stages of developing a post-merger plan and implementation (30% and 31%, respectively). Significantly, 14 per cent did not have an IT plan at all.

Only 25 per cent of respondents were able to say that they found no problems in dealing with the newly acquired company's systems. Slightly fewer than this did not know, and just over 50 per cent found problems and obstacles. These figures make the case for a careful appraisal of IT before the deal is signed. Obviously the need is greatest when the intention is to fully integrate the two organisations, but it is important in all situations. Although the real costs of processing information have fallen over the years, the size and complexity of organisations has increased, and the impact of new elements like ecommerce mean that the factors for consideration are numerous. The costs of developing new systems are significant, while failure to develop them means that the opportunities for synergy are reduced. The impact of IT on M & A success is considerable.

STRATEGY TO INFORMATION FLOWS

Apart from checking that the organisation is fulfilling the legal requirements of information generation and handling, it is useful to let any MIS audit start by focusing on the firm's business strategy. As depicted the information audit should aim to allow for maximum alignment between the company's business strategy and the information generating, processing, and decision impact of the MIS. In a research study of 124 companies, it was found that the highest performing firms had the best alignment between the distinctive competencies, dictated by the pursued strategy and the company's information systems. This follows the logic that managers implementing different strategies have different information needs; similarly, different information systems have different information generating capabilities. Thus, the more closely information is aligned with the desired strategy, the more likely managers will be to use the most appropriate levers in the formulation and implementation of the appropriate decisions.

The first requirement for the analysis is therefore a strategic audit of the firm and an assessment of goals and objectives. The alignment of the MIS with the business strategy and goals of the firm must therefore be evaluated. In small and medium-sized firms, it is our experience that one rarely finds formal MIS plans, however. It is therefore necessary to extract whether or not the firm actually has a plan for the current and future information systems requirements. In addition, the various systems are rarely integrated (which can make transitions to more developed applications somewhat easier compared to highly integrated MIS structures). In the past, MIS professionals have focused on tailoring the information systems requirements of the company to its business strategy. More recently, academics and other savants have questioned this adage, by arguing for more standardised solutions. The more of these that can be found to fit the firm's general needs, the more cost efficient and flexible the firm will be when upgrading or changing vendor for its information resources. This has recently been taken to new extremes with the advent of so-called application software providers, which sign-up companies to have standardized software run and operated not on the company's own computing system, but on large "server farms" where the connections to the firm are established via the Internet. Over the next five years, it is anticipated that 65-80 per cent of standardised software for small and medium-sized companies will be changed over to application software providers. (However, there remains a need to seek the best fit possible between the various standardised solutions on offer and the business strategy.)

This is a natural consequence of the evolution in information technology. According to Semiconductor if you were to put 64 MB of DRAM in your PC today, you could do it for about $100 using one module containing 8 chips. If you had put the same amount of DRAM in your computer in 1974, it would have cost you more than $3,000,000 and you would have needed more than 130,000 chips to do it. To take it even further, if we extrapolate the trend in memory price and capacity from 1975 to 2000 and then add another 25 years, in 2025, we will pay $100 for 2,500 gigabytes of RAM. These technological developments not only create challenges in evaluating the current information systems of the firm, but they also add serious challenges to the assessment of the firm's marketing and channel strategy, its purchasing processes, outsourcing strategy and even the organisational structure and personnel practices.

The transition induced by the advent of new technologies, such as Internet protocol applications, broadband telecommunication technology etc., is leading to new ways of organising business transactions and markets. E-business ventures are not only displaying business models not known ten years ago, but also dictating rules of engagement not foreseen by the incumbents in industry after industry; for example:

- Car dealers: Auto-by-Tel, CarPoint
- Real estate brokers: Visual Properties
- Newspapers: CNet, Excite, Yahoo!, AOL
- Stock brokers: E*Trade, eSchwab, Ameritrade
- Insurance agents: Quicken Financial Services

In addition, we are seeing new firms anticipating efficiency and scale in ways which, only five years ago, were not predicted by most strategic plans. The point is that discussions about information systems are today not a question of merely reflecting on processes, procedures and data warehousing, but have now moved to be an integral part of strategic dialogue and design of the enterprise.

When undertaking the appraisal of the MIS for strategic review purposes, it is useful to try to get a fix on what sorts of problems there may be. The questions below, used as a form of simple survey among managers at various levels, can help to identify the perception managers have of the MIS. By all means modify the questions to suit your own situation. You will notice that although some of the questions ask managers about whether they are getting the information they need, there is also exploration of the timeliness of that information. Good information which always come too late to be useful may be as useless as having no information.

Questionnaire:

These questions will help you obtain a broad feel for whether there are problems with the information system.

Possible answers, from "no competitive advantage for the firm"

1. to "excellent or significant competitive advantage for the firm" (4), are given below each question. They are examples derived from various firms. Use them as an aid in assessing the questions.

- To what degree is the firm's administrative system organised to satisfy the internal as well as the external demands of a modern firm?

In light of your assessment, how do you evaluate its competitive impact on the organisation?

Examples:

1. The administration is quite disorganised to the extent that it is hard to get required information for both internal and external needs.
2. The administration is satisfactorily organised in that it fulfils the legal demand for information. Internally, the administration is nearly exclusively organised to provide the firm's top management with the most necessary pieces of information.
3. Our administration interacts well with public authorities, vendors and customers, and through constant effort we try to improve its effectiveness and relevance to our needs for information.
4. We have a highly effective and efficient administrative system which provides the necessary and relevant information in a timely manner.

- How effective is the firm's information and reporting system?
- In light of your assessment, how do you evaluate its competitive impact on the organisation?

Examples:

1. Not effective. Necessary information is unavailable to managers when they need it. Most frequently, top management makes decisions on a loose basis because they cannot get the necessary information.
2. It is informal in structure. The top management has the full general picture and can find the current information they need. There is no talk of a more formal system.

3. We try to uncover the required information, and all information is accessible for managers so they can use it if they wish.
4. Required information is discussed at regular intervals. Necessary new information is provided and the superfluous information is discarded; this ensures that the information is available to those who need it, when they need it.

   — To what extent is the firm's reporting system suitable for its information requirements?

In light of your assessment, how do you evaluate its competitive impact on the organisation?

Examples:

1. We have no reports apart from the accounting department's annual report.
2. As long as everything is running normally, we don't do much reporting, but when something goes wrong, a report is made to management.
3. Besides short periodic accounts, management receives frequent production and sales reports.
4. Reporting takes place according to a firm plan and is essentially tied to budget follow-up. For instance, the reports address actual activity in relation to plans and also the development of budgetary consequences.

   — How much information is available on a daily basis?

In light of your assessment, how do you evaluate its competitive impact on the organisation?

Examples:

1. None is available the day it is needed. It takes at least a day to pull together the information you need.
2. Not very much, because information is usually too old.

3. The daily management is based on existing plans; they are drawn up and altered on the basis of available and current information.
4. We have built up our organisation and information system such that information of current interest is used extensively in the daily management of our firm.
5. What are you doing to improve the administration?

In light of your assessment, how do you evaluate its competitive impact on the organisation?

Examples:
1. The present plan is to continue to move very slowly in changing current methods.
2. We didn't change anything last year because it is expensive to alter the system. We did a few years ago and, on the whole, it was useful.
3. We always encourage employees to voice their suggestions for improvement. If their proposals are cost effective, we implement them.
4. Under the direction of a committee, we have an ongoing process to improve the firm. Tasks are routinely automated if the outcome simplifies administration and satisfies workers' demands.

It may be desirable to supplement this broad questionnaire with a more specific survey, which asked managers details of the internal and external information sources they use, the information they themselves generate, and their information and communication needs. Examples of survey questionnaires of this type can be found in, among others, Stanat.

Although the answers to our questionnaire can be very helpful and will often pinpoint specific deficiencies, it would be wrong to assume that a top score means there are no problems. This is because the organisation may have made do with a deficient system for so long that the absence of key information is taken as an acceptable normality. In one consulting assignment the managing director of a subsidiary company had to provide one figure every day to the corporate chief executive: that for the previous day's sales. This was given so much importance in the organisation that neither the managing director nor his marketing director gave much thought to other information that would have been more useful. Although the system could print out a periodic analysis of sales by customer by product categories, this was not seen as important information and had never been requested. When the consulting assignment led to a demand for this information, it was found that one of the major products had a customer profile which having a leading position with major construction companies, the firm had a minimal position here, and most sales of this product were to small builders.

The fall-off in total sales had been blamed on the recession prevailing at the time: the fact that the major customers were still buying other products from the company masked the changes, in the absence of any analysis by product. The problem was even more serious because lack of knowledge of the pattern of sales of this product had concealed a major strategic problem and a total shift in how the market was served. Had they been asked, the management at subsidiary and head office level would have said that the information received was what was needed. Although a more detailed survey would have identified the information each manager received, there would still have been no perception that anything critical was missing.

We provided a view of the integrated organisation, and showed the inter-relationship or strategy, structure and other factors with information. You may wish to refer back to this, as it is as relevant for IT as it is for HRM, the topic under which we introduced it. This could be applied to IT, with minor modification.

Set 1: The three related elements in this set are business strategy, critical success factors, and competencies, capabilities and processes. Initially the audit can only be carried out against the existing strategy, but after the complete appraisal is finished, and new strategic decisions taken, it may be necessary to examine the situation to see if changes need to be made. This is when the integrated organisation model is most useful, because it helps ensure that all aspects of a new strategy are thought through. Critical success factors are the limited number of factors which if done well should enable the strategy to be implemented successfully. For our purposes here we need only stress the links between the key processes, competencies and capabilities which enable the business strategy to be implemented. If we can define these, we have a basis to compare the information that is provided with that which is needed.

Set 2: The four elements in this set are informational fit, information generation, processing and the decision making impact. We have just touched on the first of these, which is the way the information we currently have fits with what is really needed. As we mentioned earlier, this is a question of timeliness as well as relevance, and it also covers frequency and format. Information generation is about the way in which the required information is obtained. It is worth stressing here that not all important information is internally generated, or in a form that is suitable for a repetitive corporate-wide information system. So there are things to consider about how information like competitor data or market analyses is obtained and stored. Although IT may play a part in this in various ways, we should not overlook important information which may be held in filing cabinets and company libraries. Processing covers not only the technical aspects of the equipment for collecting, collating, storing and distributing information, but also the degree of centralisation and decentralisation. When auditing an established system, the up-to-date (or otherwise) nature of the computers, applications software and networks is also important. There is also an integration issue of the hardware and software for MIS and that used for operational needs (for example word processing, email, and day to day management analysis and decision making).

We should also audit the security practices and assess the vulnerability of the organisation to hackers and virus attacks. Linked to this are the various internal policies and procedures which exist to reduce the risk of external raids on the system, and to protect the organisation against legal claims (for example, defamation actions arising from emails sent through the corporate system, even when these are unauthorised). Decision making impact is an assessment of the value of the various elements of the MIS to the organisation.

Set 3: This set consists of organisational matters and structure/systems. Here we are back to our integrated organisation model. The effect of the MIS on the elements in this set may be because of the way information is obtained, or the way it is made available. In fact, as we have pointed out in the discussion on the integrated organisation, it is a two-way influence. If, for example, control information is produced in a way which does not match organisational responsibilities, the management of the affected units will be impaired in their role. So either responsibilities have to be changed to match the MIS, or the MIS has to adapt to the organisational needs.

FORMAL VERSUS INFORMAL INFORMATION FLOWS

As the analysis of the company's information system develops, the audit team will also be encouraged to examine the social structures of the firm to uncover the flows of vital informal information streams. Although the formal flows can be identified from an upto-date organisation chart, interpreted in relation to the organisational style and the policies in place, much of the information flow is across informal groupings. Information rarely flows up and down within the confines of the little boxes and arrows of the formal chart, and most managers work closely with managers from other units, with whom there is a need to share information. This type of work-related informal grouping is vital to the effective management of the organisation.

However, informal groups go a stage further than this, and occur through the social interaction of people from different parts of the organisation: those, for example, who see each other regularly in the company restaurant, or in the lifts and passages, or who may be the smokers who can be found at various times clustering outside the doors of premises which have no smoking rules, or who have other opportunities for both planned and unplanned contact. Informal groups of this nature disseminate information, not always accurately, and may also be a source of new information. The audit should examine the policies and procedures for communicating information to the whole organisation. The best way to reduce distortion and rumour is not to be over secretive, and to ensure that there are ways in which information about what the organisation is doing, its results, and to a degree its intentions are passed on to employees.

However, the other side of the coin is looking at the main informal sources of new information, to see which of these can be captured and disseminated more effectively. For example, competitor information systems frequently include ways of capturing and analysing information brought in by sales people and functional managers, who may pick up information from contact with customers, suppliers and competitors. At the other extreme there is information which in theory contributes to the collective knowledge of the organisation, but which in practice resides in the brains of various individuals, goes home in the evening with them, goes on holiday when they go on holiday, and leaves the organisation when they resign, retire or when their employment is terminated for other reasons.

MANAGEMENT OF KNOWLEDGE

This takes us nicely into another important and difficult part of the audit: knowledge management. In one sense this is a recent concept, growing out of the 1990s concept of the learning organisation. In another sense, it is as old as the hills, in that knowledge has always been important to organisations, and the modern problem is caused by the size and complexity of organisations, and in many cases a management view that people are disposable resources.

Mayo stresses the importance of the intellectual capital of the organisation. He divides this into three categories:

- Customer (external structural) capital (e.g. customer contracts, relationships, loyalty, satisfaction; market share; image; reputation; brands).
- Organisational (internal structural) capital (e.g. systems, methodologies, patents, know-how, databases, knowledge, culture).
- Human capital (e.g. individual competence and experience, judgement, wisdom; team competence; leadership and motivation).

To try to analyse and record all of this would result in more information than could possibly be used. To our personal knowledge some large organisations attempted to do this as far back as the 1970s, and possibly earlier, with questionnaires sent out to all managers in order to record their knowledge and skills. Although this might have worked in a few situations, such as enabling an organisation to locate quickly experts in a subject who also had a particular language competence, in general these broad attempts were never updated, resulted in information overload, and what we might also call information "underload": information that was really wanted had never been included in the questionnaires. Mayo suggests controlling overload by concentrating on the components of knowledge management that relate to three questions:

- Is this component clearly linked to the achievement of a major strategy?
- How significant is this component in driving today's value?
- How significant is this component in driving tomorrow's value?

Knowledge management is partly an IT matter. However, it is also much more to do with how the whole organisation is managed, and how people are recruited, retained and developed. So among other things, it also relates to HRM. In auditing the intranet and database systems which are the IT component, it is also important to consider the HRM elements of knowledge management. The IT side may provide data capture, storage and dissemination methods, but does not determine the policies and procedures which recruit people with the right knowledge, hone and develop knowledge, and encourage people to share it. The purpose of the appraisal is not to design a knowledge management system, but to examine what the organisation has, what it costs and how appropriate it is.

When it has nothing, the facts are easy to record, although answering whether the organisation would benefit from such a system may be more difficult. Where there is such a system in place, there is more to audit. First, the running costs should be identified. Although it may be tempting to want to record the development costs of the system being used, this is not really helpful information as the costs are sunk. It should be remembered that the costs incurred by the IT department are only one element: the other is the time people throughout the organisation spend inputting data into the system. This should be compared with an estimate of the value gained, which is to do with how the system is used and what benefits flow from that use. Newell and Swan tell an interesting story of how a simple question can bring a revealing answer:

This company has spent a considerable amount of money on developing an intranet to promote knowledge sharing. When members of the organisation were asked for an example of the useful knowledge that was on the intranet, the example given was the company bus timetable. This provides information on the time the company bus will be at one of three locations within the particular city. Given that 20 minutes is the maximum time between buses, and that this does not change from day to day, this is unlikely to really contribute to developing and using the intellectual capital within the organisation! The final task is not just to mark the system as good or bad, but to indicate what, if anything, needs to be done about it.

COMPUTER-BASED TECHNOLOGY

The terms "information technology" and "information systems" tend to misdirect our thinking about the new directions that we are moving into. The advent of affordable personal computers has transformed the way many people do their daily jobs. It is now unusual to go into any manager's office and not see a computer by the desk or somewhere in the background. But although the penetration of the PC has been fast, it has built on familiar ground. It changed how things are done, put greater power for effectiveness in the hands of many people at all levels, but in a way was a continuation of the things that had traditionally been done. Before word processing there was typing. Before spreadsheets there were calculators and analysis paper. Certainly computers, email and voicemail have broken the pattern which says that people have to be concentrated in offices This has enabled large businesses to reduce office space by encouraging some home working, and has allowed self-employed people to have better communications and to offer large-organisation levels of quality in letters, reports and home-produced promotional materials.

These things have changed what is done, but have not been astonishing. We are now in a period when the new computer technologies are beginning to produce step changes in business. Instead of stepping off a rather slow escalator for something faster, we now have to work out ways of getting to the next floor when there is nothing tangible to slide on to. E-commerce is one of the big innovations, which is still largely in the question mark box, but with the queries gradually disappearing with the growing acceptance of things like Internet banking. While we would not suggest that any organisation should set up a dot-corn operation just because it does not have one, we feel that the audit should look at the way the technology is changing, the potential implications for the organisation, and the mechanisms by which the organisation monitors the directions that the technologies are taking.

TAKING A PROCESS VIEW

We suggested that among the various ways of moving from a function-by-function analysis was the examination of processes. These may stretch across departments within a function, and/or across functions. A study of processes avoids the classic problem of thinking of the organisation as a series of watertight compartments, and falling into the trap of believing that optimising performance in each of the parts will automatically lead to the optimal performance of the whole organisation. Here we will look at processes in three ways, by exploring the idea of benchmarking, adding some remarks on business process re-engineering, and exploring the value chain approach.

BENCHMARKING

Many organisations compare their performance ratios with those of their competitors, and this is a good thing to do. It can prevent complacency, allow a more accurate assessment of whether the results achieved show a strength or a weakness, and stimulate action. Many people call this benchmarking. However, useful though this process is, it is not benchmarking.

It may be an essential first step to deciding to benchmark, but it is only a first step. So what is benchmarking? Watson quotes the definition given by the American Productivity and Quality Centre:

Benchmarking is a systematic and continuous measurement process; a process of continuously measuring and comparing an organisation's business processes against business process leaders anywhere in the world to gain information which will help the organisation take action to improve its performance.

This definition moves benchmarking a long way from ratio comparisons. It is very clearly about comparing processes, with a view to finding ways to improve. So the emphasis is not just on what the other organisation achieves, but how it does it. It does not take much pondering on this to realise that in order to benchmark against someone else's process, you have to understand your own. Watson suggests that benchmarking has evolved to a fourth generation of the concept. He saw the first generation as the product level, with a main tool being reverse engineering. The idea was to study competitors' products. Xerox was the leading organisation in this field, and in much of the future development of benchmarking.

The second generation was competitive benchmarking, which made comparisons of the organisation's processes with those of competitors: "Xerox developed this capability after finding that the manufacturing cost of its products equalled the sales price of competitors' products". There are obvious difficulties in benchmarking processes of competitors, if one is to stay within the bounds of legal and ethical behaviour. Watson's third generation was a logical development from the second. As many processes are applicable to a wide range of industries, there is much that can be learned from organisations which are not competitors. There are two advantages to moving this way. First, the best performance from a particular process may well be achieved by an organisation which is not a competitor; second, there are fewer legal and business limitations to cooperation between organisations which do not compete. Once an organisation determines to compare its key processes with whoever is best in the world at each, it has moved a long way from just thinking about being as good as competitors. The fourth generation is strategic benchmarking, which is also the title of Watson's book. This fits very well with modern concepts of strategic alliances, and is the exchange of information for benchmarking between organisations which are formally working together to achieve some strategic purpose. Because not all organisations have strategic alliance partners, this approach cannot be universal. Its advantage is that the close relationship makes it easier for organisations to collaborate to a much deeper extent. We should add internal benchmarking to the types mentioned above. This can bring improvements in performance, although not necessarily taking the organisation to world class performance standards. It has the advantage that data is more easily available, and benchmarking is relatively simple to organise. In our experience the obstacle is a defensive attitude. This means that when a subsidiary in one country has a better performance in a particular area than a subsidiary in another, the "explanation" is spontaneous and given off the cuff. It focuses on the differences between circumstances rather than looking for commonalities. These differences are of course sometimes relevant, but not always, and large organisations in particular can gain much from the units in the group which are the leading performers in particular processes. The British Government may have learned this lesson, as it is now making efforts to identify best practice in various activities within the network of hospitals of the National Health Service.

ROLE OF BENCHMARKING

Clearly, to undertake benchmarking takes time and organisation, and it would be difficult to fit external benchmarking within the time scale of the typical corporate appraisal. However, organisations which take benchmarking seriously have units set up to undertake it, which means that there is already a source of information, however incomplete, which may provide useful insight. The first phase of benchmarking, identifying areas where performance needs improving, and comparison with the ratios from other organisations, is a valid and usually manageable activity of the corporate appraisal, which will help give a different insight into the assessments collected by other means. Internal benchmarking should be considered as part of the appraisal process if there are appropriate benchmarking partners within the total organisation. It can be organised faster than external benchmarking, and, provided the processes are considered wisely, can be a manageable part of an appraisal exercise.

Both internal and external benchmarking are worth considering as a follow-up to an appraisal. This is to enable improvements to be made in various operational areas which may have been identified as having problems, and also means that when the appraisal is revisited, there are additional elements that can be brought within it. The health warning is that benchmarking is not a substitute for a strategy. Continuous improvement is an important aim, and the organisation may fail if it neglects it, but improvement alone will not guarantee success. Similarly, just copying what other organisations do, without adding any creative thinking of your own, will not take you to the forefront of performance. Benchmarking has to be a dynamic activity.

CORE PROCESSES

Although BPR in its total concept is beyond the scope of the corporate appraisal, the identification of the core processes is not. In fact there is a strong affinity with the value chain, and the concepts of core competencies and core capabilities, which we will discuss later.

Johansson et al state: 'A process is a set of linked activities that take an input and transform it to create an output". And: "By thinking about businesses as processes rather than as functions, managers can focus on streamlining processes in order to create more value for less effort rather than focusing on reducing the size of functions in order to simply cut costs. Cost cuts will naturally occur as non-value adding activities are removed from the processes and as the processes increase in their level of effectiveness". Organisations have thousands of processes, and identifying every one would be like one of those interminable tasks in the Hades of mythology. Even if identified and defined, we would be left with the problem of what to do with the information. Core processes are different. Normally a business may have between 5 and 10 of these, and because they are critical to the competitiveness of the organisation, there is valuing in identifying them, and charting each.

The core processes are those which have an impact on customers, so what processes are core can only be defined in the context of the market and customer needs and expectations. A good starting point for defining them is the value chain.

PROBLEMS WITH BPR

BPR is not easy to apply. The identification of the core processes can be difficult, but is a pushover compared to the task of developing something different to replace them. Coulsen-Thomas found in his research across Europe that most so-called BPR activities examined were process simplification rather than re-engineering, and were driven by a desire to reduce costs and not for longer term strategic benefits. He observed: "What is clear is that many of the BPR solutions being adopted are yielding cost benefits today at the price of inflexibility tomorrow. Thus paths and options are being limited and prescribed in order to 'speed things up' in ways that can reduce the scope for creative thinking and innovation".

If you ally the misunderstanding of what BPR is to the difficulties of doing it well, and the quick-fix mentalities of too many managers, the fall in popularity of the approach is easier to understand.

THE VALUE CHAIN

The value chain concept was originated by Porter. He argued: "To diagnose competitive advantage, it is necessary to define a firm's value chain for competing in a particular industry". He also maintained that 'Competitive advantage cannot be understood by looking at a firm as a whole. It stems from the many discrete activities a firm performs in designing, producing, marketing, delivering, and supporting its product. Each of these activities can contribute to a firm's relative cost position and create a basis for differentiation". In other words, you have to work at a micro level to identify what is important. Although the term is widely used by managers in general conversation, the Bain research showed that it was applied in only 26 per cent of the sampled organisations. This could be interpreted as a signal of success for a method which was identified some 14 years previously, but it is clearly not at the top of the popularity list.

Value Analysis

Porter envisages an organisation as having five generic primary areas:

1. *Inbound Logistics.* This involves all the activities connected with the receipt, storage and handling of materials, components and supplies. In the case of a retailer this would be the finished goods for resale. Under this heading Porter includes inventory control.
2. *Operations:* These are all the activities involved in converting inputs into their final form. It is easiest to visualise this by thinking of a manufacturing or processing business, but of course there are operations in service businesses. Think of an airline, a hotel and a hospital. After that it is easier to visualize operations in the context of other service businesses, like management consulting, banking or insurance.
3. *Outbound Logistics:* This includes the physical distribution of the product, including order processing as well as the physical handling of the product.
4. *Marketing and Sales:* Porter defines this as "Activities associated with providing the means by which buyers can purchase the product and inducing them to do so".
5. *Service:* This includes the service activities provided to increase the value of the product, such as after-sales service, spares availability or training the customer's employees. Each and all of these is potentially capable of delivering unique value to the customer, which provided the economic equation is satisfactory, can create competitive advantage.

The primary activities do not cover the whole of an organisation. Porter sees four additional activities at the support level:

1. *Procurement:* Purchasing tends to be a mainly centralized activity, but with many exceptions. For example, the purchasing department may order most

components and materials, but not usually legal and similar professional services. What is purchased is affected by the managers from whom the purchase is made, and the quantities obtained will be influenced by the inventory control policies. However, the purchasing function has a great effect on the costs of inputs, and therefore on the value that can be passed on to customers. It affects every area of the organisation.

2. *Technology:* This affects the whole organisation. As we saw there is the technology of process as well as the technology of products and services. Functionally, technology may be centred on R&D and engineering departments, but in practical terms it influences everything the organisation does.

3. *Human Resource Management:* People are recruited, trained, promoted and paid, and every primary and support area employs people. The activity may be centralised or decentralised; it may be in the hands of specialist functions, or split between HR specialists and line managers. In some organisations the whole activity may fall to line managers. However it is organised, HR will affect every area of the organisation.

4. *Infrastructure of the Firm:* The infrastructure activities in Porter's classification could be taken as whatever has not been discussed so far, but this would be to imply that the infrastructure has no effect on value. It implies as a minimum the functions of general management, finance and accounting, legal services and public affairs. How functions are divided between head offices and business operations has an effect on how they are able to contribute value. Support activities may not be visible to the customer, but nevertheless can create or destroy value. For example, the comprehensive training given by an

airline to its cabin staff may create value, not because the customer knows about the training, but through what he or she experiences, the behaviour of the in-flight staff. The accounting conventions may make some areas seem to be unprofitable, when in fact they are contributing to overall success. Performance targets and reward systems may drive behaviour in one direction or another, and not always in the way management wants. The idea is that a chain of value exists inside every organisation, and understanding this and building on it is a way to build a strong competitive position.

However, Porter's thinking goes beyond the boundaries of the firm, and argues that the industry company is only one of a series of links in a much larger chain which stretches from the raw materials to the ultimate buyer. Many of the value-creating opportunities lie at the interfaces between the organisations which make up this chain. Therefore there is considerable merit in working closely with suppliers, customers and through them the customers' customers, to seek areas of overall improvement. Collaborative work of this kind is, of course, a feature of modern approaches to quality management, and appears in much of the literature on business process reengineering, and it is no longer considered stupid to give up an activity which is not performed as well as it could be, and to transfer it to a supplier.

Value is created, according to Johansson et al, in four broad ways, alone or in combination: improved quality, service, reduced cost to customer and reduced cycle time. The starting point for an assessment of the value chain may be to establish what the *organisation* believes are the processes which deliver value to the customer, but by itself this may be dangerous and inadequate. It is the customer that is the key, and to make any sense of the value chain there is a need to establish what the customer is looking for. However, there are limitations to this, such as when the organisation is considering an innovation that has never been done before, and therefore customers may have no experience or even understanding of it.

Although Porter's framework may be helpful as a peg on which to hang various ways in which the organisation provides value, it has some drawbacks. It tends to mirror the organisation chart's labelling of functions, rather than the processes. JIT or MRP processes, for example, may link the inward logistic, operations, finished stock and procurement in a way that is not apparent from the way the functions are set out. But perhaps this could be a strength of the framework, if it led to the understanding that processes will overlap his headings, and that value may be created by this as much as by what goes on within each group of functions.

A second problem was hinted at in our introduction. Porter uses an arrow-shaped diagram to illustrate the value chain, and this has become world famous. His nine headings fit into this diagram. However, we have seen many so-called value chain reports which do little more than break down the organisation chart into subheadings, which are then listed under the nine headings on an enlarged version of the arrow-shaped chart under each heading. Often, this gives no more information than could have been read off the organisation chart, does not indicate the processes that enable value to be created, and does not show the costs or benefits of what is done.

It is useful, as we said, to begin with an internal view of the processes which create value, and to separate these from the processes which are essential to serve a customer, but which are doing nothing special for that customer. In the first stages we may begin with what it is that we are providing the customer: for example, immediate access to technical advice; any product can be delivered next day; enabling the customer to reduce wastage rates; loan replacement immediately available if equipment breaks down. We can rate which of these things we think we are doing better than competitors, and which we believe give customers that extra element of value.

This part of value chain analysis is about self-inspection, but it will be meaningless unless it has customer inputs. Market surveys may yield some of this information, but greater depth may come from focus groups of current and potential customers. Such marketing research methods can also yield valuable information about the value chains of competitors. A focus on these formal ways of obtaining information should not obscure the important information that is gained when the organisation is always in close contact with its customers, enjoys good relations with them, and discusses their needs with them almost continuously. Unfortunately, comparatively few organisations have such a close relationship with their customers so that they are really in each other's confidence and, in any case, knowing a customer well may not help you understand why their competitors do not buy from you.

Remember that customers do not all obtain value from the same thing, or that value may not be for the same reason. For example, many small businesses deal with stationery suppliers that offer a good mail order service, one feature of which is next-day delivery. This gives potential benefits to customers, such as reducing the stock levels that have to be carried, and helping to avoid emergencies: none of these is particularly important to a business run mainly from home. The benefit to such businesses is the ability to know that the order will be delivered on a particular day, so that it is possible to ensure that someone is in the office to receive it. If this promise were unreliable, the supplier would be changed. For a larger organisation, which always has staff available to receive orders, the main value may be in obtaining the highest volume discounts, and having the benefit of being able to reduce stocks of stationery supplies to reduce the money tied up. The benefit from the offering is thus quite different for different customer situations.

The information obtained has to be specific. Generalised comments from customers like 'good service' are not specific enough. What is it about this service which is seen as good, and what is the benefit that the customer perceives? When both the internal and external information has been put together, it is possible to sort out what is giving the customer value, and to move to the processes which enable that to be achieved.

The example makes two important points. The first is that the customers see the outcome, not all the elements of the process that creates that outcome. The second is the need to look at the costs of the processes which bring a customer benefit. Management consulting firms measure the time their employees spend on different activities, and these systems make it easier to look at the costs of what is done. And in the example given there are no fixed assets exclusively dedicated to providing this particular value.

Unfortunately this is not true of the majority of organisations, where little record is kept of how much time is spent in indirect areas of activity, and assets are distributed within functions rather than processes. To make real sense of value chain analysis, it is necessary to look at the costs of providing the benefits to customers, and the fixed and working capital that enables the benefit to be provided. But it is not easy, and in a large organisation can be very difficult indeed.

The analysis described so far gives a snapshot of the current value chain of the organisation. It may have been enhanced by an examination of the value chain of the whole industry. This may have been made even more useful if an attempt is also made to under stand the value chains of key competitors, to the degree that it is possible to do this from outside. This information gives a platform for a number of strategic considerations, such as:

- Is it possible to modify a process to provide the same benefit to customers at lower cost?
- Can we change a process economically so that it delivers greater value to customers?
- Would it be sensible to negotiate with suppliers, so that a process in the value chain is either passed back to them, or brought on board by us, in order to provide greater overall value?
- Are there areas where we do not provide a value to customers that they can obtain from competitors, or will require in the future?

The purpose of the corporate appraisal is not to answer these questions, although the options may be identified as part of the analysis. It is to see that the importance of the questions is understood, and in a form which can be given proper attention when strategies are formulated.

CORE COMPETENCIES AND RELATED METHODS

Core competencies and its relations, critical success factors and core capabilities, are among those methods which stretch across the whole organisation. Apart from the usefulness of the approaches themselves, as a way of thinking about strategy, they also have value in the integrated view which they provide. But they are not easy concepts to use. In corporate appraisal, there is merit in identifying what the organisation possesses that is core or critical, both as a foundation for corporate endeavour, and to ensure that these attributes are maintained and developed. This makes it possible to analyse the gap between what the organisation has and what it needs.

There is a real difference between these methods and the more traditional approaches that were discussed earlier. It is possible to analyse the sources of profit, the risks from reliance on too few customers, and many other such matters without very much awareness of the vision of the organisation, or knowledge of the view it holds of the future. When we come to critical success factors or core competencies, we move into new territory. We can look backwards and say this is what has been core or critical to this organisation in the past, or that we have suffered because we lacked a particular attribute possessed by competitors. Indeed, most examples we have seen in books on core competencies have given their examples through this use of hindsight, and we have yet to see well-documented work which demonstrates that such core competencies were predetermined by far-sighted managers, based on their perception of what the future might be. But looking backwards can provide lessons, and will establish a platform of where the organisation stands today.

However, identifying what critical success factors or core competencies are needed for the future can only be done if those undertaking the appraisal have a clear sense of what the organisation believes is the vision for the future. This may be available in some organisations, in which case it can be used to assess what is needed and the gap with what exists. Where the view of the future is unclear, or if the current view is suspect, the forwardlooking part of the process becomes part of the strategic decision process and moves outside the boundaries of the corporate appraisal.

In describing three different, but related concepts we are not urging any organisation to use them all, nor would we press any organisation to use any that they did not see as relevant to their problem.

CRITICAL SUCCESS FACTORS (CSFS)

The critical success factors approach is well established, and has been particularly useful in helping top managements define their management information needs. CSFs are "the limited number of areas in which results, if they are satisfactory, will ensure successful competitive performance for the organisation". They relate to the basic internal or external conditions for the firm's strategy (e.g. customer acceptance, competitive moves), or those competencies or resources (e.g. human, financial) it must attain.

Jenster expanded this notion into a more comprehensive and strategic concept, suggesting that the definition and monitoring of CSFs differs for various strategy types. His study of 128 firms in mature manufacturing industries found that the firms which had a higher return on equity:

1. Formally identified their CSFs,
2. Used these factors to monitor their progress in the implementation of strategic changes,
3. Benefited from formally integrated reporting and information systems.

Miller found that CSFs, when formally identified, implicitly communicate the top management's priorities and thereby direct organisational efforts in the desired direction. The desired direction is attained through the motivation of the organisation's employees, by providing a framework against which they can make sense of priorities, assumptions and environmental conditions, so that they are able to contribute better to the execution of corporate plans.

For example, consider a company which views the introduction of new products as one of its CSFs. Beyond communicating that top management views the organisation's future as hinging upon being a product innovator, this clearly conveys to individuals where their most significant contribution can be made. Most members of management are strongly motivated to excel in relation to the expectations of corporate leadership. They will adapt to meet those expectations provided that top management's wishes are clearly and consistently communicated. Effective leadership necessitates the clear definition of success factors, the ideal organisational performance in relation to them, and the explicit communication of these factors to all appropriate levels of management in a structured manner.

In addition to providing a bridge between the firm's objectives and management's strategy, the isolation of critical factors also provides a vehicle for the design of an effective system of performance measurement and control. This way, the design of CSFs becomes more than just identifying the areas which "must go right", but assumes a powerful strategic role in which the specific efforts of top management and the employees are joined and aligned in a manner consistent with the firm's vision. In summary, the factors identified as essential to the organisation's success serve as the primary integrating mechanism between management's long-range goals and the channelling of resources and executive attention. Explicit recognition and use of such CSFs provides, therefore, a planning process/system through which strategy formulation can be made operational and controlled within the firm.

Determine the Elements which Affect Success: The first step in determining CSFs is to audit the forces which are relevant to the firm's present and future position.

Strategic areas may include:

- *General Environment:* Factors which influence the firm and over which it has no control. Included here may be issues such as general socio-demographic trends, interest rates and exchange rate fluctuations.
- *Industry Characteristics:* Features of the firm's industry and related industries. In general, it appears that each industry has a set of common dimensions to which individual firms need to adhere. For example, supermarket chains will have one set of dynamic factors and banks another.
- *Competitive Forces:* Postures of competitors, suppliers, customers and potential new entrants, as well as those elements which firms following similar strategies in related industries need to be alert to. These may include certain quality standards, product mix, cost control etc.
- *Company-specific Characteristics:* Factors derived from the unique aspects of a particular firm's competitive position (i.e. its strengths and weaknesses as well as opportunities and threats), traits of the management team, and/or time elements.
- *Personal Values of key Players:* The demand, wishes, needs and capabilities of key players, executives and other personnel must be examined. For example, the personal preferences of the major stockholders should not be neglected.
- *Resource Availability:* Availability of financial, as well as physical and human resources, will have an impact on the strategic success.

These strategic characteristics may form the basis for defining the firm's sensitivity to the influences or changes along the various dimensions. It shows how the firm's sensitivity can be examined using a weighting scheme where 1 equals no effect, and 10 implies substantial or critical impact.

The impact grid can also be used in the design/review and integration of a firm's strategic plans, as well as to assess reversibility of resource commitments. Moreover, this evaluation is used to create the list of potential elements from which management selects the firm's 5 to 10 CSFs. The dimensions may also be used to develop alternative result scenarios and for the identification, achievement and evaluation of management's objectives, as well as in the subsequent transformation of ideas into action.

Some of the identified factors affected by the various elements are *strategic* in nature, in that they relate directly to the way senior personnel interpret situations and carry out plans. Other success factors are *operational* and not necessarily directly useful to the tasks and activities of key personnel. Although they are important to the way lower personnel define and integrate particular tasks, they may receive management attention on a less frequent, ad hoc or by-exception basis.

Review the Current Strategic Plan: The next step is to look at the information from the current strategic plan, if one exists, or to deduce the vision and strategy from the organisation's actions (and from the other approaches to the appraisal which have already been discussed) if no such plan exists. Later it may be necessary to repeat this action if new strategies are made following the appraisal. Essentially what we are doing here is to establish a baseline to record the current situation.

The information we extract from the plan should give the present perception of the answers to questions such as:

- What type of firm do we want the organisation to be?
- What type of activities do we want to engage in?
- What markets do we want to pursue?

Although these questions sound simple and straightforward, answering them can be a long and tedious affair. Validation of the answers by panels of experienced managers will help to ensure that the appraisal is not wandering in the wrong direction.

Identify the Current Critical Success Factors: CSFs are the limited number of factors important to strategic success. They are the limited number of areas which must be monitored to ensure successful execution of the firm's strategic programmes. These factors can be used to guide and motivate key employees to perform in the desired manner, and in a way which will ensure successful performance throughout the strategy. The use of these factors in discussions and planning within the firm will clearly and succinctly communicate critical elements of the strategy to members of the organisation. More importantly, the CSFs direct the attention of key managers to focus on the basic premises of the firm's strategy.

The selection of proper strategic dimensions is essential, inasmuch as they will serve as motivation for those whose performance is being measured. Thus, the CSFs must:

- reflect success of the defined strategy,
- represent the foundation of this strategy,
- be able to motivate and align the managers as well as other employees,
- be very specific and/or measurable.

A manufacturer of cutting tools has as its major strategic theme "Shipping of orders within 24 hours". The board of directors identified timeliness of shipments and industry market share as two of their CSFs.

A diversified organisation will have a family of CSFs, as the requirements of the centre and each SBU will be different. On the other hand, a global single business organisation may have a common core of CSFs which are applicable to subsidiaries in all countries, although they may need to be supplemented by others which reflect the different local market situation.

Measure the Degree to which the Organisation Fulfils the Current CSFs: The fact that a CSF has been identified does not mean that the organisation is able to meet it. The next step is to audit performance against each of the CSFs. Ideally this should be on the basis of objective criteria, which is easier if the CSFs have been used as the basis of strategic performance indicators. Strategic performance indicators (SPIs) should be used to measure the short-term progress towards the long-term objectives. The SPIs are the indicators specifically used to measure and monitor key individuals' short-term progress towards achieving good performance along a critical dimension. SPIs provide motivational information which must be explicit enough to allow managers to understand how their actions influence strategic success, even though they may not have a full understanding of the underlying strategy.

SPIs must strive to satisfy six specifications. They should be:

- *Operational:* They must focus on action and provide information which can be used for control.
- *Indicative of Desired Performance:* Indicators must be measured against a desired level of performance.
- *Acceptable to Subordinates:* Subordinates should have significant input into determination of the indicators during the design/review process.
- *Reliable:* Most phenomena cannot be measured with precision, but can be described only within a range or as a degree of magnitude. It is up to the steering committee to think through what kind of measurement is appropriate to the factor it is meant to measure.
- *Timely:* This does not necessarily imply rapid reporting. The time dimension of controls should correspond to the "time span" of the event.
- *Simple:* Complicated strategic performance measurement systems often do not work. They confuse the organisation's members, and direct attention towards the mechanics andmethods of control, rather that towards the targeted performance results.

After being selected, the indicators should be analysed in terms of the information required to measure their achievement. Performance indicators will generally require information from a wide variety of different sources, both internal and external, in order to enable management to monitor progress in the different functional areas of the organisation. Where SPIs of this type do not already exist, it will be necessary to use what data is available. Where hard data is totally lacking, one method that can be used is to get groups of key managers together, to rate performance against each CSF on a scale of 1 to 10. Although judgements of this type may be helpful, remember that they may also be tainted.

Reassess the CSFs If Vision or Strategy Changes: The CFSs only have validity in relation to a specific situation. Any change in the vision for the organisation, or the strategy, should trigger a re-examination of the CSFs. This may not, strictly speaking, be a part of the corporate appraisal, but is an essential step to remember.

CORE COMPETENCIES

As a popular strategic approach, core competencies came to the fore with the publication of a *Harvard Business Review* article. Among their later publications was a much acclaimed, but somewhat evangelical, book. In fact, the originators of the idea, in so far as it is ever possible to track a business concept to its starting point, were Learned et al: "A central idea was distinctive competence - the concept that every firm has its own uniqueness which is crucial to developing its strategy Andrews/Christensen/Learned were the originators of the notion of core competencies that was rediscovered in 1990".

It may be of passing interest that management consultants Bain & Co. found in their 1998 annual survey of management tools and techniques that core competencies was ninth in terms of popularity (63% of their sample of companies were using it). In 1993, when they began this annual survey, the figure was 52 per cent, reaching a peak of over 70 per cent in 1996. Of course the figures must be interpreted in relation to the sample, and cannot be extrapolated to the universe of all companies, but the trends are significant.

"A competence is a bundle of skills and technologies that enables a company to provide a particular benefit to customers. At Sony that benefit is 'pocketability,' and the core competence is miniaturisation. At Federal Express the benefit is on-time delivery, and the core competence, at a very high level, is logistics management." "In the long run, competitiveness derives from an ability to build, at lower costs and more speedily than competitors, the core competencies that spawn unanticipated products. The real sources of advantage are to be found in management's ability to consolidate corporate-wide technologies and production skills into competencies that empower individual businesses to adapt quickly to changing opportunities."

From these quotations, we can see a competency as a bundle of skills and technologies which can be used for the benefit of the organisation. Identification of these bundles builds naturally on the audit of the technologies but competencies are more than technological know-how: they include the skills built up across the organisation that enable the firm to provide a product or service which customers want, and which builds into a defensible competitive position.

Prahalad and Hamel use an analogy of a competence tree when thinking of the diversified company, which has many similarities with the technology tree. The main roots, which feed the tree and give it stability against storms, are the core competencies: there are usually between 5 and 15 of these (we might suggest that the minor roots are those competencies which, although not core in the particular sense used here, are still required to enable the organisation to function). The trunk of the tree is made up of the core products. The branches are the different businesses that have grown to exploit the core products, and the leaves, flowers and fruit are the end products, many of which could not be foreseen when the core competencies were developed. There are warnings hidden in this analogy. The roots have to continue to grow and develop, and expand. A tree that grows top heavy will fall. Second, leaves, flowers and fruits mature and fall off, therefore there has to be a continual process of renewal if the tree is to survive. We will assume that our tree is not deciduous.

But what makes a competency core? In order to qualify, Hamel and Prahalad argue that a core competency must:

- give access (or potential access) to a wide variety of markets,
- deliver a clear benefit to the customer (or more accurately, a benefit that the customer perceives),
- be hard for competitors to copy, so that it provides a clear basis for differentiation.

A core competence is *not*, therefore:

- a single skill,
- a competence that all competitors have,
- a product,
- Something possessed by only one small area of the organisation.

THE CONCEPT

The corporate appraisal task is to answer two questions:

- What are the competencies of this organisation?
- What are the current core competencies?

Hinterhuber et al suggest a number of steps in the identification of core competencies, which we have built on, adding to them some ideas from Klein and Hiscocks. What is described below thus draws from the views of both authorities, plus some of our own experiences. It is not meant to reflect the full views of any particular authority, and if you want to look at these you will need to go to the original sources. The separation of the steps into appraisal and strategic tasks is ours, to fit the needs of this book.

- The appraisal task:
  — determining current competencies

- assessing the relative strengths of the competencies
- identifying those which deliver value to current customers.
* The strategic task:
- establishing which are needed for the longer term
- examining the portfolio of competencies.

THE APPRAISAL TASK

At this stage we are trying to assess all the competencies of the organisation, many of which will not prove to be core. This is where a classification like that suggested by Hamel is helpful, to try to get some order into what can otherwise appear to be a daunting task. Four starting points are suggested. It is recommended that all of them be used, as the whole truth is unlikely to emerge from any one of them.

1. What can be interpreted from the organisation's structure (for example, if the organisation has a telephone sales operation, it is likely to have some competencies in this area). At this stage it may not be possible to define these precisely, but we can at least note them for further consideration.

2. Interviews with key people inside the organisation. Who is key will vary with the organisation, but a good rule is to cast the net wide, as important competencies may be buried inside departments of the organisation, where they are invisible to top management. This part of the process is likely to work better if the interviews are structured.

3. Competencies which are obvious from an examination of the activities, products and services of the organisation. Often the intangible elements are taken for granted within the organisation, although the competencies required to achieve them may be among the most important for the organisation.

4. What can be learned from customers and suppliers, both from market research reports, and from discussions and focus group interviews.

At this stage the organisation will have a long "laundry list", which will probably contain individual skills that need to be grouped into competencies, and will certainly include many competencies which are neither strategic nor core. Before moving on, it is sensible to try to validate this list, possibly through focus group discussions with key managers. Even though as a validation method this has drawbacks, it does mean that there is involvement of others, both in assessing the facts and making judgements on them.

Relative Strengths of the Competencies

The internal perception of the extent to which a competence is possessed may not be the reality. We can make what is meant here somewhat clearer by using an individual competence with which everyone will be familiar: writing. Everyone who uses this book has a technical ability to read and write. However, our individual competencies at writing will vary with the purpose, and if there were an objective way of scoring how good we all were there would certainly be differences.

- To write an occasional academic article requires knowledge of vocabulary and grammar (including the correct use of the apostrophe!), technical knowledge of the subject and an ability to organise thoughts. There is usually no real time pressure on the author, and many go through several drafts before they are satisfied, and have to make further changes after peer review. Yet if we think about articles of this type we know that some are more interesting to read than others, and not all have the same high quality of thought. For many occasional authors like this, the task does not come easily.
- To write a book on, say, a management subject requires mastery of more aspects of the subject than is needed for the single article, and the ability to hold

to a clear objective, and to coordinate many different topics. An author of such a book will find it very hard going if writing is a struggle, and if he or she is working under a publisher's contract there is a deadline to be met. And from your own reading you know that you could rate the overall competency of the author by using a simple classification like clarity, readability, relevance and practicality. You would not consider all authors with the competence to produce a book to have equal strengths in that competence.

- A journalist has to add other skills, among which is the ability to write quickly, to a predefined length and to a tight deadline.
- A novelist requires many of the skills of the management book author, plus creativity and insight into what makes people tick. And for most novels not even the authors would claim to have the same level of competence as a literary giant (and not all need it for the market for which they are writing). Although it is possible for any one person to have all four competencies, it is unusual. We have never met such a paragon. Using this analogy, we can see why we need to spend time trying to plumb the depths of the corporate competencies we have identified. Are we strong, average or mediocre, and how appropriate are the strengths of the competencies for the objectives we have to fulfil?

Sometimes a closer correlation between truth and beliefs can be achieved through further internal assessment, performed by a panel of managers from within the organisation who have knowledge of customers and competitors. Scoring the organisation against each main competitor can sometimes help assess the strength relative to competitors. External expert knowledge may be used to perform a similar function. The most objective method is benchmarking, against direct competitors, against other firms which are high performers in one or more areas of competence, and internally across the organisation to assess the extent to which the competence is truly shared.

By definition, any competence which is common to all in an industry, and which every competitor is good at, cannot be a core competence (although it may still be important).

Competencies that Deliver Value to the Customers

A competence should deliver value to at least a significant segment of the market. The next stage is therefore to examine what each of the competencies we have identified does for the customer. Johnson and Scholes suggest that this part of the analysis should begin by asking customers what is important to them, which gives primary reasons for success. Management should next consider the secondary reasons for success: what lies behind the things that the customers value. So if one of the customers' reasons was "good service", the secondary definitions might include "flexibility". The hardest task is to move below this to a third set of reasons - in this example, what the organisation does to provide flexibility. Hinterhuber et al recommend identifying "the articulated, and if possible non-articulated customer wishes concerning product characteristics and product-related services".

With this information, and the CSFs discussed earlier they suggest that it is possible to move on a two-phase evaluation chain to identify what is important, and to show visually the relative strength of each element analysed. The first matrix they propose enables each CSF to be compared with the performance characteristics the customers are seeking. Symbols are used to indicate the organisation's strength (or otherwise) in each of the cells in the matrix. The second matrix compares the same performance characteristics with the competencies needed to support them, using a similar system of symbols. Both matrices include weighting and scoring, one use of which is to aid the positioning of each competence in a portfolio of core competencies.

Both of these methods have strong links with the value chain and if this has been analysed effectively its results can be coordinated with the competency analysis. It would be possible to establish the historic core competencies that support the present position, from the analysis so far, and the appraisal itself should end at this point. In practice some thought should also be given to the next steps, which move into strategy. For the sake of completeness, these are mentioned below.

If an aim is to use core competencies to change the industries in which an organisation operates, it follows that some attempt should be made to think beyond the current range of products and services, and to explore what may be core in a more futureoriented manner. Klein and Hiscocks offer one method for doing this, although this is built on an analysis of skills rather than competencies. They call it the opportunity matrix, a method which requires the use of an appropriate computer database. Skills are listed and scored, and entered as one axis in the database. Possible diversification and potential future products are then listed, and scored for the level of skill needed. A five-point scale is used, varying from "skill not required" to "world class capability essential". The database may be programmed to identify opportunities which match skills, and which could represent opportunities for the organisation.

However, there is a strong argument for a more visionary approach, perhaps looking at a number of scenarios of how the organisation might change its market, and working back to the skills needed to achieve this. Skills still need to be clustered into competencies.

However, the approach could also be used to analyse current products and services, and the resultant matrix used as a basis on which they may be grouped into competencies. The assessment of all this evidence can help to determine which competencies are indeed core.

Portfolio of Competencies

Hinterhuber et al use the scores from their correlation chain to position the organisation's competencies. The matrix is reproduced and positions could be plotted judgmentally, provided there is some evidence to support the contentions.

The three most interesting positions are quadrants ii, iii and iv. Quadrant ii may indicate areas of weakness which the organisation should either correct, or render unimportant by changing its activities. Quadrant iv contains the core competencies, which require management if the organisation is to be able to sustain and develop its competence. Quadrant iii may provide opportunities to use some of these competencies to develop products which the customer would value. The danger of this quadrant is that these competencies may include those needed for the future rather than the present, and that a more dynamic assessment might decide that some of them are really core.

Although the portfolio examination of competencies has a lot of appeal, and indeed is following suggestions made by Hamel and Prahalad, there is one weakness. The fact that a competence has high customer value and is an area of high corporate ability misses out one key dimension: uniqueness. This could be solved when competencies are listed on the chart, by showing with a symbol against each the degree to which the organisation shares the competence with competitors. The quadrant would be renamed critical and core competencies.

7

Industry Analysis

It included industry analysis as one of the key elements of the corporate appraisal. This can be thought of as the first stage in competitor analysis, the understanding of the arena in which the organisation operates. Basically, industry analysis is a study of the forces within the industry which affect profitability. The line of thinking we have followed came from Porter although it has been modified as a result of our experiences in applying the concept. Here we concentrate on industry analysis as a tool of the corporate appraisal. Hussey and Jenster shows how to progress from this to in-depth competitor analysis. Strategic thinking is a creative, innovative process. Sensible strategies should be based on a thorough understanding of the industries in which the firm operates.

Creativity unsupported by analysis is likely to lead to poor strategies; analysis unsupported by creative thinking is likely to lead to a copycat strategy. We can visualise the industry as being made up of eight centres of competitive forces affecting profitability, which operate within the context of the business environment. This is three more than in the famous Porter five-forces model, although we should add that only one of these is fundamentally new: the others clarify certain aspects of the Porter concepts. The analytical process is described and is supported by a questionnaire which can be used to facilitate the work. The creative thinking is what you as managers must bring as you work through the various stages of analysis in your own organisation.

DEVELOP A BLOCK DIAGRAM

A useful first stage in industry analysis is the drawing of a block diagram which gives a framework for thinking about the industry, and helps to move from the broad concepts to the specific situation in a real industry. For example, *suppliers* is a very general heading, and it is more useful to think in terms of more specific groupings of suppliers. It may also be that, in the industry being analysed, it is sensible to consider different stages in the supply chain, and to represent these in the diagram. Similarly, few industries have only one type of buyer, and a more typical flow might be through a chain of distribution. A fast moving grocery products company is likely to reach its final consumer by selling to different types of wholesalers and retailers.

A company making industrial components might sell to an original equipment manufacturer, which sells on its product to industrial users. It may sell direct to those final customers, or reach them through dealers and wholesalers in order to offer spares. There may also be a reconditioning sector, which has a requirement for the components. Mirroring this reality is an important step to understanding (the term *intermediaries* might be used to indicate the organisations that stand between the industry and the ultimate customer).The industry itself may not be homogeneous. The lift industry, for example, has at least two activities, manufacture and installation of lifts, and servicing and repair. Some firms do both, but many others only operate in the service and repair side. Representing these essential differences on the block diagram is important, because the forces of competition may not be the same for all.

There are also what can be termed contractual specifiers and influencers, and if these exist in the industry under analysis they should be reflected in the block diagram. An example is the general practitioner or consultant who is not a distributor of ethical Pharmaceuticals, but who determines what the patient obtains from the pharmacist. Specifications for sewage treatment plant may be laid down by a consulting engineer, whose role may shut out some competitors, or provide opportunities for others. The *contractual influencers* are one of the additions made to the original Porter concept.

Why is this important? First, this thinking about the outline structure of the industry will make it easier to apply the principles of industry analysis to the particular situation. Second, it will give a basis for an approach called industry charting, which is an analytical and communication tool. Third, industry charting can be used in a dynamic way, to help think through how the industry might change. But remember, the block diagram and subsequent analysis should give a picture of the whole industry, and not merely reflect what a particular company in the industry actually does. The fact that your company does not deal directly with consumers, for example, is no reason to exclude this option if others in the industry do operate in this way.

UNDERSTANDING THE INDUSTRY FORCES

Industry analysis is about understanding the forces which shape the profitability of all the organisations in the industry. However at the outset we should stress that advantages may be neutralised by disadvantages elsewhere, and that we need to take a balanced view using the whole model to reach sound conclusions.

Buyer and Intermediary Power

There are two reasons for studying the structure of the industry through the chain to the ultimate consumer. The first is to ensure that the whole of the present structure is known, as this may reveal new strategic options, including the all-important one of changing the "rules of the game" by finding another way to get the product to the ultimate consumer. A second reason is to determine the relative influence over profits exercised by the various stages in the chain, and the way power is likely to shift in the future. It is not necessarily the industry itself which determines its own margins and profitability;

sometimes the greater power is in the hands of the buyers. Factors which influence the relative location of this power and influence include:

- *Relative Size:* If the industry includes firms that are considerably larger than their customers, sheer weight of resources may put them in the dominant position. The converse may apply when the buying organisations are the larger. This is not a universal truth, as other factors may outweigh size in importance. For example, in the UK grocery products are largely controlled by supermarket chains, which not only have most of the retail outlets, but also have developed ownlabel products that they can adjust in volume and price if the brand manufacturers do not toe the line. In this way they may determine the profitability of manufacturers, whose organisations may be considerably larger than those of the supermarkets.

- *Dependencies:* Bargaining strength may lie with the least dependent of the two parties. This is a composite of the number of industry firms contrasted with the number of buying firms (what flexibility does each have?), and the importance of the product to the profits of each party.

- *Profitability of the Buying Industry:* The industry firms are likely to be in a healthier position when they are selling to a profitable industry. Where buyers are unprofitable or have low profits, there is likely to be stronger resistance against price increases. This resistance will increase when the buyer is facing an elastic demand curve, and cannot easily pass on its extra costs.

- *Experience of Buyers:* Buyers purchasing from a mature industry are likely to have more experience than those dealing with a new industry. Thus, the more mature the industry, the weaker its bargaining position may become (subject, of course, to other factors). Where the buying industry is also mature, there may be a tendency for the degree of product differentiation to fall, making it more difficult for the industry to sustain high margins.

- *Threat of Integration:* The industry firm that patently has the capability and strength to integrate into its buying industry possesses a key bargaining point. If the buying industry thwarts its profit aims, it has the potential to remove the blockage. The opposite applies when the buying industry can offer a credible threat of backwards integration. In either case the credibility of the threat is enhanced when both parties are aware that such a move would be economically viable. Do not forget that the actions of *your* customers may be affected by the power of *their* customers.

The key factor in successfully analysing the intermediaries and customers in a particular industry is segmenting them into groups and distinguishing them either by the reason they buy or how they buy. Criteria for segmenting customer groups include the following:

- Industry or market segment
- Product application
- Geographic location
- Size of purchase
- Frequency of purchase.

A key task is to define the main groups for each intermediary and to classify the customer groups by buying characteristics, and to analyse each of these groups in terms of the relative power they exercise against companies in your industry and the implications of that power for you and your competitors, and for the success of their own businesses.

CONTRACTUAL INFLUENCERS

This term covers those who have a contractual role in the buying process, although this may not always be obvious to the industry. We previously gave the example of the general practitioner or medical consultant who prescribes an ethical pharmaceutical, which the patient then obtains from a pharmacist (this industry is complicated in the UK by the role the National Health Service plays in paying for prescriptions, and exercising some influence on what doctors may prescribe). If the doctor knows nothing about the drug, it will not be prescribed and therefore a sale is lost, despite the fact that the doctor is not a stockist of the drug. Similar examples occur in the construction industry, where an architect may specify, for instance, a lift, and that specification may exclude some lift companies from bidding. Another example is plant and machinery, where the buyer may rely on specifications drawn up by a consulting engineer.

The term does not include informal and non-contractual influencers, such as the neighbour who recommends a particular brand of lawn mower, the magazine article which draws attention to a slimming pill, or the teenager's peer group who strongly influence his or her choice of clothes. These types of influence are important for marketing purposes, but are not part of the structure of the industry. Contractual influencers, on the other hand, are part of the industry. It would be impossible to make sense of the ethical pharmaceutical industry without including the role of the medical profession. Do contractual influencers exist in the industry you are studying and, if so, who are they?

Suppliers

It is traditional for an industry to believe that it holds the edge over both its buyers and its suppliers, a statement that patently cannot always be true since the industry itself is a buyer to its supplier. Relations with the supplying industry are not always seen as a matter of strategic importance. In reality the analysis of suppliers is the converse of the analysis of buyers. The factors to consider are therefore the same: industry or market segment, product application, geographic location, size of purchase and frequency of purchase. If you doubt this, consider the change in the personal computer industry. Initially it was the manufacturers of the hardware which were in the position of power in the overall industry. Over the past 15 years or so this power has moved into the hands of two of the supplying companies, Intel, which provides most of the world's chips, and Microsoft, whose domination of the operating system and software puts them in a dominant position to dictate what happens to the hardware manufacturers. Would you rather own shares in IBM, Apple or Microsoft?

Suppliers exercise power in an industry in a number of ways: by lowering the quality of goods for a given purchase price, by tightening payment and service terms, and so on. To the extent that suppliers in general, or particular supplier groups, exercise significant power, industry costs increase, profitability diminishes, and the industry competitors may lose control over the future direction of new product developments. As is the situation between the industry and the buyers, there are countervailing sources of power that the industry can exert on suppliers. The actual balance of power between the industry and particular suppliers is a result of considering the net result of all the factors. An early step in industry analysis is to cluster suppliers to your company and your competitors into meaningful groups, according to the most significant characteristics of supplier behaviour (e.g. size, type of product, distribution channels). You should then analyse those groups to identify the power they exert on the industry and what that means for a company participating in the industry.

Entry Barriers

The entry barriers will affect the profitability of an industry and the way in which competitors behave. If it is easy for new firms to come into the market competition may be fiercer, as organisations have to battle against known and unknown competitors. Entry barriers can only be interpreted in relation to the attractiveness of the industry. Relatively low barriers will deter firms from entering low-profit/low-growth industries. The barriers may have to be very high to keep a new entrant out of a highly attractive industry.

Examples of entry barriers which *raise the costs* of a new entrant are:

- Economies of scale or the experience curve factor may raise the capital costs of entry to a very high level (e.g. electronic calculators).
- Highly differentiated products may require extensive advertising support before a newcomer can break in (e.g. household detergents). This may raise costs to prohibitive levels.
- The nature of distribution may require entry at a high level of output (e.g. supermarkets will not stock brands which are slow moving and have low market shares). Other entry barriers may create a *legal restriction* to entry, or in some way *deny access* to a critical part of the market.
- Patents.
- Legal controls (e.g. auditors, television broadcasting companies).
- Control of distribution outlets (e.g. the British film industry until recently).

Where entry barriers are very low the industry may become fragmented and competition fierce, with new competitors regularly coming into the market. Industry profitability is to a large extent dependent on market imperfections, and one element of corporate strategy might be to find ways of raising the entry barriers. It should be noted that there are four types of possible new entrants, and the barriers will not have the same effect against all of them.

1. Competitors that are already in the industry, but not in the country being studied.
2. Those in related areas, such as a bank which has acted as an insurance broker, and now wishes to move into the insurance industry.

3. Firms which are new, but which have been set up by people who have operated in the industry as employees.
4. Firms which are totally new to the industry.

Exit Barriers

Exit barriers are the factors which tie a firm to the industry and make it difficult or impossible for it to leave. These conditions are relevant when firms would like to leave because of low earnings and poor prospects, and because of the nature of the industry there are few organisations willing to acquire the business at an acceptable price. If the industry is successful, there are usually potential acquirers who make exit possible. Where the barriers occur, firms will hang on, trading as best they can, and depressing profits in the industry. Exit barriers may be the need to write off high-value specialised assets for which there is no buyer. Examples are petrochemicals, steel works, oil refineries and mines. Any firm may be tied to its industry through particular contracts, or legal requirements which make it costly to meet severance payments to employees. There may also be government pressure on the firm to stay in the business. In businesses of low capital intensity, and low entry barriers, small firms may remain in the business because the owners may prefer to take lower earnings instead of facing unemployment if they close down. In certain countries, exchange control regulations may make it impossible for a company to repatriate any capital sum realized on the sale or closure of a business.

Industry Firms

It is normal for analysts to examine such factors as market shares and to pay some attention to the different positioning of each firm in the marketplace. Industry analysis tries to identify all the factors which affect the intensity of competitive behaviour. The competitiveness of the industry is not revealed by brand shares alone, although these are important. Competitive behaviour is also influenced by many other factors, including:

- *Growth Rates of the Industry:* Competitive behaviour tends to be less aggressive if industry growth rates are relatively high, because each firm can increase its sales without necessarily increasing its market share. This statement is considerably modified by the position on the life cycle curve. In a new industry high growth rates may bring in new competitors, which will tend to lead to aggressive behaviour. In almost all industries, a fall in the growth rate will tend to intensify competition. Often it is the change that causes new patterns, rather than the growth rate itself. Other things being equal, one would expect to find more aggressive behaviour in an industry whose annual growth rate has fallen suddenly from 10 per cent to 3 per cent than in an industry whose growth has stabilised at 3 per cent.
- *General Level of Profits:* Lack of profits among the industry (or significant firms in the industry) will tend to make competitive behaviour less predictable. Where profits are high for all, there may be a measure of tolerance of competitors. A change to lower profits may trigger a more aggressive attitude.
- *Level of Fixed Costs:* Where investment is large and highly specialised, and fixed costs are a relatively high proportion of total costs, competitors tend to "hang on", selling at less than full costs, when the market slumps or there is over-capacity for some other reason. Shipping, oil refinery and petrochemicals all provide examples where competitive behaviour may lead to low profits or losses over a very long period of time, because the alternative is plant closure when assets cannot be realised.
- *Economies of Scale/experience Curve:* Competitive behaviour is likely to be more aggressive when there are clear advantages to being big. This may happen

when cost levels are dependent on high volumes, or when the experience curve effect means that progressively higher volumes will lead to progressively lower costs. Lower costs mean prices can be reduced, which in turn means that even higher volumes can be gained. In a growth market, where demand is elastic and the product subject to mass production (e.g. motor cycles, calculating machines, electronic components) the experience curve effect can bring dominance to the firm that gets far enough ahead. Competitive behaviour is likely to be very aggressive during this period.

- *Degree of Differentiation:* Market imperfections give a degree of protection to individual firms and reduce the impact of competition. Thus it is reasonable to expect the fiercest competition when all firms are offering products of commodity status, and the most peaceful behaviour when each firm offers such a highly differentiated product that it is almost unique.

- *Number of Firms and Market Shares:* A fragmented industry, with no one firm having a significant market share, tends to be more competitive than one which has a clear market leader that is in a dominant position. To some degree, these tendencies may be modified by the position on the product life cycle. It is unwise to assume that mature markets will all have gone through the shakeout period. Some are highly fragmented because the economic circumstances do not favour large firms (many service industries).

- *New Entrant:* In long-established industries, firms often reach an unspoken form of accommodation with each other, softening the aggressiveness of competition. This will often change with the entry of a new firm which either does not know or chooses to ignore these implicit "rules" (for example, the emergence in the UK of the insurance company

Direct Line, which over a decade or so has caused many competitors to change their strategies). A similar effect may occur if one of the companies appoints a new chief executive from outside the industry.

- *Nature of Product:* A perishable product (e.g. airline tickets, fresh produce) is likely to be more susceptible to random price cutting than one which can be stored easily and cheaply.

PLOTTING STRATEGIC GROUPS

The analysis of the industry requires much detailed knowledge about the competitors. Understanding may be improved if we can cluster competitors into groups that have similar strategic characteristics. This may be essential in an industry where there are hundreds of competitors and it is impractical to study every one of them in detail. It may be desirable when the numbers are manageable, but it is helpful to get a fix on who is competing and where. Porter developed the idea of "strategic groups", which could be plotted on a diagram to show the variations in competitive activity. One value of this is that it may show up which are the real competitors to a particular company, and which are in the same industry, but are not really a threat.

Porter suggested a matrix with specialisation (narrow to full line) on one axis, and vertical integration (high to assembler) on the other. However, this is illustrative, and what he advocates is a matrix which shows the way in which the firms are similar to other firms in the competitive strategy they are following. The two sides of the matrix might in another industry be quality brand image and mix of channels. The groups are illustrated by circles which diagrammatically represent the collective market share of the firms in the group, and the names of the firms are written in each circle.

Questionnaire

The forgoing points have been put into a questionnaire form to help you undertake industry analysis in your own organisation. It is possible to make a useful analysis with the aid of this. However, we have found it useful to supplement this with one further analytical approach, the development of industry charts, which provide a helpful way of recording the detailed information that should lie behind the answers to the questions.

CHARTING THE INDUSTRY

The charting approach described here has been used in many companies and industries. It develops from the block diagram of the industry, which is used as an outline onto which all the relevant facts about the industry are noted. The points we have gone through so far should be supported by hard facts about the industry, and the charts record that data in a way that enables us to see it all together and helps us to understand the full situation. The industry charting approach in a real situation is usually done on A3 paper, with one page for the map and another for drawing together the implications of the analysis. It is sometimes necessary to use part of the second sheet as a note pad for information which does not easily fit on the main map, but at the end of the exercise the aim should be to have everything that matters about the industry structure on a couple of sheets of paper. This aim may change when an organisation spans more than one industry, or in a global industry when it is necessary to look at the industry on a world as well as a country-by-country basis.

Of course it is possible to interpret an industry without drawing an industry chart, but the two main advantages of this method are that the exercise helps ensure that the right questions are asked, and the resultant chart communicates a great deal of information in a compressed way to other persons. Strategies to respond to what is discovered rarely emanate from only the analyst, and information has to be shared with, and the issues fully understood by, other key managers. The charting approach helps do this, and also provides a framework for keeping information up to date. Another benefit found from this approach is that it reveals where information is lacking, and often shows up other problems.

It is not uncommon for different parts of an organisation to be using different figures for the market or market shares, and this approach makes these differences very clear. Our experience is that the method often shows that a piece of information that the organisation has relied on in the past is inaccurate, occasionally dangerously so. Market size, for example, may be calculated from a variety of sources, not all of which are as complete or as accurate as they might be. It is rarely easy to take market information from several overlapping sources, without exposing some areas of doubt. Any mechanism that shows that if "fact" A is correct, "fact" B has to be untrue is potentially very helpful, and may reveal that assumptions that have been used in the past are unreliable.

The charting approach becomes an early stage in competitor analysis, and if each competitor is profiled, can become the basis for developing scenarios of how an industry could change, and who might be likely to initiate changes.

THE INDUSTRY AND THE BUSINESS ENVIRONMENT

The past, present and future of any industry is affected by the forces of the business environment. Technological development has, for example, been a driving force in the merging of what used to be the separate industries of typewriters and computers, and, more recently, in extending the "new" industry to telecommunications and video.

It provides a classification for thinking about the trends in the environment. The connections between all the points remind us that a change in one factor may affect all or any of the other factors. Positioning the industry in the centre stresses the importance of these external changes, and that they should not be neglected. We should also recognise that an industry may be a driver of changes to the environment: technology, in particular, is strongly influenced by how businesses try to exploit it. Although there is much that will affect a whole industry, a word of warning should be given. It is wrong to believe that every organisation in an industry is affected to the same extent by a change in the environment. So although a general view is helpful, we should accept that it has limitations.

It uses the same broad classifications as the figure, but provides space for them to be expanded into subfactors. Equally important is the space provided to record the implications of these factors.

FINDING THE REAL STRENGTHS AND WEAKNESSES

The Systematic Approach we Have Outlined will Result in the Uncovering of Four Types of Facts About the Organisation: There are those that indicate strengths and weaknesses which have a strategic importance. Such weaknesses include lagging behind in a key technology, relying for most of the profits on products in declining markets with no successful new products to take their place, or having a portfolio of SBUs all of which require more cash to develop their potential than the organisation can generate. Such strengths might be a true leadership position in a key technology, and preferred supplier status with customers for 60 per cent of sales.

- It is probable that there will be matters identified which have immediate operational significance, such as a cost saving opportunity or a change in the promotional material to emphasise a particular aspect of the product or service which gives value to customers.

- There will also be some supporting information which is useful in identifying the absence of a weakness, and which may need to be used when strategies are considered, but is not otherwise helpful. Of course in some situations the absence of a weakness can be a strength, but in many other situations it is no more than giving the ability to play the competitive game.

- The fourth category is all the information which has yielded no findings of any significance. This includes the blind alleys that have been explored, and also various facts uncovered which have no obvious importance.

A book has to be written in sequential chapters, which implies a chain relationship between the various elements of the appraisal, with item neatly following item. Of course reality is not like this at all, and the key elements have a sort of spider's web relationship, with a tangle of crossed lines and a pattern of mutual dependency. We have heard it called a can of worms, but although this may describe with some accuracy the feeling induced through having to pull together numerous facts from the various parts of the appraisal, it is erroneous because each worm in a can is independent of every other worm. We are trying to imply that in any organisation what is found from one element of the appraisal is unlikely to be totally independent of what is found in other elements. Something needs to be done to draw the whole appraisal together, and to concentrate on the things that matter. How this task is tackled will depend on the purpose of the appraisal.

If it was undertaken as part of a due diligence report in an acquisition situation, there are four groups of things that should be clear at the end:

- Evidence that aids a decision about whether to proceed with the acquisition.
- Identifying serious weaknesses and the implications of these should the organisation make the acquisition.
- Highlighting where strategic decisions would be needed in order to obtain synergy between the organisations.
- Providing information which enables decisions to be made on how the two organisations should be merged operationally.

This would be a somewhat different conclusion to the appraisal than if it had been undertaken as part of a strategic review. It is the strategic review use that will be examined in more detail.

INVOLVING MANAGERS

We were critical of the way SWOT is used in many organisations. This does not mean that we undervalue the knowledge and insight managers have into their businesses.

The issue is how to tap into this in a sensible way. The appraisal itself may have been undertaken by a single person, but is more likely to be a team effort. Or there may have been several teams to look at different aspects, whose work has been planned and coordinated from one central point. It is possible that management consultants have undertaken all or part of the appraisal, or that outsiders have been involved in some way with the internal teams. To some degree various managers will have played a part in getting the information together. But this will not necessarily mean that managers have had any opportunity to see the conclusions or to discuss them in a collective way.

Although it may occasionally be inappropriate, in most situations it is important to widen the involvement of managers across the organisation in drawing out the strengths and weaknesses, and the implications of these. One way to do this is to organise focus groups at various levels, with the membership of each being people with appropriate knowledge and experience. The agenda would be modified to the scope of contribution that those attending are able to make. Each group meeting should be based on those facts from the appraisal which are relevant to the group attending. Instead of asking people to think of strengths and weaknesses, we suggest that the meeting approach the subject more obliquely, and for each group of related findings follow a sequence something like this:

1. Here are some facts which seem to us to be important.
2. What implications do these have for the organisation?
3. How important is each grouping of findings to the organisation?
4. What are the causal factors for each state of affairs?
5. What actions do we need to take to correct things we do not like, or to build on things that we do like?

The equilibrium analysis approach discussed is particularly helpful when discussing item 4. What this approach should do is to make people aware of things they may not have considered. For example, people may be feeling quite satisfied with the performance of the organisation based on year on year comparisons, but would not have this feeling if they were shown that the rest of the industry was doing much better. In addition, there is the chance to gain extra background and insight. One thing that frequently happens in the way SWOT is often used is that the same fact is identified as both a strength and a weakness, which is hardly logical. Many of us were brought up on traditional legends and adventure stories, and in this context it is easy to see how the helplessness of the maiden rescued from the dragon by the gallant knight could be the factor that increases her attractiveness to him and leads to the "happy ever after" ending.

But was the helplessness ever a weakness? With this stereotype character, it is this which is the strength, as our damsel's aim in life is to gain a gallant husband. Of course, it would have been unfortunate if she had been roasted and eaten by the dragon, but this would be a mischance rather than a fundamental weakness! We might reach a different conclusion if a real-life modern woman were unable to deal with her personal dragons, but again our answer would depend on her aims and ambitions. The mix of underlying hard facts and management insight, related to an understanding of what the organisation is trying to achieve, should prevent the simultaneous classification of something as both a strength and a weakness. "Our 90 per cent market share is a strength, but it is also a weakness because we cannot defend it against new entrants who might be attracted to the market." Does this sort of statement mean that you should remove the weakness by reducing market share?

The real issue we want to get at is that "Our present rate of profitability is potentially vulnerable, because it depends on an unsustainable 90 per cent market share". Looking at it in this way takes us into a number of different actions we might consider, as it takes us to the heart of the issue. We can even make estimates of how profits would be affected by various reductions in market share to help clarify our thinking. The insight of managers who are helped to see the facts in an appropriate way can lead to a very different understanding of what is the real issue. The minimum result that might come out, which can still be useful, is that managers do not see as critical something which the team believes is very important. This is useful information because an issue which is ignored does not go away.

There are some cautions over the involvement process. Managers have vested interests in the future of their own activities, or in resisting what might be seen as a criticism of past decisions. It is not just that careers may depend on how something is seen, but that subconsciously we want to defend something in which we have invested our hearts and minds. There may be rationalization of the status quo, the introduction of unsupported "facts", or attempts to play down a particular fact. The motivation is not necessarily obstructive, and may come from a heartfelt belief. So when you involve managers in this way, you need some skill to separate fact from erroneous belief and wishful thinking.

CREATING A PICTURE FROM THE PIECES

By this stage there is a dossier of the things that have been discovered, plus the results from the various focus group meetings. The appraisal team should put all of this together in a report, so that the facts and the interpretations are readily available. However, if this is all that is done, top management is passed the whole task of making sense of what has been found. This would not be particularly helpful, so there is a need to pull out from all this the information that the team believes is relevant, and the supporting key facts. This is the second most important result of the appraisal: the most important result will be the strategic decisions which are taken in the light of the findings. We will first give some indications of how the findings might be written up, if we were undertaking a corporate appraisal of a business. Later we will look at some of the special requirements if we were sitting at the top of a diversified multi-SBU company. With some adaptation on your part, we hope that this will enable you to think about the position in your own organisation.

CORPORATE APPRAISAL OF A BUSINESS

You may have a very thick file as a result of your appraisal, now made thicker by the outcome of the various meetings. While this should be available to top management, it should be used to *support* the conclusions of the appraisal, and not to *be* those conclusions. The suggestion here falls into two parts: an analysis of what seem to be the important facts, and some key figures which enable a clear picture of the organisation to be seen. How this report is put together will depend on the organisation. It can be prepared and presented as a report to top management, and this is what is most likely to happen if management consultants are used. However, it may be more effective if the chief executive is involved in going through the information with the team, so that his or her insight is gained, and that ownership of the report is established where it should be, right at the top.

The threads of the appraisal may be drawn together in the form of a series of factual statements about the organisation, together with the strategic implications and some of the possible strategic options that might be investigated. There are of course numerous ways in which this document can be written, and it is not something that we should be dogmatic about. However, it is important that the statements *are* written, since in most companies there are likely to be areas of dispute (in fact, it is almost possible to say dogmatically that if everyone agrees with the report, the job has not been done properly), and emotions will be involved.

It is much easier to make an objective decision if all the evidence is fully documented. The reports may not always be pleasant. Few people enjoy trying to convince their chief executive that an area of the company which is dear to his or her heart is not right for the organisation, or of similar unpopular measures. But this sort of study must be approached with integrity, for without a genuine attempt at honest appraisal the whole exercise may become a meaningless gesture. The final report should show clearly the strong and weak points of the organisation. It should assess the vulnerability of the internal factors to external changes, and should establish what we like to call the organisation's "risk balance" (which, put simply, is the number of baskets it has to keep its eggs in!).

Our example is somewhat simpler than a real situation (for most organisations this is a gross understatement). Too complex an example would add more to length than elucidation. Our aim is to illustrate that only the key findings need appear in the summary, and that each key finding should be based on evidence which must be recorded and available if required to justify the statements (cross-references could be included to the pages in the dossier). Simple lists, however accurate and insightful, only do part of the job, and we recommend adding a column to show the strategic implications. It would be possible to go one step further and suggest various strategic options that might be considered.

SCHEDULES OF KEY INFORMATION

Pieces of information uncovered in the appraisal may be interesting in themselves, but often have more value if they can be related to each other. Summarising a lot of information about each product in a table, such as the classification of the product, its annual sales and profit contribution, market shares, expected growth rates of the market, the various types of resources needed to obtain this (assets, percentage of factory capacity, working capital, percentage of sales force time devoted to this product, and whatever else is relevant) can give a clearer view of the issues than a series of functional analyses. The headings suggested are indicative, and it is important not to let each table get so large that the wood is concealed among the trees.

CORPORATE APPRAISAL OF A MULTI-BUSINESS ORGANISATION

At the business level the requirements would be much as above. The diversified organisation, divided into a number of SBUs, has an additional requirement. At corporate level the interest is certainly on total corporate performance and the role of each SBU in contributing to this. However, at this level it is unlikely to need to know all the detail that appears. There is a need to understand the businesses, but corporate-level strategy requires a somewhat different way of seeing the information.

TABULAR PRESENTATIONS

Arraying information in a tabular format is always helpful in comparing the different parts of a multi-business organisation. At the centre there is a specific concern about the overall finances of the whole organisation, and the ability to finance the growth of SBUs. In fact it was the inability of conglomerates to be able to support all the needs of healthy growth businesses which was one reason why, beginning some 20 years ago, there was a move to float off many businesses, and reduce to a core of businesses that could be supported. A further pressure when organisations did not realize the issue themselves was the spate of takeover bids where the aim was to release value by breaking up the organisation. Clearly it is a corporate weakness for a conglomerate not to be able to provide the finance that its businesses need.

PORTFOLIO ANALYSIS

A second approach which is useful, although less fashionable than it once was, is portfolio analysis. This approach is very helpful in enabling a view to be gained of all SBUs in the organisation, or sometimes all products. Our view is to avoid the prescriptive labels attached to some portfolio charts which imply a strategy, and instead to use the chart to help think of the relative value of each area plotted to the organisation, and its likely future cash using or cash generating potential. We have touched on portfolio analysis both the business portfolio and others for comparing competencies and technologies. It is also possible to add an exploration of relative risks to a portfolio chart.

Hussey provides a description of the basic approach and the enhanced method showing risks, and provides full scoring rules. Segev are also recommended, and compare various methods. The 1995 books are related. They give detailed scoring rules for several different portfolio approaches, and have the added value of software with the second book to facilitate use on the computer. For SBU comparisons we would normally use a method which has market prospects on one axis and competitive position on the other, but not the simplistic Boston Consulting pioneer matrix. For comparison of products it might be better to use one of the methods which uses life cycle stages and competitive position as the two axes.

The decision should be based on what gives most insight into the company, and what facilitates communication of the findings to others. Once SBUs are plotted the matrix can be used to show a different perspective of the organisation. By adding the totals of the key financial figures of all the businesses entered in a particular cell of the matrix, it is possible to show the sources of earnings by matrix position, together with the amount of assets attributable to those businesses, and the positive or negative cash flows of each. It is also possible to make the analysis more dynamic, by indicating likely movements in the matrix position of each SBU.

SOURCES OF SHAREHOLDER VALUE

The question of whether and how value is added through being part of a corporate family was addressed by Porter and it is his thinking which is largely followed here. Some additional insight was provided by Buzzell and Gale who drew their conclusions from the PIMS database. The appraisals at business level can be used to help assess whether the corporate whole is adding or reducing shareholder value by its ownership of various SBUs. This requires grafting additional knowledge of the organisation on to various elements of the basic analysis. If value is not created by membership of the whole, the position of any or all of the businesses may be weakened, and the total business may become a takeover target. The stock market frequently values diversified organisations at less than the sum of their parts. Obviously there is a strength if shareholder value is added, a possibly fatal weakness if it is not, and an opportunity if the situation could be improved.

There are at least five aspects of the creation of shareholder value that should be considered:

1. *How the Centre Manages:* Goold, Campbell and Alexander argue that value can be created or destroyed depending on how the parent manages. There are no black and white answers, as the skill lies in fitting the parenting style to the particular circumstances of the businesses. There is value in examining the appropriateness of the corporate planning, decision making, and control processes and systems in relation to the nature of each of the businesses.

2. *Shared Resources/activities:* Map how the different businesses add value by sharing resources and activities. For example, common physical distribution facilities may give a cost and service advantage to all the businesses in the portfolio. If there are no benefits from this aspect, is this because sharing is not possible, or because it would have a negative impact on results?

3. *Spill-over Benefits Like R&D:* Are businesses benefiting from inventions and technologies developed in other parts of the group. Is there a mechanism to allow such sharing to happen? Does this mechanism work well?

4. *Shared Knowledge and Skills:* What synergy is gained from shared knowledge: for example of markets, common customers and suppliers? Is there any transfer of skills between businesses?

5. *Shared Image:* What is gained or lost from common brands and the overall image?

Corporate appraisal is complex, but we hope that we have also shown that it is important and essential. It is indeed the foundation of strategy, and the only sure way of identifying and understanding the capability of the organisation. The decisions that can emerge from it may be far reaching. It should lead to different perceptions, and it is not enough to make it a one-time exercise. In fact the experience of the first occasion may lead to setting up systems for collecting information that was not available at the start, but which will lead to different insights in the future. This was the case with two of the organisations described earlier and of course with many others in our experience.

There are limitations. Organisations are dynamic, moving and evolving. An analysis of the type discussed here cannot be stretched over too long a period before conclusions are reached, because if this happens the first pieces of the puzzle may no longer be connected to the last pieces. Therefore, in practice there is need to compromise, and to concentrate on what seems to be the most important. But all this is an argument for ensuring that the appraisal is undertaken regularly. The findings from the analysis become the foundations for strategic thinking. They may not themselves be enough to make sound strategic decisions and we would argue that there is much more to strategy than this. But we would draw an analogy with a building. A building is something different from its foundations, and it is this difference which brings admiration or dissatisfaction. But if it has no foundations it may be physically impossible to build it, and if by chance it is built on faulty foundations it has a high chance of falling down. Foundations matter.

Bibliography

A. Hussaiy, 2001. Creativity, innovation and strategy, in Hussey, D. (ed.) *The Innovation Challenge*, Wiley, Chichester.

Aamel, R. 1994. The concept of core competence, in Hamel, G. and Heene, A. (eds) *Competence Based Competition*, Chichester, Wiley.

Aandler, R. 2002. *Value-Based Strategic Management: A Survey of UK Companies*, London, Harbridge Consulting Group.

Bedingham, K. 1999. The measurement of organisational culture, *Journal of Professional HRM*, 14, January.

Buzzell, R. D. and Gale, B. T. 1987. *The PIMS Principles*, New York, Free Press.

Cannon, F. 1987. A note on organisational change, *Management Training Update*, July, Harbridge Consulting Group Ltd, London. Reproduced in Hussey, D. and Lowe P. (eds) 1990. *Key Issues in Management Training*, London, Kogan Page, p. 159.

Channon, D. F. 1997. Activity based costing, in Channon, D. F. (ed.) *Blackwell Encyclopedic Dictionary of Strategic Management*, Oxford, Blackwell.

Christensen, C. R., Andrews, K. R. and Bower, J. L. 1978. *Business Policy: Text and Cases*, 4th edn, Homewood, II, Irwin.

Coulsen-Thomas, C. J. 1994. Business process re-engineering and strategic change, *Strategic Change*, 5(3).

Drucker, P. E, 1964, *Managing for Results*, London, Heinemann (page references are to the 1967 edition, Pan, London).

Ford, D. 1988. Develop your technology strategy, *Long Range Planning*, 21(5), October.

Gluck, F. W. and Foster, R. N. 1975. Managing technological change: a box of cigars for Brad, *Harvard Business Review*, September/October.

Goold, M, Campbell, A. and Alexander, M. 1994. *Corporate Level Strategy: Creating Value in the Multi Business Company*, New York, Wiley.

Grant, J. H. and King, W. R. 1983. *Topics of Strategic Planning*, Boston, MA, Little, Brown.

Hamel, G. and Prahalad, C. K. 1994. *Competing for the Future*, Boston, MA, Harvard Business School Press (page references are to the 1996 paperback version).

Hayes, R. H., Wheelwright, S. C. and Clark, K. B. 1988. *Dynamic Manufacturing:Creating the Learning Organisation*, New York, Free Press.

Henry, J. P. 1990. Making the technology-strategy connection, in Hussey, D. (ed.) *International Review of Strategic Management*, vol. 1, Chichester, Wiley.

Hollensen, S. 1998. *Global Marketing -A Market Responsive Approach*, Hemel Hempstead, Prentice Hall.

Hussey, D. 1996. *Business Driven Human Resource Management*, Chichester, Wiley.

Jenster P. V. and Jaworksi, B. 2000. Driving forces in market orientation: a study of industrial firms, *Strategic Change*, 9(6), 357-62.

Johansson, H. 1, McHugh, P., Pendlebury, A. J. and Wheeler, W. A. 1993. *Business Process Reengineering*, Chichester, Wiley.

Jones, T. P. 1972, *Creative Learning in Perspective*, London, University of London Press.

Kaplan, R. 1995. *Building a Management System to Implement Your Strategy: Strategic Management Survey*, London, Renaissance Solutions.

Klein, J. A. and Hiscocks, P. G. 1994. Competence-based competition: a toolkit, in Hamel, G. and Heene, A. (eds) *Competence Based Competition*, Chichester, Wiley.

KPMG 1998. *Colouring in the Map*, Mergers and acquisitions in Europe research report, London, KPMG.

Learned, E. P., Christensen, C. R., Andrews, K. R. and Guth, W. D. 1965. *Business Policy: Text and Cases*, Homewood, IL, Irwin.

Leonard-Barton, D. 1992. Core capabilities and core rigidities: a paradox in managing new product development, *Strategic Management Journal*, 13,111-25.

Lindsay, J. 1994. The technology management audit: a company self assessment, in Buckner, K. (ed). *The Portfolio of Business and Management Audits*, Uster. Strategic Direction Publishers.

Maslow, A. H. 1943, A theory of human motivation, *Psychological Review*, 50, 370-96 (reproduced in abridged form in Vroom, V. H. and Deci, E. L., *Management and Motivation*, Harmondsworth, Penguin, 1970).

Owen, P. 1990. Fostering innovation in organisations, in Lorn, C. (ed.) 7990 *Technology Strategy Resource Book*, Zurich, Strategic Direction Publishers.

Pendlebury, A. J. 1990. Manufacturing strategy for competitive advantage, in Hussey, D. E. (ed). *International Review of Strategic Management*, vol. 1, Chichester, Wiley.

Porter, M. E. 1980. *Competitive Strategy: Techniques for Analysing Industries and Competitors*, New York, Free Press.

Prahalad C. K. and Hamel, G. 1990. The core competence of the corporation, *Harvard Business Review*, May/June.

Reimann, B. C. 1987. *Managing for the Shareholders: An Overview of Value-based Strategic Management*, Oxford, Blackwell/The Planning Forum.

Rigby, D. 1999. *Management Tools and Techniques*, Boston, MA, Bain & Co. (copy of presentation dated 19 April).

Rockart, J. F. 1979. Chief executives define their own data needs, *Harvard Business Review*, March/April.

Rowe, A. J., Mason, R. O. and Dickel, K. E. 1994. *Strategic Management: A Methodological Approach*, 4th edn, Reading, MA, Addison-Wesley (summarized in Channon, D. (ed.) *Blackwell Encyclopedic Dictionary of StrategicManagement*, Oxford, Blackwell).

Segev, E. 1995a. *Corporate Strategy: Portfolio Models*, London, International Thomson/Boyd & Fraser.

Skinner, W. 1978. *Manufacturing in the Corporate Strategy*, New York, Wiley.

Stalk, G., Evans, P. and Shulman, L. 1992. Competing on capabilities: the new rules of corporate strategy, *Harvard Business Review*, March/April. 92(2).

Watson, G. H. 1993. *Strategic Benchmarking*, New York, Wiley.

Index

A

Acquisition Assurance, 60.
Acquisition Organisation, 59, 64.
Audit, 15, 17, 18, 25, 27, 28, 40, 60, 61, 69, 70, 135, 163, 164, 165, 167, 168, 169, 170, 171, 175, 184, 188, 189, 190, 191, 192, 193, 194, 195, 197, 200, 201, 222, 223, 226, 239, 245, 247, 248, 250, 251, 265, 268, 271.
Auditing Technology, 185.

B

Benchmarking, 178, 252, 253, 254, 255, 275.

C

Capability Customer, 7, 8, 9, 18, 28, 31, 37, 40, 49, 55, 67, 69, 72, 76.
Capability Perspective, 16, 17, 39.
Central Representative, 9, 12, 32.
Commercial Perspective, 16, 18, 19, 20, 21.
Competence Frameworks, 82, 86, 87, 88.
Core Processes, 255.

D

Defence Equipment, 8, 11, 44, 49, 70, 75, 76, 78.
Defence Policy, 5, 6, 13, 47, 48, 52, 65.
Doctrine Centre, 9, 12, 31, 34.
Dominant Organisational Culture, 133.

E

Employee-Customer-Profit Chain, 99.
Entrepreneurial Skill, 127.
Ethnic Minority Groups, 89.

F

Financial Perspective, 16, 21.
Financial Resources, 151, 152.

H

Human Resources, 59, 77, 78, 80, 208, 266.

I

Improve Acquisition, 44.
Industry Firms, 282, 287.

J

Joint Capabilities Board, 18, 31, 37, 67, 71, 72.

L

Leadership Capability, 81, 82, 83, 85, 88, 98, 107, 128.
Life Capability Management, 5, 10, 11, 38, 45, 47, 57, 73.

M

Market Valuation, 150.
Matrix Techniques, 197.

O

Opportunity Analysis, 25.
Organisational Strategies, 113.

P

Performance Management, 4, 56, 57, 75, 76, 88, 100, 101, 102, 103, 230.
Portfolio Analysis, 152, 300.

R

Research Perspective, 16, 24.

S

Science Innovation Technology, 8, 10, 32, 49, 79.
Strategic Layer, 42.
Strategic Plan, 139, 197, 207, 221, 267.
Strategic Situation, 136, 140.
Sustainable Development, 59, 60.

T

Tabular Presentations, 300.
Technology Management, 42, 78, 79.

V

Value Analysis, 256.
Virtual Team, 16, 27, 38, 39.

W

World Class Production, 178.